We Can
Have
Revival
Now

We Can Have Revival Now

John R. Rice

SWORD of the LORD
PUBLISHERS
P.O. BOX 1099, MURFREESBORO, TN 37133

Table of Contents

Foreword......................................7

1. Mass Evangelism and Defeatist Voices That
   Despair of Revival..........................9

2. The Bible Foretells Greatest Revivals
   Yet to Come................................33

3. False Teaching About the Last Days...........47

4. "The Last Days," a Blessed Age of Revival.....71

5. Great Revivals in Bible Times Prove
   We Can Have Revival Now.................89

6. We Can Have Revival Now Because of God's
   Infinite Resources, Freely Available
   for Soul Winning.........................109

7. Present-Day Wickedness, Apostasy and Modern
   Civilization Cannot Prevent Revival.........133

8. The Revival Harvest Is Always Ripe
   Among Lost Sinners......................155

9. God's Way to Mass Revival.................183

Foreword

Dr. John R. Rice, one of America's greatest evangelists and Twentieth Century's Mightiest Pen, was invited to inaugurate the Bob Jones University Lectures on Evangelism with a series of ten addresses presented during the month of February, 1950. In our opinion, no man in America was more qualified, not only because Dr. Rice was one of the great evangelists of his day but because he also was editor of America's Foremost Revival Publication, THE SWORD OF THE LORD. Through this paper and his books, Dr. Rice constantly promoted soul winning and revival. In addition, he held Sword of the Lord Conferences on Revival and Soul Winning all across America and an annual National Conference at least once a year for the last 7 years of his life.

We have heard some well-meaning preachers claim that the days of revival are past; but in these lectures, Dr. Rice proves from the Bible that we can have revival now. I wish every preacher in America would read this book at least once a year. It would encourage his heart regarding the important matter of soul winning and revival. Every evangelist especially should read this book at least once a year.

Here are unanswerable scriptural arguments that the day of revival is not past. May God use these lectures in their printed form to inspire pastors and evangelists as well to pray for, work for, and plan for revival.

Curtis Hutson, Editor
THE SWORD OF THE LORD
Box 1099
Murfreesboro, TN 37133

Mass Evangelism and Defeatist Voices That Despair of Revival

We can have revival now! That is the sense of what Jesus said to His disciples and followers again and again.

In Matthew 9:36-38 a statement of Jesus to His twelve disciples is given just before He sent them out, giving them power over unclean spirits.

"But when he saw the multitudes, he was moved with compassion on them, because they fainted, and were scattered abroad, as sheep having no shepherd. Then saith he unto his disciples, The harvest truly is plenteous, but the labourers are few; Pray ye therefore the Lord of the harvest, that he will send forth labourers into his harvest."

Jesus saw the multitudes and had compassion on them. Oh, if only He had Spirit-filled and prepared workers to teach them, win them, save them! So He said to His disciples, "The harvest truly is plenteous, but the labourers are few; Pray ye therefore the Lord of the harvest, that he will send forth labourers into his harvest." There was no trouble with the harvest; it was great and plenteous. There was a shortage of laborers!

That is contrary to all of our excuses, all of our unhappy efforts to avoid blame for our powerlessness and fruitlessness. The trouble is with the laborers, not with the harvest! So Jesus beseeches the twelve to pray the Lord of the harvest to send forth more laborers into His harvest!

After these twelve had been sent out to preach and teach and heal, Jesus appointed seventy other workers and told them the same thing. Read the record in Luke 10:1-3:

"After these things the Lord appointed other seventy also, and sent them two and two before his face into every city and place, whither he himself would come. Therefore said he unto them, The harvest truly is great, but the labourers are few: pray ye therefore the Lord of the harvest, that he would send forth labourers into his harvest. Go your ways: behold, I send you forth as lambs among wolves."

The twelve are gone forth to preach, but these are not enough. The harvest truly is great, but the trouble is with the laborers. Again these seventy are commanded, "Pray ye therefore the Lord of the harvest, that he would send forth labourers into his harvest." These were only new converts. They were not even grown "sheep," only "lambs"; but Jesus said, "Behold, I send you forth as lambs among wolves." They were all He had, and with yearning heart He sent these new converts out to win souls.

Again we see that there was no trouble with the harvest but with the laborers. God had a man-power shortage then; He has one now. They could have had a revival then if they had workers who meant business, workers with the power of God upon them, workers who would pay God's price for revival.

But a third time Jesus speaks on this same theme. It is an entirely different place and occasion. Jesus is at the well of Sychar in Samaria. He has just won to loving trust and surrender the poor, shabby woman whom He met at the well. The disciples seemed wholly indifferent about the concern of the Saviour for sinners. They had been to the town to buy food, and they won no one. They told no one that the Son of God, the Creator of the world, the Wonder-working Jesus, sat at the well down below the city! They want Jesus to eat, but He has been so blessed in the salvation of this poor woman that He is too full of joy for her and too full of concern for others to want food. And here we read what Jesus told them:

"My meat is to do the will of him that sent me, and to finish his work. Say not ye, There are yet four months, and then cometh harvest? behold, I say unto you, Lift up your eyes, and look on the fields; for they are white already to harvest. And he that reapeth receiveth wages, and gathereth fruit unto life eternal: that both he that soweth and he that reapeth may rejoice together." — John 4:34-36.

Here is that plaintive strain again! Oh, if people would only see the white harvest as Jesus saw it! Here are lost people, but they can be won! Here are men and women steeped in sin, depraved, blinded, but dear to the Lord; and, having immortal souls, they must be won. They are like the ripe harvest which may waste at the first wind or rain, and the Saviour says, "Lift up your eyes, and look on the fields; for they are white already to harvest."

It was wrong then, it is tragically and criminally wrong now, to suppose that some other time will be the time of revival, or that the time for revival is already past. The harvest is white now. Some people can be won now who will be forever lost unless we act soon. And one who will work at this blessed business shall reap his sheaves and receive his wages.

Oh, blessed harvest! And oh, blessed are the reapers! And oh, happy and blessed will be the wages, when "they that be wise shall shine as the brightness of the firmament; and they that turn many to righteousness as the stars for ever and ever" (Dan. 12:3).

All these Scriptures should burn in our hearts, for they are as applicable today as they were when Jesus uttered these principles, thrice repeated. They could have revival then; we can have revival now. The harvest was white then; it is white now.

Souls were lost then and away from God; many likewise are lost now. Then the people of God could have God's power, could use His Word, could have the blessed anointing of the Spirit of God, could claim God's promises and see great revivals. Now, God has not changed, and men have not changed, and the Word of God, which lives and abides forever, is still good! We can have revivals now! The harvest is white.

Will we again see great revivals, mass revivals? Will multitudes gather again, as in old time, to hear the preaching of the Gospel? Will there be a deep moving of the Spirit of God upon His people, renewing their love, cleansing their lives and giving them passion and power for soul winning? And will whole towns, cities, countries be moved mightily by such revivals? Will thousands of sinners in each of many cities hear the Gospel, be convicted, repent of their sins and be converted in mass evangelistic efforts? I say that we can and will in proportion to the way God's people meet His requirements.

When I say that we can have great revivals now, all over America there are great groups that say no.

What do we mean by revival? Some would make a distinction between revival of the saints and evangelism—winning the unsaved. But all the great soul winners have used the word "revival" to include not only the stirring of Christians and winning them to a new consecration, a new cleansing of heart and life and a new obedience, but the winning of the unconverted.

These two greatly-to-be-desired results cannot be far separated; for the primary work of the church is evangelism, soul saving. The Great Commission, the basic charter of the church, includes a command for soul winning and then a command to teach the baptized converts the same basic soul-winning duty. It is impossible for a Christian to be really revived, to get a fresh vision of the will of God in his life and a new and a more abounding zeal to do the will of God, without honestly setting out to obey Christ in this soul-winning matter.

All the successful evangelists have known this. And when Spurgeon, Finney, Moody, Torrey, Chapman, Gipsy Smith or Billy Sunday spoke of revival, they meant not only a blessed refreshing for Christians, but a great campaign of evangelism for the unsaved.

"What God hath joined together, let not man put asunder." And God has immutably joined Christian surrender, devotion and faithfulness with soul winning. For one to know Christ better is to catch His soul-winning passion and be about His main business.

So when we say "revival" we include evangelism. When we say that we can have revival now, we mean that we can have the mighty power of God to win multitudes to Christ.

Let us say further that when we say we can have revival now, we mean the same kind of revival which God has graciously given in all ages, that is, mass evangelism, the preaching of the Gospel in power to great multitudes by men especially called and anointed, men whom the Bible calls evangelists.

Many these days say we cannot have revival now. They say we can win souls in Sunday schools and in personal work, but that we cannot have mass evangelism. Some claim that the age has so changed that God can no more use evangelists.

The voices that say no more great revivals, may not say it in those words. They may say it by criticizing evangelists, like the ultradispensational seminary president who said that evangelists are "false forces in evangelism." They may say it like a prominent pastor in an N.A.E. committee: "We don't want any of this Billy Sunday stuff." They may say it by charges of "sensationalism" against evangelists, or "money-grabbing."

Some say we are in the last days, that Jesus is coming very, very soon; therefore, great revivals are impossible. Some say that we have a new day, a great new modern world which cannot be reached with the old-fashioned ways.

Modernists say the old-time *message* will not do. Some Bible believers say that the old-time *methods* will not do. In actual fact, God has given in the Bible the old-time method of revival in the pattern of Elijah, John the Baptist, Jesus, Peter, Paul, Barnabas, Apollos and Stephen, as He has given the message.

I for one am persuaded that God has no more changed His essential method of preaching the Gospel to great multitudes than He has changed His message. It is still true that "it pleased God by the foolishness of preaching to save them that believe" (I Cor. 1:21), just as it is still true that "Christ died for our sins according to the scriptures." We had as well face the fact that radio evangelism, rescue missions, house-to-house visitation soul winning, child evangelism and soul winning in colleges all flourish when there is powerful mass evangelism like that in the days of D. L. Moody and Billy Sunday; and diminish when mass evangelism diminishes.

And God's people had as well be reconciled to the scriptural fact that evangelists must be included with evangelism. Ephesians 4:11, 12, 16 says:

"And he gave some, apostles; and some, prophets; and some, evangelists; and some, pastors and teachers; For the perfecting of the saints, for the work of the ministry, for the edifying of the body of Christ. . . maketh increase of the body unto the edifying of itself in love."

Evangelists are a gift of God to the church. The office of the evangelist is as definite as that of pastor or teacher. And the office of an evangelist comes before that of a pastor in the divine order and importance, as they are named here. One who says that God will not use evangelists as He has used them before is really saying that there can be no more of the Bible kind of revivals.

When we say that we can have revivals now, we mean we can

have all the blessing that God Himself has attached to the ministry of evangelists. If we can have revivals now with the work of mighty Spirit-filled evangelists like Spurgeon, Moody, Torrey, Finney, Chapman and Sunday, then we can have pastors' colleges, Bible institutes, universities, rescue missions, and great upsurges of missionary zeal and work.

You see, the key work of evangelists in the kingdom of God involves not only soul winning but, in the words of Scripture, "the perfecting of the saints, for the work of the ministry, for the edifying of the body of Christ. . . " so that all together may make "increase of the body." Let us face this thing honestly. Those who say "no more great revivals" really say "no more Christianity in the power and vigor of New Testament times."

I say that we can have great revivals now, as great revivals as the world ever saw. I mean we can have mass evangelism, shaking whole cities, with thousands saved in a single campaign. I say that the Gospel can again grip whole communities, whole areas, and affect the moral standards, the philosophy of life of the general public. I say that as a result of such mass revivals we may have a new and mighty missionary impetus that will win millions of souls around the world, that will build and support great Christian institutions like those that came with the ministry of great evangelists. I mean an evangelism led by men called of God as evangelists, anointed with power from Heaven; men with the gifts needed for mighty mass movements, backed by Bible-believing pastors and people.

Who are these who doubt that we can have great revivals? Whose are these defeated voices that despair of great revivals, these voices which discourage faith, these defeated voices which withhold support from those who would do what Jesus commanded in getting the Gospel to every creature?

The defeated voices that teach that the vigor and glory of New Testament Christianity cannot be reproduced are the voices of modernists who do not believe the fundamentals of the Faith; the voice of worldlings who are not willing to give up sin and the favor of the world; the voice of the backslidden who have lost faith, lost their first love, lost their Christian joy; the voice jealous of evangelists and their boldness, their crowds and popularity; and the voice of the ultradispensationalists whose wrong understanding of the Bible hinders their belief in the possibility and probability of great revivals.

Let us discuss these defeated voices which despair of revival.

I. Modernists, Unbelievers in Fundamental Christian Doctrine, Say No More Great Revivals

It is true that modernists who deny the inspiration and reliability of the Bible, deny the deity of Christ and His blood atonement, deny the need for the new birth and other fundamental Bible doctrines, encourage what they call evangelism. But modernists habitually and deliberately change the meaning of historic Christian words and use them in another sense entirely foreign to their original meaning.

A modernist may speak of Jesus as the Son of God or say that Christ is divine when he does not believe in the virgin birth of Christ, nor His bodily resurrection, nor that He is deity incarnated. These infidels in the churches simply mean the false doctrine that all men are the sons of God by nature, and that Christ in that is not essentially different in nature than other men, though perhaps better in degree.

The modernist may speak of the Bible as the Word of God when he does not believe it is God's infallible revelation at all, but only that there are some good things in it from God.

When a modernist speaks of salvation, he does not mean personal regeneration, a new birth by personal faith in Christ.

You see, modernists are deceivers. As the Scripture says, these are false teachers "who privily shall bring in damnable heresies, even denying the Lord that bought them...." And again the Scripture says, "Through covetousness shall they with feigned words make merchandise of you" (II Pet. 2:1, 3). Discerning Christians must beware of the "feigned words" of modernists who intentionally deceive by using the language of historic Christianity when they do not believe in historic Christianity. So modernists speak of "evangelism" when they really mean house-to-house calling to enlist people in church membership, often without regard to repentance and the new birth.

Actually modernists oppose evangelism and old-time revivals. In discarding New Testament doctrine, they have discarded New Testament methods and aims. And modernists say that now a grand new day has come, in which people are too intelligent to be influenced by the old Gospel.

Dr. Harry Emerson Fosdick, typical modernist, in a letter often published, said that he did not believe in historic Christian doctrines and did not know a single intelligent minister who did! In other words, modernists proudly believe their learning is so far advanced and that modernists have so gained control in the churches that old-time doctrines, as preached in mass evangelism, will not be heard nor accepted by intelligent and enlightened people.

Fosdick preached and published a sermon on "The Peril of Worshiping Jesus" (*Hope of the World*, Harper). In that sermon Fosdick plainly denounces those who worship Jesus, says we should not call Him Lord, should not pray to Him, should not enshrine Him on our altars, should not sing, "In the Cross of Christ I Glory."

Of course if you take away from the evangelist the deity and Lordship and worship of Jesus Christ, you have no revivals. Well, modernists do not believe in revivals, do not want revivals, and finally, hope they have forever killed revivals in the Bible sense, in the old-fashioned sense of mass evangelism.

The American Unitarian Association of Boston, Massachusetts, has published a pamphlet, *The Relation of the Liberal Churches and the Fraternal Orders.* Elijah Alfred Coil, minister of the First Unitarian Society, Marietta, Ohio, is the author. He roundly rebukes lodge men whose orders plainly teach salvation by character and the universal fatherhood of God and the brotherhood of man, without a need for being born again, and yet go to hear evangelists preach. He quotes Billy Sunday as saying, "The fatherhood of God and the brotherhood of man are the worst rot ever dug out of Hell." He properly reminds his modernistic friends that evangelists and all Bible believers hold in spirit the creed, "We are accounted righteous before God only for the merit of our Lord and Saviour, Jesus Christ, by faith and not for our own works or deservings." This modernist, this Unitarian minister, this Master of the Masonic Lodge, denies the doctrine of salvation by the blood of Christ and urges his infidel friends to stay away from preaching like that of Billy Sunday.

You see, modernists, all unitarian Christ-rejectors, do not want revivals, do not believe in revivals and think they are gone forever among intelligent people. But that is only because they believe Bible Christianity is out of date.

Even the milder modernists fear evangelism. For example, Dr. A. Earl Kernahan, in his book, *Visitation Evangelism; Its Methods and Results,* with a foreword by Methodist Bishop Edwin H. Hughes, pioneered a method much used among modernists for increasing church membership by house-to-house visitation. Kernahan says many fine things. It is evident that he believes in some kind of conversion, though he says that "every child on earth is a Christian." But he is afraid of mass evangelism. He says on page 40:

> Too often the professional evangelist brought in to lead a campaign of mass evangelism, is reactionary in his theological

outlook. Oftentimes he is eccentric, and his eccentricities are exaggerated for publicity purposes. Oftentime he is a past master in the creating and directing of a dangerous mob psychology. Often the people who are won by this method are won to a certain theological interpretation of the Bible, which is mechanical and out of date.

Again, on page 56 Kernahan says:

> We have been driven to attempt a new method because we are in a new day of evangelism. Mass evangelism has very largely served its day and is gone, or is going.

Modernists, those who believe that the evangelist in a "campaign of mass evangelism, is reactionary in his theological outlook," and that the converts of revivals are thus often "won to a certain theological interpretation of the Bible, which is mechanical and out of date," naturally believe that "mass evangelism has very largely served its day and is gone, or is going." God forgive all the fundamentalists who join in this modernist propaganda against old-time revivals.

Let us face this voice of defeat which says there will be no more such great mass revivals. It is the voice which hates the Bible, which would take the crown of deity from Jesus Christ, which denies historic Bible Christianity. If the modernist's viewpoint is right, then Bible Christianity itself is doomed along with mass evangelism. Thank God, we know better than that!

Let me restate it: Bible evangelism, mass evangelism, that is, old-time revivals, are offensive to modernists who hope and believe that they are out of date. The emphasis on sin is offensive to modernists who are not willing to repent. The emphasis on God's grace, on the blood of Christ as the only hope of sinners, is offensive to the modern infidel who worships man and believes in salvation by merit instead of by saving faith.

Evangelism is based on the authority of the Bible as God's infallible revelation. Such faith in the Bible is essential to Bible evangelism, essential to great revivals, but is utterly abominable to modernists. The voice of modernism, unbelief in the churches which says there can be no more great revivals in the historic and old-fashioned sense, speaks as the enemy of the Bible and as the enemy of New Testament Christianity itself.

II. The Voice of Worldliness Says
No More Great Revivals

All the best and most fruitful evangelists fight sin, and this is offensive to the worldly and to the friends of the worldly. Sensible, experienced evangelists and other Christian leaders know that, until God's people humble themselves and pray and seek God's face and *turn from their wicked ways*, God cannot hear from Heaven and forgive His people and heal their land (II Chron. 7:14). Psalm 66:18 says, "If I regard iniquity in my heart, the Lord will not hear me." God will not hear the cry of Christians for revival power, for the convicting and saving of sinners, except as they confess and forsake their sins. So it is the divinely appointed method for those who would help to bring about revival that they should preach to Christians on their sins, their failures, their worldly ways.

Likewise, in preaching to the unsaved, one soon finds that it is impossible to get sinners convicted of their sins and bring them to repentance without making them conscious of their lost estate. It is true that one is not saved by keeping the law, but "the law was our schoolmaster to bring us unto Christ" (Gal. 3:24). When preachers condemn sin and preach on the wages of sin and show how God hates sin, how God will judge and punish sin, the Spirit of the Lord can bring sinners to see their need of a Saviour.

A young evangelist, preaching in his third revival and seeing drunkards and other hardened sinners wonderfully saved, told me with great joy, "I have found out that, if I can get people lost enough, I can get them saved!" Of course he meant that, if he could get sinners to know how far they are from God, how terribly wicked their hearts, how fearful their ultimate fate if they do not repent, he can get many of them to flee to Christ for refuge and trust Him for mercy.

With this in mind, the reader should remember the great moral revolution brought about by the evangelical revival under Wesley's leadership in England. The great book, *This Freedom Whence*, by J. Wesley Bready (American Tract Society) gives documented proof that prison reform, the Sunday school movement, the end of the slave trade and an enormous raising of moral standards throughout England and America were all largely brought about by the influence of this revival and such preaching as that of John Wesley and Whitefield.

Older people in America remember that the preaching of Billy Sunday and of other evangelists like him had more to do with the bringing of prohibition in America and a moral revulsion against drinking than any other single factor. When the churches in America turned their backs on mass evangelism, they lost the prohibition cause.

Students of revival will remember how plainly and powerfully Finney preached against every kind of sin—from profanity and secret orders, to vanity in dress. Sermons of D. L. Moody on sowing and reaping and kindred subjects brought tremendous conviction. He preached against slavery, against drink, against secret societies. He preached restitution and repentance.

So honest, Bible-preaching evangelists today speak out boldly against the moral rot in the movies, against increasing drunkenness, the terrible drug problem, against divorce, against the lewdness of the dance and the looseness and immorality of necking and petting among modern young people. Such preaching is unpopular with worldly people.

We must not suppose that the opposition of worldly people to mass evangelism is always insincere. People who rationalize and excuse their worldly living or who defend the worldliness of others come to dread the division, the sensation produced by such preaching. They fear that worldly people will be driven from the church, that the income of pastors will diminish, that pastors and churches will thus lose the favor of influential people. Such opposition may be sincere, but we must face it for what it is— the voice of worldliness, the voice of unsurrendered, unconsecrated people.

One should note that many who oppose mass evangelism and speak against evangelists and feel that the methods of mass evangelism are out of date, are fundamentalists. Some preachers who believe the Bible and all its principal doctrines are not willing to take the costly stand for holy living which great revivals demand.

I was called to a church for revival services. The pastor seemed to be orthodox in doctrinal position. He had from time to time called in well-used evangelists each year, obviously because of the new converts added to his church through revival efforts. But he went privately among his people to minimize my plain preaching against worldliness and sin. When I talked to him about it, I found that he himself attended picture shows and did not teach Christians to live a separated or consecrated life.

But some Christians who are themselves willing to avoid worldly amusements and habits are yet unwilling to have worldliness rebuked in the pulpit. Plain preaching may alienate some of the best paying members. Many pastors have not the courage to face the scorn of leaders in secular education, the newspapers and social leaders.

In a large, historic Eastern church fundamental in doctrine, the deacons' board was largely dominated by members of the Masonic fraternity. Obviously, for the popular pastor to attack this evil would bring serious opposition; so he did not do it. Later he resigned the church to go into "evangelistic and Bible conference work." In his public announcement he assured the public that he would preach only "a positive gospel," by which he evidently meant that he would not denounce sin. It was not surprising that he had little results in his evangelistic campaigns and soon accepted another pastorate.

This man is a good man. He believes the Bible; he loves Jesus Christ and wants to see people saved. But he would be against old-time evangelism with its preaching on sin, its mighty call to repentance, its rebuke of the world and the reproach of Christ which falls on Christians who are true to Christ in great revivals.

Many a born-again Christian does not want any preaching that will offend his picture-show-going, cigarette-smoking, dancing son or daughter and his worldly neighbor.

Almost always such people say that such revivals are out of date. They rationalize their own cowardice and in contrast say evangelists are sensational and uncouth.

One of the voices of defeat, which says, No more great revivals, is the voice of worldliness.

III. Spiritual Backsliding Opposes
and Discredits Revival

Related to the voice of worldliness, yet distinct, is the voice of backsliding. Many are indifferent to revivals and do not believe revivals are possible simply because they are backslidden.

Some truly born-again Christians do not have faith that God really answers prayer. They do not have any deep confidence in the power of the Word of God to convict and save sinners as preached by Spirit-filled men. They do not pray for revival with any enthusiasm because spiritually their faith has grown cold and small.

This is the voice of spiritual backsliding. Many Christians, truly born again, have found their love for Christ has grown cold. Such Christians have no deep compassion for lost sinners, no holy urge in their hearts to win people to Christ.

The thought that there can be no more great revivals comes naturally to one who does not much care about revival. There are obviously so many difficulties and so many problems in connection with a great revival that one who is backslidden and cold in heart does not want to believe the Bible.

Such Christians have often grown to neglect secret prayer because they find no real joy in talking to God and have no deep burden for His help. Often they do not enjoy the Bible, and many who claimed to have been converted never seriously read the Bible to find out the will of God.

These Christians with cold hearts, with no mind for prayer and no time for the Bible, are not prayer-meeting Christians. They do not delight to hear the Word of God preached. Often they do not have family worship, or have only a perfunctory kind. Backslidden in heart, those whose love has grown cold and whose devotion to Christ has wavered, do not long for great revivals and often do not believe in them.

And if backsliders do not want revivals, then the converse naturally suggested is that one who does not want revivals is backslidden in heart.

The Christian who is defeated about other matters would be defeated about revivals, too. In their unbelief, in their lack of compassion, in their lack of intimate touch with Christ, those spiritually backslidden despair of seeing great revivals again. This voice of defeat comes from a defeated life and a defeated heart.

IV. Jealous Christian Workers Often Consciously or Unconsciously Oppose and Fear Revivals

One of the voices which cries out that the old-time revivals are out of date, that new methods must be used, is the voice of jealousy.

God set in the church pastors and teachers, as is plainly taught in Ephesians 4:11. God also gave evangelists, but He put the evangelist before the pastors and teachers!

"And he gave some, apostles; and some, prophets; and some, evangelists; and some, pastors and teachers."

Just as apostles and prophets are placed before evangelists, so evangelists are placed before pastors and teachers in this divinely-inspired order. Evangelists are called and ordained of God to win more souls than pastors and ofttimes to have larger crowds, have more influence with Christians, gain a better hearing from outsiders and perhaps receive better remuneration than many pastors.

Now Christian workers are only human beings. As Diotrophes was jealous of John the Beloved, as enemies of Paul preached the Gospel from envy, we may expect the same spirit sometimes to appear today.

In Christian colleges, instructors are sometimes envious of full professors, and heads of departments are often jealous of the powers of the college president. Assistant pastors often seek to compete with the pastors in the affections and leadership of people in the church. The organist is frequently jealous of the choir leader.

So, many a pastor when he sees the evangelist preaching to larger crowds, preaching with greater boldness, seeing more converts than he himself has seen, often finds it difficult not to envy the evangelist.

Pastors have often criticized evangelists as being sensational when actually they regretted they could not be as bold and preach to as large crowds. A pastor has often criticized an evangelist as being a money-grabber when actually the evangelist put far less stress on financial remuneration than the same pastor.

Pastors usually will not accept a pastorate without a definitely promised salary, and often haggle for a free parsonage and a paid vacation. I have known a number of ministers to refuse a call to a pastorate because they said the salary promised was not adequate. Yet I have never known a reputable evangelist to set a price on his service, or ask a minimum guarantee. I have known a number of well-known Bible teachers to do so.

The reason such pastors criticize an evangelist is not that the evangelist *asks* for more money but that he sometimes *gets* more! For the very same reason, poorly-paid pastors criticize well-paid pastors. That is simply old human nature playing a familiar part.

Denominational leaders are often jealous of the influence of evangelists. Pastors are in position to raise money for the denominations while evangelists usually are not. Pastors will usually cooperate more fully with the denominations than will evangelists. Pastors often have annuity or life insurance at stake, and often expect to need the recommendation of the denominational secretary or the good will of the bishop, while evangelists are usually independent in such matters. Evangelists are usually not made trustees of denominational colleges or seminaries.

This jealousy and natural antipathy of pastors and other Christian workers toward evangelists who get bigger crowds is natural, but it is carnal.

A great church asked me to come for revival services. The pastor said, "We always pay Bible teachers $100 a week and evangelists $150 a week. Will that be satisfactory?" I replied that any amount the church set would be abundantly satisfactory, that I would not be a party to any agreement whatever on the salary matter. It was to be left to the pastor and church since I never made any demands.

After a blessed revival, with the church auditorium packed out night after night and with many saved, including prominent businessmen, the church paid me considerably more than the $150 a week intended. A short time before, the church had had a well-known and beloved Bible teacher and had paid him $100 a week. He had spoken to not more than a third as many people per night, I suppose, and I could well see the viewpoint of the church which was willing to pay more for larger crowds, more souls saved and greater blessing.

But I can imagine how that Bible teacher would feel about evangelists! And the thoughtful reader will see why Bible teachers have complained that evangelists are sensational, that they play on people's emotions, and that they harshly condemn sin. Such people criticize evangelists, not because evangelists are wrong, but because they are right. Men who do not win souls criticize those who do. Men who have small crowds criticize those who have large crowds.

I can see how a defeated man, resenting the crowds or the popularity or the income of some greatly used evangelist, can come to believe that all such evangelism is out of date and that it would be better to win souls in the Sunday school, in child evangelism, or in Youth for Christ, without great mass revivals led by evangelists.

One of the defeated voices which despair of revival is the voice of jealousy among Christian workers.

V. Ultradispensationalism Is a Voice of Defeat Despairing of Revival

Some Christians overemphasize the dispensational teaching in the Bible. Of course there is a dispensational difference between the old covenant and the new covenant, between the ceremonial law and the Gospel. But ultradispensational people say that the Acts of the Apostles is a record of a transition period and that the Christianity of the book of Acts is not to be a pattern for present-day Christianity. Such people sometimes say that the Sermon on the Mount was for Jews only, not for us, that even the Lord's Prayer is "a kingdom prayer" not suitable for us. They say that the miracles, power and gifts manifested among Christians in the book of Acts are now out of date. Such people usually say that the only "baptism of the Spirit" there is now is what one receives at conversion.

These ultradispensationalists say that we are in the last days, that the Saviour must come very soon. They say that "the great apostasy" is on so that a great revival is impossible. They usually think that a number of signs prove that from the time of the first World War on to the present should be called "the last days" and that many signs indicate the Saviour must come at most in a few months or years.

The ultradispensationalists do more to discourage revival than many because they are not infidels but Bible believers. They are not amillennial but premillennial. They believe in the verbal inspiration of the Bible and believe it literally true. These ultradispensationalists are usually followers of John Nelson Darby, one of the founders of the Plymouth Brethren movement. They have had tremendous influence in the notes of the Scofield Bible; they have infiltrated the Bible institutes built by the evangelists, and substituted their own pet doctrines for the teaching of Moody, Torrey, Spurgeon and Finney on the fullness of the Spirit.

The ultradispensationalists generally say that no more great revivals are likely, that it is much harder now to win souls because of the great apostasy which, they say, now marks the closing days of the age.

This teaching is subtle, it is respectable, but it is deadly in its effect on evangelism.

Ultradispensationalists have not turned out a single great evangelist. They turn out many Bible teachers.

Typical of that teaching is the book called *True Evangelism* by Lewis Sperry Chafer, which calls evangelists "false forces in evangelism," which says that "a revival is abnormal rather than normal" and not to be "a sanctioned method of work" (p. 7). He says that evangelists place "false or undue emphasis on methods" by demanding "some public action in connection with conversion, such as standing or going forward in a meeting." Chafer especially opposes sending "out workers to plead with individuals in a miscellaneous congregation," and desires evangelists not to preach on sin.

Many ultradispensationalists accuse every evangelist of compromising who works with churches of any denomination but Plymouth Brethren.

Many kindly Christian people, influenced by ultradispensationalists, feel that it is hopeless to expect revival. They are defeated. They feel so critical of worldly people that they cannot help them, so critical of evangelists that they do not trust them. Such people have a tendency to enjoy technical study of the Bible more than soul winning, to be more interested theoretically in Jewish missions than in great citywide campaigns, though only a handful of Jews are saved each year in all the Jewish missions in America and frequently one single citywide campaign will show more converts than all the Jewish missions in America will show in a year.

Another full chapter will be given to show from Bible prophecy that great revivals are yet to come and that this ultradispensational viewpoint about revivals is utterly unscriptural. But here let us mark this ultradispensational voice for what it is—the voice of defeat, the voice of failing Christians. The doctrine of the ultradispensationalists is heresy. The attitude of criticism and division is sinful. It discourages revival and brings reproach on premillennial truth. It puts out the fires of soul winning.

Let us make a clear distinction between the premillennial doctrinal position and ultradispensationalism. I am a premillen-

nialist, which simply means that I believe Jesus may come at
any time, just as He promised, and certainly must come before
there can be any millennium on this earth. I take the Bible
literally and believe that the same Jesus who went away shall
so come in like manner as the disciples saw Him ascend into
Heaven, and in accordance with the plain promise of the angels
who stood by (Acts 1:11).

Premillennialists simply take the Bible at face value when
it teaches that the Lord Jesus Christ Himself will one day return
for His own, raise the Christian dead, change the Christians who
are alive and take us with Him to Heaven, then a little later
will reign literally on the earth. It happens that evangelists
generally take the Bible literally, and so nearly all the great
soul winners have been premillennial in faith. Spurgeon, Moody,
Torrey, Chapman, Billy Sunday, Bob Jones were all premillennial. As far as I know, all the widely-used interdenominational
evangelists in America today are premillennial in doctrine; that
is, they believe that the Saviour may come at any moment, just
as He said.

But to set dates or years for the Saviour's return, to say that
we cannot take the examples of the New Testament as our pattern in soul winning, to say that Christians should never pray
for the power of the Holy Spirit and that the times themselves
forbid revival, is a voice of defeat, the voice of a false dispen-
sationalism.

You hear the cry of defeated voices which despair of revival.
Some of these do not want revival. Those who wish to have
revival do not have the faith for it and perhaps are unwilling
to pay the price for it. They are the voices of modern unbelief,
liberalism; of worldliness; of spiritual backsliding; of jealousy
among Christian workers; the voice of ultradispensationalists
whose wrong interpretation of the Bible makes them believe
great revivals are now unlikely, if not impossible.

Say what you will—these voices are voices of defeat, not of faith, not of victory. Their spirit is not the spirit of the Acts of the Apostles, not the spirit of the Apostle Paul. Their spirit is not true to the promises of Christ, nor to the implications and obligations of the Great Commission. Defeated Christians are not Spirit-filled Christians, are not faith-filled Christians, are not Christians in the glory and power and joy of the Lord.

We must not believe these defeated voices. They are wrong! And in succeeding lectures we earnestly hope to show that we ought to have and can have now, if Christians will meet God's requirements, as great revivals as ever blessed this earth.

Does the Bible justify the pessimism of those who think there will be no more great revivals? Absolutely not. How happy some would be if they could find in the Bible justification for their false alibis and excuses, justification for their powerlessness and fruitlessness. If there were a verse in the Bible which said there would be no more great revivals, which said that soul winning would become harder and harder, you may be sure that it would be shouted from the housetops by preachers and teachers who win few souls and have no revivals.

I assure you that the Bible has not a single word to the effect that soul winning will get harder and harder, that revivals will become more difficult or impossible—not a single prophecy that the day of great revivals will pass away before Jesus comes. All that is in the minds of defeated, backslidden, powerless Christians.

In fact, the whole trend of the New Testament teaches that we are in the age of great revivals. Jesus promised the disciples to whom He gave the Great Commission and to us who should follow them in their work, "Lo, I am with you alway, even unto the end of the world" (Matt. 28:20). When Jesus said, "He that believeth on me, the works that I do shall he do also; and greater works than these shall he do; because I go unto my Father" (John 14:12), He did not even hint that that promise would little by little fail, and that fewer and fewer results could be expected.

The great promises of fruit-bearing, of answers to prayer, of enduement of power with the Holy Spirit, are all given to be in effect throughout this whole gospel age. There is not a word in the Bible, I say, to indicate that the Gospel will become less effective, that sinners will be harder to win, that revivals will become more difficult or impossible. The contrary is true. And in the next lecture I shall go more fully into that blessed truth that we are now in the age of revivals, in the age of the pouring out of the Holy Spirit, and that all the promises about revival and soul winning fit as well for us as they did at Pentecost and in the times of the apostles and in other eras of great revivals. We are in the revival age, and great revivals may be had anytime God's people meet God's requirements. But that is a subject I will later discuss.

In this lecture I must show you that the greatest revivals the world is ever to see are yet future. Greater revivals are to come than any the world has ever experienced is plainly taught in the Word of God. What a comfort it ought to be to our hearts! When we find that God has plainly promised greater revivals than any the world has yet had, that will certainly prove that the day of revivals is not passed.

1. The Great Tribulation Revival

Jesus told of a coming time which He called the "Great Tribulation." In Matthew 24:21, 22, He said, "For then shall be great tribulation, such as was not since the beginning of the world to this time, no, nor ever shall be. And except those days should be shortened, there should no flesh be saved: but for the elect's sake those days shall be shortened." Note that the time coming will be more terrible than any the world has ever seen up until then.

Later in the Olivet Discourse, Jesus gave us a key as to when this Great Tribulation will be. In verses 27 to 31 He said:

"For as the lightning cometh out of the east, and shineth even unto the west; so shall also the coming of the Son of man be. For wheresoever the carcase is, there will the eagles be gathered together. Immediately after the tribulation of those days shall the sun be darkened, and the moon shall not give her light, and the stars shall fall from heaven, and the powers of the heavens shall be shaken: And then shall appear the sign of the Son of man in heaven: and then shall all the tribes of the earth mourn, and they shall see the Son of man coming in the clouds of heaven with power and great glory. And he shall send his angels with a great sound of a trumpet, and they shall gather together his elect from the four winds, from one end of heaven to the other."

Here we see that the Lord Jesus was particularly speaking to Jews, and so He told them of the time when He would send forth His angels and gather together His elect (Israelites) from the four winds of the earth. It will be when Jesus is seen visibly, bodily, coming in the clouds of Heaven with power and great glory (vs. 30).

But verse 29 tells us that this is to be "immediately after the tribulation." So it appears to me that, after the rapture of the saints (when we who are saved will be caught up to meet Him in the air), Jesus will later return with us to the earth, this time to regather Israel and save them and reign on the earth. But the period after the rapture of the saints, while we shall be in Heaven with the Saviour just before He returns to reign, will be the time of the Great Tribulation on earth. This is the teaching of the best premillennial scholars. This is the position of Moody, Torrey, Scofield (in the Scofield Bible), James M. Gray, H. A. Ironside, William Pettingill and Arno Gaebelein. Hence, the Great Tribulation time is yet to come.

After every saved person shall be taken away with Jesus and when the Antichrist himself will rule on the earth, will come the Great Tribulation. There will be so much persecution and trouble and war that it, above all the periods in human history, is to be called the Great Tribulation. The Antichrist will refuse people who do not take his mark the right to buy and sell. Those who get converted under these conditions will surely risk their lives for Christ. Yet the Bible tells us that in this Great Tribulation there will come the most marvelous revival.

Revelation 7:9-17 gives us a beautiful picture of the converts of the Great Tribulation revival gathered in Heaven.

"After this I beheld, and, lo, a great multitude, which no man could number, of all nations, and kindreds, and people, and tongues, stood before the throne, and before the Lamb, clothed with white robes, and palms in their hands; And cried with a loud voice, saying, Salvation to our God which sitteth upon the throne, and unto the Lamb. And all the angels stood round about the throne, and about the elders and the four beasts, and fell before the throne on their faces, and worshipped God, Saying, Amen: Blessing, and glory, and wisdom, and thanksgiving, and honour, and power, and might, be unto our God for ever and ever. Amen. And one of the elders answered, saying unto me, What are these which are arrayed in white robes? and whence came they? And I said unto him, Sir, thou knowest. And he said to me, These are they which came out of great tribulation, and have washed their robes, and made them white in the blood of the Lamb. Therefore are they before the throne of God, and serve him day and night in his temple: and he that sitteth on the throne shall dwell among them. They shall hunger no more, neither thirst any more; neither shall the sun light on them, nor any heat. For the Lamb which is in the midst of the throne shall feed them, and shall lead them unto living fountains of waters: and God shall wipe away all tears from their eyes."

Here in Heaven are people praising God for salvation. Who

are they? Those who will have been saved during the Great Tribulation.

Two verses here are specially important.

Verse 9 tells something of the number of these saved: "After this I beheld, and, lo, a great multitude, which no man could number, of all nations, and kindreds, and people, and tongues, stood before the throne, and before the Lamb, clothed with white robes, and palms in their hands."

Verse 14 is also important: "And he said to me, These are they which came out of great tribulation, and have washed their robes, and made them white in the blood of the Lamb."

In the first part of this same chapter, we have a discussion of 144,000 Israelites from twelve tribes who will be converted during this time of the Great Tribulation. But aside from the Israelites, here is "a great multitude, which no man could number, of all nations, and kindreds, and people, and tongues. . ." who are saved. These will have come out of the Great Tribulation, when we see them assembled in Heaven. They will have washed their robes in the blood of the Lamb.

It is suggestive that the scene is laid in Heaven. Most of these converted in the Tribulation Period will have been martyred on earth. No such mighty assembly of Christians can be gathered on earth in those awful days when it will mean death not to take the mark of the Beast. But when these multiplied, uncounted thousands and millions who will be saved during the Great Tribulation are later assembled in Heaven, they will be given the honor due to martyrs, due to those who came to Christ in spite of such temptation and persecution and trouble.

These to be converted in the Great Tribulation Period will not be allowed to buy nor sell. Many of them will starve. But now we are told that "they shall hunger no more, neither thirst any more; neither shall the sun light on them, nor any heat. For the Lamb which is in the midst of the throne shall feed them, and shall lead them unto living fountains of waters: and God shall wipe away all tears from their eyes" (vss. 16, 17).

Oh, my heart leaps within me as I think of that revival! I am not against numbers. At Pentecost they were counted and found to be about three thousand. But in this blessed revival to come and spread over the whole earth during the reign of the Antichrist, when true preachers and Christians will have been carried away to Heaven in the rapture and the churches will have been taken over by unbelievers, and when it may mean death to turn to Christ—then uncounted multitudes that no man can number from every nation and kindred and tongue and tribe will turn to God.

What a revival! Nothing less than millions could be meant by these terms, "a...multitude, which no man could number." Past counting will be the converts in the marvelous revival yet to come in the Great Tribulation.

The Great Tribulation revival, so clearly prophesied in Revelation 7:9-14, proves that the day of great revivals is not passed, shows that the greatest revivals are yet to come.

And this blessed revival also proves that whatever the outward distress, God's people can seek His face and have His power. Whatever the human limitations, we can have revival.

We can have revival when it means persecution and death for Christians. We can have revival when the government is wicked and anti-Christian. We can have revival when modernism is everywhere in the saddle. We can have revival, provided God's faithful few pay God's price to have His mighty power!

Thank God for this wonderful revival when such multitudes will be saved in every nation of the world that they will be uncountable! Thank God for the 144,000 Israelites saved to witness for Christ in that period! But thank God still more for the multitudes, the uncountable multitudes, to be saved in every nation, saved among every heathen tribe, every language and dialect! What a revival God will give in the Tribulation time!

2. The Coming Great Revival in Israel

But another great revival, in which millions are to be saved, is plainly foretold for the future.

Throughout the Bible there runs a story of God's love for Israel. Often He has punished His chosen people. They are even now scattered through all the world because of their sins. But again and again, in both Old Testament and New Testament, God has promised that He will bring the nation Israel back to Himself.

One of the clearest statements in the Scripture about the coming conversion of the Jews who will be left alive on the earth is in Romans 11:25-31:

"For I would not, brethren, that ye should be ignorant of this mystery, lest ye should be wise in your own conceits; that blindness in part is happened to Israel, until the fulness of the Gentiles be come in. And so all Israel shall be saved: as it is written, There shall come out of Sion the Deliverer, and shall turn away ungodliness from Jacob: For this is my covenant unto them, when I shall take away their sins. As concerning the gospel, they are enemies for your sakes: but as touching the election, they are beloved for the fathers' sakes. For the gifts and calling of God are without repentance. For as ye in times past have not believed God, yet have now obtained mercy through their unbelief: Even so have these also now not believed, that through your mercy they also may obtain mercy."

Everybody knows that blindness in part has happened to Israel. How difficult it is now to win a Jew to Christ! I see a few Jews saved in my large union revival campaigns, but it is difficult to win Jews. They are usually spiritually blinded and prejudiced, and not many of them are saved.

But it is God's plan that the blindness that has happened to

Israel will be taken away. When is that? It is, verse 25 says, after "the fulness of the Gentiles be come in." After this gospel age has run its course, after Christ comes and receives His own into the air, after the Tribulation when He returns to reign on the earth and restore the kingdom to Israel on David's throne in Jerusalem, then the nation Israel is to be saved. The statement is, "And so all Israel shall be saved."

At present Jews are our enemies for the sake of the Gospel, but they are beloved for the Father's sake. The gifts and callings of God are without repentance—that is, God cannot turn away from the promise He made to Abraham. God cannot turn away from the choice He made of Jacob. God will not go back on His promises to David. So one of these days, after the fullness of the Gentiles is come in, God will turn away ungodliness from Jacob, and the nation Israel will turn to their God and be saved. So is the plain teaching of the Word of God.

We Gentiles have obtained mercy through the unbelief of the Jews. God turned to the Gentiles with the Gospel. But one blessed day when the fullness of the Gentiles be come in, then God will take away the blindness from Jewish minds and hearts, and they will turn to Christ.

This marvelous conversion of Israel is foretold back in Deuteronomy 30:1-6:

"And it shall come to pass, when all these things are come upon thee, the blessing and the curse, which I have set before thee, and thou shalt call them to mind among all the nations, whither the Lord thy God hath driven thee, And shalt return unto the Lord thy God, and shalt obey his voice according to all that I command thee this day, thou and thy children, with all thine heart, and with all thy soul; That then the Lord thy God will turn thy captivity, and have compassion upon thee, and will return and gather thee from all the nations, whither the Lord thy God hath scattered thee. If any of thine be driven out unto the outmost parts

of heaven, from thence will the Lord thy God gather thee, and from thence will he fetch thee: And the Lord thy God will bring thee into the land which thy fathers possessed, and thou shalt possess it; and he will do thee good, and multiply thee above thy fathers. And the Lord thy God will circumcise thine heart, and the heart of thy seed, to love the Lord thy God with all thine heart, and with all thy soul, that thou mayest live."

We see here that, when the people of Israel turn with all their heart to obey God and seek Him, the Lord will bring Israel back to Palestine, gathering Jews out of every nation where He has scattered them. God will bring them into the land of Palestine, and they will possess it and multiply.

Then verse 6 promises, "And the Lord thy God will circumcise thine heart, and the heart of thy seed, to love the Lord thy God with all thine heart, and with all thy soul, that thou mayest live." That means regeneration. That means that God will make Christians out of those Jews who will be regathered from all over the world.

The Prophet Ezekiel also foretold this regathering and conversion of Israel. In Ezekiel 20:33-38 we are told that God will bring the nation Israel out into the wilderness and plead with them as He did with their fathers in the days of Moses. Then He will purge out the rebels, all who will not be converted, and settle the rest into the land of Canaan.

Ezekiel, chapter 36, tells also of this wonderful regathering of the nation Israel from all the heathen countries when God brings them back into the land of Palestine. And Ezekiel 36:26-28 says:

"A new heart also will I give you, and a new spirit will I put within you: and I will take away the stony heart out of your flesh, and I will give you an heart of flesh. And I will put my spirit within you, and cause you to walk in my statutes, and ye shall

keep my judgments, and do them. And ye shall dwell in the land that I gave to your fathers; and ye shall be my people, and I will be your God."

That is a wonderful picture of a saved people with new hearts, with God's Spirit dwelling within them. That is what will happen to the Jews when Christ returns to reign and regathers them and saves them.

One of the most moving descriptions of this marvelous revival among the Jews is given in Zechariah.

Zechariah 12:10 says, "And I will pour upon the house of David, and upon the inhabitants of Jerusalem, the spirit of grace and of supplications: and they shall look upon me whom they have pierced, and they shall mourn for him, as one mourneth for his only son, and shall be in bitterness for him, as one that is in bitterness for his firstborn."

When Jesus returns and delivers Israelites from the persecution and trouble of the Great Tribulation and destroys the Antichrist and his armies, then Jews will know this is the Saviour.

Zechariah 13:1 says, "In that day there shall be a fountain opened to the house of David and to the inhabitants of Jerusalem for sin and for uncleanness." That fountain was not opened at the crucifixion. It will be opened at a future time when the nation Israel will have their hearts opened to the Gospel, in Jerusalem, and will turn and be saved.

Then verse 6 tells us, "And one shall say unto him, What are these wounds in thine hands? Then he shall answer, Those with which I was wounded in the house of my friends." When Jesus shall appear among the Jews and rescue them, they will see the wounds in His hands and ask Him questions. He will reveal to them that He is the Saviour the Jews hated and crucified before—the Lord and King of the Jews, the Prince whom the Jews have so long despised. And when they see these wounds and know who Jesus is, they will mourn in repentance and turn to God.

Again I remind you of Paul's inspired word in Romans 11:26, 27, "And so all Israel shall be saved: as it is written, There shall come out of Sion the Deliverer, and shall turn away ungodliness from Jacob: For this is my covenant unto them, when I shall take away their sins."

There have been some great revivals in the past.

I should like to have stood at Mt. Carmel when Elijah prayed down fire from Heaven and when all the assembled people fell on their faces and declared, "The Lord, he is the God! the Lord, he is the God!"

I should like to have seen the crowds that heard John the Baptist and repented of their sins and were baptized in Jordan.

I should like to have seen the "multitudes" who heard Jesus and turned from their sins. (That term *multitude* or *multitudes* is used more than twenty times in the book of Matthew about the crowds who heard Jesus.)

I should like to have seen the great revival at Pentecost when three thousand turned to God in a day and other thousands of men and women in the days that followed.

I should like to have been in the revivals where D. L. Moody preached, and Finney and Torrey and Chapman and Billy Sunday.

But bless God, I will be in a revival far greater! I will be there to see it, and so will all the Christians, all the saints of God, when Jesus regathers the nation Israel, so long despised—the blinded nation yet so beloved for the Father's sake—and shows them His hands and has them repent of their sins and turn to Him, a whole nation in a day! What a blessed revival!

I think this wonderful revival to come at the beginning of the millennium, when Christ returns to reign and gathers Israelites out of every nation under Heaven, is good evidence that the day of great revivals is not done. God is the same, His plans run on toward their climax and victory. How wicked for us to be defeated and unbelieving!

3. Christ Delays His Second Coming
That Others May Be Saved

We have shown that a mighty revival, with unnumbered millions of converts, will occur in the Great Tribulation time, and that after that, when Christ returns to reign and regathers the nation Israel, all Jews left alive after some rebels are purged out, will turn to Christ and be saved at once. Those revivals are wonderful, but what about the immediate future? What is God's will for these days?

It is the same as it was for the days of the apostles. Christ Himself today longs to see souls saved more than anything else. And the Scriptures teach us that Jesus delays His return on earth so that people may be saved.

Second Peter 3:3-9 has a wonderful picture of the heart of Christ and His intense longing for the salvation of sinners:

"Knowing this first, that there shall come in the last days scoffers, walking after their own lusts, And saying, Where is the promise of his coming? for since the fathers fell asleep, all things continue as they were from the beginning of the creation. For this they willingly are ignorant of, that by the word of God the heavens were of old, and the earth standing out of the water and in the water: Whereby the world that then was, being overflowed with water, perished: But the heavens and the earth, which are now, by the same word are kept in store, reserved unto fire against the day of judgment and perdition of ungodly men. But, beloved, be not ignorant of this one thing, that one day is with the Lord as a thousand years, and a thousand years as one day. The Lord is not slack concerning his promise, as some men count slackness; but is longsuffering to us-ward, not willing that any should

perish, but that all should come to repentance."

Scoffers are to arise who shall doubt the return of the Saviour. Their argument is that, "since the fathers fell asleep, all things continue as they were from the beginning of the creation." And believers naturally wonder why Christ does not come again and put an end to the present wicked world system, resurrect and gather His saints and close up the present tragic age.

But why does Christ not quickly return? Verse 9 tells us: "The Lord is not slack concerning his promise, as some men count slackness; but is longsuffering to us-ward, not willing that any should perish, but that all should come to repentance."

The Lord Jesus is not slack in His promise about coming again, but His long-suffering heart wishes to delay until others may be saved. He is "not willing that any should perish, but that all should come to repentance." This is given as the reason for the delay in the Saviour's coming. This Scripture shows what the Lord Jesus has on His dear heart.

The "Bible teachers" who spend their time principally in speculation about the time of the Lord's coming, about the mark of the Beast and signs of the times, and the men who preach from newspapers as much as the Bible would do well to prayerfully consider what the Lord is concerned about. Instead of spending their time on speculation and guessing and date-setting about the Lord's return, they would be spending their time far better in soul winning and making glad the heart of the Saviour.

We have shown in this chapter how God will give mighty revivals during the Tribulation time and then when Jesus comes from Heaven to set up His throne, as promised, at Jerusalem. But we should remember that the Lord Jesus is now waiting for us to have revivals. The Saviour delays His coming because He is not willing that sinners should perish. In other words, the Lord is as much concerned about revivals and as willing to give them now as at any other time. It is not fair to draw any inference from this Scripture contrary to this: the Lord Jesus, before He returns for His saints, still longs for multitudes to be saved and willingly will give great revivals when His people pay the price.

This age is an age of revivals. We still have the Great Commission. We still have the promise, "Lo, I am with you alway, even unto the end of the world." All the promises of answers to prayer are ours. In Heaven they still rejoice more over one sinner that repents than over ninety-nine just persons. And Jesus is longing continually to have souls saved—in fact, He delays His return for one purpose—to give us time and opportunity to have more revivals and win more souls!

Those who say no more great revivals ignore the clear teaching of the Word of God concerning great revivals yet promised for the future.

| **False Teaching About the Last Days** | **3** |

Thousands of tracts, magazine articles, sermons and radio messages tell the people, "Jesus is coming soon!"

"These last days of this dispensation" and similar phrases are very common in Christian magazines.

"Time is running out!" writes one Christian, by which he means that in a very short time Jesus is certain to come.

"The last great mission opportunity before Jesus comes" is the way one mission field is described.

A widely-known seminary professor on the West Coast is quoted as saying, "I believe we are seeing the very closing days of this dispensation."

Some Christian writers regard the nuclear bomb, the rise of Russia, the founding of the new Israel state, World War II (as they regarded World War I), as evidence that we are in the very last days before Jesus comes.

All these people, usually faithful Bible believers and earnest Christians, have been influenced and misled by a heresy that has become widespread in recent years. This mistaken teaching holds that we are now, according to what are regarded as definite signs, in the very last few weeks or months or years before Jesus must come; that this period which they call "the last days" is more difficult than ever. They believe that sinners are harder hearted, that Satan deceives people more than ever, that world conditions make it harder to reach people with the Gospel, and that for all these reasons great revivals are less likely than ever, if not impossible.

A noble and greatly used man of God says about the Billy Graham revival in Los Angeles late in 1949: "For these three thousand we are profoundly grateful to God, and our confidence in the power of mass evangelism to sweep folks into the kingdom of God has been restored."

Our brother agrees that the day of mass evangelism has not passed, though it took the Los Angeles revival to prove it. But it is noteworthy that many others like this noble brother have been led to feel that mass evangelism has been outdated and is no longer able "to sweep folks into the kingdom of God."

We need to face the false teaching, so prevalent, which has undermined the confidence of the people that great revivals and mass evangelism are possible today.

Again and again godly men have asked me how the work in the revival field goes. "Isn't it getting harder to have revivals?" They are astonished when I tell them that it is not. Many others who are defeated lament that they cannot get the publicity that evangelists could once get, that local conditions, like the competition of movies and television, radio and sports and the grip of modernists on the churches, are unfavorable to revivals. And in the case of literally thousands of preachers these thoughts are connected with the teaching they have absorbed that the Lord Jesus is certain to return soon, and that in the immediate period before His return, we will be unable to have great revivals.

"The great apostasy is on," they say. They mean that they think the modernism of today proves that the end of gospel opportunity is about at hand, forgetting that great waves of infidelity have come to the world and even to the church down through many centuries, as it was in England before the Wesleyan revivals, as it came in France before that, and as it came even in the early church in the first centuries of the Christian era.

The defeatism of Christians, who are not bold in preaching nor bold in prayer because they believe that Christian work is less effective than ever before, that the Gospel does not bring the results that it did before and that great revivals are less likely than ever before, is tragic indeed. And it is especially sad to see this defeatism springing up because of misinterpretation of Scriptures by Christians who really believe the Bible and love Jesus Christ.

This ultradispensational teaching that Jesus is certain to come soon, that certain signs prove the age is rushing to an early end, that the apostasy, world conditions and increased activity of Satan make gospel efforts less fruitful and revivals more difficult and unlikely, is a distressing perversion of a great truth.

It is true that Jesus may come at any moment, but the ultra-dispensationalists do not preach the emphasis that Jesus urged, "Watch therefore, for ye know neither the day nor the hour wherein the Son of man cometh" (Matt. 25:13) and the Bible doctrine often stated and inferred that Jesus might have returned anytime since Pentecost and may return now at any time. Instead, they emphasize world conditions and so-called signs and spend their time in study of the technical details of prophecy and speculation rather than on the soul-winning work which Jesus bade us do until He returns.

Jesus would have us watch for His coming simply because He commanded us to watch. However, the custom has grown up among a lot of premillennial Christians of looking for Christ's return because we have had World Wars I and II or of looking for Christ's return because Zionists and infidel Jews have established the modern national Israel in Palestine. Some are moved more by newspaper accounts than by the plain command of the Lord Jesus.

Earnest Christians ought to recognize that this ultradispensational outlook is largely a retreat from alarming conditions which Christians are not willing to face and for which they think the Gospel is not sufficient. Too many Christians see the wickedness of the human heart, as expressed in Hitler's murderous career and in the far worse wickedness of communism, and their faith wavers. Instead of an attitude of aggressive evangelism with the Gospel which is really the dynamite of God, sufficient for any generation, they declare that such a generation as this is too hard for God, that Satan is too active, that the apostasy is too great and conditions too unfavorable for a revival.

Let us face this defeatism for what it is. Let us recognize the lack of faith, the powerlessness for the retreat of Christians from the battle which seems hard.

Indeed, some Christians rationalize the situation and subconsciously evade the facts of their powerlessness and unbelief with the doctrine that, since we are in the last days, it is impossible to win souls in any great numbers. That is bad enough, but many such Christians are actually not much concerned about soul winning, preferring to examine the Scriptures with a kind of morbid curiosity, hoping to be thought wise, when really they shed no tears for souls and never wait before God pleading for revival or His mighty pentecostal power.

Learned men say to the people, "Let us gather around the Word"; then they examine the Word of God as if it were a museum piece. It is as if, in a museum, soldiers gather around a sword, talk with interest of its history, how it was made, who wielded it, and tell what exploits were wrought with it in the past, yet never take this same sword to battle. So do many "Bible teachers" and "Bible students" use the Word of God.

The Bible is not simply to be the object of dispassionate, technical interest and investigation. It is not a museum curiosity!

It is the sword of the Spirit which ought to be used to cut sinners to the heart. It contains the Gospel, the dynamite of God which is the power of God unto salvation to everyone that believeth. "Is not my word like as a fire? . . . and like a hammer that breaketh the rock in pieces?" (Jer. 23:29), the Lord asks.

So all the searching of the Bible and the searching of the daily newspapers to find some "signs" that prove Christ will come within a certain specified time is contrary to the spirit of the Scriptures and does dishonor to the Lord Jesus Christ who left us here simply to get the Gospel to every creature.

1. That Christ's Return Is Imminent Cannot Be Reconciled With the Teaching That He Could Only Return After Modern Events

There are two theories about the premillennial coming of Christ which are contradictory. Both cannot be true.

One theory is that Jesus will not come until certain signs have appeared. Some think Jesus cannot come until the Gospel is preached again to all the world. Some think Jesus could not come until what they call "the budding of the fig tree," the reestablishment of the nation Israel as it has recently been reestablished in Palestine. Others think that Jesus could not return until the so-called "great apostasy," the wave of modernism in the church which has occurred in America in the last fifty or sixty years and is now possibly past its climax.

Many would say that World Wars I and II are signs of the soon coming of Christ. If that be true, then Jesus could not have come before these wars. Others believe that earthquakes, that famine following the wars, that the present capital-labor controversy encouraged by socialists and communists everywhere are signs of Christ's coming; therefore, Christ could not have come before these clashes occurred and communism and socialism reached their present popularity.

I want you to see that this first and popular theory I am discussing is simply that Jesus was to come only after certain definite signs should appear.

The other and contradictory theory is that Jesus might have returned anytime after Pentecost. No one knew when He would return, so it would have been possible for Him to have returned before World Wars I and II, before the evolution theory became widely prominent and the present great rage of modernism developed. He might have come before the modern missionary movement. Or He may come now at any moment. This theory, or doctrine, is the doctrine of the imminency of Christ's return.

But note carefully that this doctrine of the imminency of Christ's return contradicts the doctrine that Jesus could not come until a certain set time in a program and that He must come after a number of specified signs are fulfilled. The teaching that Christ must come at a set time or in a particular generation and only after a certain program of signs is fulfilled is entirely different from the doctrine of the imminent coming of Christ which is clearly taught in the Scriptures.

I beg your patience as I state it again. It is important for us to see that one cannot hold to the imminency of Christ's return—that is, that He may come at any moment, that He might have come at any time since Pentecost as far as anyone then could know, and that Christians, all through the ages, were right to expect Christ to come at any moment and to watch for His coming—and believe at the same time that certain signs must come first. That doctrine—that Christ's coming is imminent, the time of His coming unknown and unknowable—is clearly taught in the Bible.

But one cannot hold to the imminency of Christ's return and at the same time believe that there had to be a first World War before Christ could return or that Christ could not return before the nation Israel was established in Palestine or that Christ could not return before the present wave of modernism and worldliness.

Every reader may take his choice: believe in Christ's imminent return, as taught in the Scriptures, or believe that Christ's coming had to await certain events. The two doctrines are irreconcilable. They cannot be harmonized. The intelligent Bible believer cannot hold to both positions. And the Bible certainly clearly teaches the imminent return of Christ, that is, that Christ may return at any moment.

That being true, it will naturally be impossible for anybody to tell when we are in the last days of this dispensation. That being true, there can be no signs which definitely show the approach of the return of Christ. If Christ has to wait until certain signs appear before He can return, then His return is not imminent.

On the other hand, if Paul was right to expect the Lord's return in his day, as he did, speaking of "we who are alive and remain unto the coming of the Lord" (I Thess. 4:15), then all are wrong who think that Christ's coming is now indicated by World Wars I and II, the great falling away of these days, the founding of the nation Israel in Palestine, etc.

Either Christ might have come at any moment, as He taught, or He could not return until certain other events occurred. Both cannot be true. If Christ cannot now return until the Gospel is preached to some tribes in the Amazon Valley, then the imminent coming of Christ could not be true.

But let me say again: the imminency of Christ's coming is clearly taught in the Bible.

To the disciples on Mount Olivet and to all succeeding generations of Christians, Jesus commanded, "Watch therefore: for ye know not what hour your Lord doth come" (Matt. 24:42).

Again He said to them and to us, "Therefore be ye also ready: for in such an hour as ye think not the Son of man cometh" (vs. 44).

Again He said to these disciples and to all Christians who come after them, "Watch therefore, for ye know neither the day nor the hour wherein the Son of man cometh" (Matt. 25:13).

Then He told them, "And what I say unto you I say unto all, Watch" (Mark 13:37).

If these Scriptures are to be taken at honest face value, then all Christians, including those first disciples and Christians of all ages, have been commanded to watch for Christ's return, since He might come at any moment.

Christ's second coming, then, does not now wait, and never did wait, on any world events.

2. No One Knows Even Approximately When Jesus Will Come

In the Olivet discourse the Saviour discusses the second coming. The clearest point in all His teaching on the second coming is that no one knows when it will be. Consider Mark 13:32-37:

"But of that day and that hour knoweth no man, no, not the angels which are in heaven, neither the Son, but the Father. Take ye heed, watch and pray: for ye know not when the time is. For the Son of man is as a man taking a far journey, who left his house, and gave authority to his servants, and to every man his work, and commanded the porter to watch. Watch ye therefore: for ye know not when the master of the house cometh, at even, or at midnight, or at the cockcrowing, or in the morning: Lest coming suddenly he find you sleeping. And what I say unto you I say unto all, Watch."

Now observe the clear teaching of the Saviour that no man can know the time.

1. The angels do not know when Jesus will come.

2. While on earth the Lord Jesus Himself did not know when He would return.

3. Jesus said His second coming was so wholly unpredictable that He illustrated it by the servants waiting for their master's return. The master might come in the evening, midnight, cockcrowing or in the morning.

In this world no one can foretell even approximately when Jesus will return and when this age will end. If the more than nineteen hundred years which have already elapsed since Christ promised to return be divided up into four watches or periods to represent evening, midnight, cockcrowing and morning, we find that Jesus is saying that no one can know even within centuries of the time of His return.

4. The all-important teaching of Jesus about His return is that He may come at any moment.

Jesus may not come for another one hundred years, for five hundred years, for one thousand years. People often say, "Jesus is coming soon." That is not what Jesus said. He said, "Behold, I come quickly" (Rev. 22:7). We know Jesus will come suddenly. Whether He will come soon or late, we do not know. Whether He will come at evening or at midnight or at cockcrowing or in the morning, we do not know. Jesus said that we are not to know. We are simply to wait. We are to expect His coming, to be ready for His coming and to be doing His blessed will in carrying the Gospel to every creature, but we do not know even the approximate time of His coming nor of the end of this age.

This same strong teaching is given in Matthew 24:36-39. Again we have the clear statement of Jesus that no one can know even the approximate time of His coming.

"But of that day and hour knoweth no man, no, not the angels of heaven, but my Father only. But as the days of Noe were, so shall also the coming of the Son of man be. For as in the days that were before the flood they were eating and drinking, marrying and giving in marriage, until the day that Noe entered into the ark, And knew not until the flood came, and took them all

away; so shall also the coming of the Son of man be."

Again Jesus states that no man can know the day or hour of His return. He repeats that even the angels in Heaven do not know the time, and then He illustrates the total lack of information which any man can have about the time of the second coming. As it was in the days before the Flood when people ate, drank, married, and gave in marriage and had no hint of the time when the Flood would come until "the flood came and took them all away," just so surprising and unforeseen will be Christ's second coming. Before the Flood they did not know even one day ahead when it would come.

So from the words of the Lord Jesus Himself, we properly infer that we cannot know even one day ahead of time when Jesus will come.

Again this question of Christ's return and the restoration of the kingdom to Israel was brought up by the disciples after Christ's resurrection. Read the discussion in Acts 1:5-7:

"For John truly baptized with water; but ye shall be baptized with the Holy Ghost not many days hence. When they therefore were come together, they asked of him, saying, Lord, wilt thou at this time restore again the kingdom to Israel? And he said unto them, It is not for you to know the times or the seasons, which the Father hath put in his own power."

Jesus had told the disciples to tarry and wait there until they were endued with power from on high. They were to be baptized with the Holy Ghost and so supernaturally empowered for soul winning.

Do you ever find Christians more concerned about the technical details of prophecy, more concerned about speculation as to the time of Christ's return, than about soul winning? Well, before the twelve apostles were Spirit-filled they had the same carnal viewpoint. Instead of rejoicing that they were to be filled with the Spirit for soul winning, they immediately jumped to the hopeful conclusion that Christ referred to His return, the restoration of David's throne and the future independence of Israel. So they said, "Lord, wilt thou at this time restore again the kingdom to Israel?"

Then Jesus in strong and emphatic language told the disciples that the time and season of His glorious return and the restoration of Israel were not within their province at all, not matters for them to know.

"It is not for you to know the times or the seasons, which the Father hath put in his own power. But ye shall receive power, after that the Holy Ghost is come upon you: and ye shall be witnesses unto me both in Jerusalem, and in all Judaea, and in Samaria, and unto the uttermost part of the earth." —Acts 1:7, 8.

It is good to remember that the carnal mind seizes on externals rather than spiritual internals. The carnal nature is more concerned with incidentals than fundamentals. Men would rather be baptized than born again. Men would rather talk in tongues than have the mighty soul-winning power of the Holy Spirit. Just so, modern, speculating ultradispensationalists prefer to look for signs rather than to obey the Great Commission and to win souls.

Let us clearly understand what Jesus taught. 'It is not for us to know the times or seasons' concerning the second coming. Not the day, nor the hour, not the year, not the era of the second coming can be foreseen. Jesus expressly said that the Father deliberately kept this secret and it is not one that Christians should seek to know.

3. Date-Setting, Speculation, an Embarrassing Heresy

How it appeals to foolish human pride for a man to think, *In my superior wisdom I have figured out something others do not know!* And, particularly, Bible teachers like to show their superior understanding of the Scriptures and the times, because: first, perhaps 'the discovery' is sensational and will help get a crowd of excited hearers and, second, perhaps it will be a good alibi for man's powerlessness and fruitlessness in soul winning.

Men try to make the headlines by predicting when the next war will begin and when the next depression will be upon us. One can arouse more excitement and attract more attention if he can give plausible evidence that he has discovered approximately when the Saviour will return. That indicates that such a Bible teacher is more spiritual, more discerning, more everything that a proud, carnal heart desires to appear to be! It is not surprising, therefore, that we have constantly recurring efforts to set the approximate date of the Lord's return.

For example, more than a century ago a farmer in New York state named Miller started to read his Bible and discovered, he thought, what the scholars had overlooked. By making a day mean a year (which it never does) he took some of the prophecies of Daniel from out of their setting and figured that Jesus must return on a certain day in 1846. Convincing many of his neighbors that he was right, these Millerites made themselves white robes and got ready for the rapture. They waited in vain on hilltops and haystacks for the Saviour to catch them away.

One day I sat at dinner with Dr. Lowe, a professor of Biblical Interpretation at the Practical Bible Training School, Johnson City, New York. He told me that his people lived in the community of Farmer Miller and many of them had been convinced that Jesus was coming on the day announced by Miller.

One uncle planted no crops. Why should he when he wouldn't be there to gather them? He showed his faith by sitting on his front porch while others toiled. But Jesus did not come, and that winter thirteen of his cows starved while he and his family barely lived on the milk from one cow and from corn meal given by a neighbor.

Seventh-day Adventists are the spiritual descendants of the Millerites, and many of them still try to figure the time of the Lord's return by misinterpretation of Daniel's prophecy.

How foolish to think that the secret of the date of Christ's return is given in the book of Daniel and that Jesus and none of His disciples knew it!

The British-Israel cult could not find the date of Christ's return in the Bible, so they turned instead to the Great Pyramid, counting it an inspired revelation like the Bible. In the ascending passage leading to the Tombs of the Kings in the pyramid they figured that one larger portion with a higher ceiling would represent the time of Christ's return; so they took a tape measure from the supposed original edge of the pyramid through the passage to the enlargement. They counted every inch a year and so began to foretell when Jesus would come!

One greatly heralded British-Israel teacher in Los Angeles predicted that Jesus would come September 16, 1936, as I recall. Needless to say, his prophecy was proved wrong, and his influence was broken. Date-setting for the return of the Saviour has always been a heresy which turns out with embarrassment.

In my boyhood I saw in the old opera house at Gainesville, Texas, a picture prepared under the direction of "Pastor Russell" of the "Millenial Dawn" cult. He predicted, "Millions now living will never die," and his books agreed that Jesus would come in 1914. When 1914 brought not the return of the Saviour but the first World War, Pastor Russell said Jesus came invisibly. The Russellites, later called Rutherfordites, now called Jehovah's Witnesses, still teach this heresy. But they still die!

Since speculation as to the date of the return of Christ has proved so foolish in the past and always is connected with heresy, it seems that Bible-believing Christians would take seriously the word of Jesus, "It is not for you to know the times or the seasons, which the Father hath put in his own power" (Acts 1:7).

Such speculations are carnal and grow out of human pride and from misinterpretation of the Bible. No one knows even approximately when Jesus will return. No one knows the day, the year, the generation when Jesus will return. He may come today. Praise His name, I would be glad to see Him! But there is no way for any honest Bible student to foretell whether Jesus will come soon or after hundreds of years.

4. No "Signs" of Christ's Coming by Which We May Know It Is Near

In my early ministry I sometimes preached on "Signs of Christ's Second Coming." I had a chapter on that subject in my book, *The Coming Kingdom of Christ.* In a second edition I was compelled to modify my teaching. I was compelled to see that the next thing on God's program, as far as Bible prophecy is concerned, is Christ's coming in the air to receive His saints when the Christian dead shall be raised and living saints changed and called up to meet Him in the air.

That event is imminent; it may occur at any time. If Christ may come at any moment, then obviously we need not wait for any signs. And any signs could not make Christ's coming other than imminent, could not prove He would come this year or day and could not prove He would not come this year or day.

The Bible teaching is that Jesus may come at any moment, signs or no signs. He could have come even in apostolic days before any recent events could have occurred.

But did not Jesus speak about signs of His coming? Jesus spoke particularly of one sign, but that was not a sign of the first phase of His coming and the rapture but a sign which will occur after the rapture, at the close of the Tribulation Period, before Christ comes visibly, triumphantly, to the earth to reign.

This sign is mentioned in the Olivet discourse of Jesus. In Matthew 24:3 we have the disciples' question, "Tell us, when shall these things be? and what shall be the sign of thy coming, and of the end of the world?"

You see, the disciples asked, "What shall be the sign of thy coming, and of the end of the world?" Or better translated, "What is the sign of thy coming, and of the end of the age?"

In Luke 21:25-27 Jesus answered about signs:

"And there shall be signs in the sun, and in the moon, and in the stars; and upon the earth distress of nations, with perplexity; the sea and the waves roaring; Men's hearts failing them for fear, and for looking after those things which are coming on the earth: for the powers of heaven shall be shaken. And then shall they see the Son of man coming in a cloud with power and great glory."

It is similar to the passage in Matthew 24:29, 30 where Jesus mentioned the sign in these words:

"Immediately after the tribulation of those days shall the sun be darkened, and the moon shall not give her light, and the stars shall fall from heaven, and the powers of the heavens shall be shaken: And then shall appear the sign of the Son of man in heaven: and then shall all the tribes of the earth mourn, and they shall see the Son of man coming in the clouds of heaven with power and great glory."

Note the following facts about Jesus' answer.

1. The sign is to be "immediately after the tribulation." I understand from the Scriptures that the Tribulation cannot begin till after the rapture, so Jesus must come into the air to receive His saints before the Great Tribulation. "The sign" is after Christ's coming for His saints, not before.

2. We see that Christ's coming referred to by the prophets was His coming to the earth to reign after the rapture. Jews would naturally look forward to the part of Christ's coming that will affect them, when Jews will be regathered from all the earth, when the "angels. . . shall gather together his elect from the four

winds, from one end of heaven to the other'' (Matt. 24:31), when Christ will destroy all the enemies of the Jews and overthrow all Gentile dominion and restore David's throne in Jerusalem and sit on David's throne.

It is this kingdom that the apostles asked about in Acts 1:6: ''Wilt thou at this time restore again the kingdom to Israel?'' Gentile Christians are naturally more concerned about the rapture, the first phase of Christ's coming. But Old Testament prophecies in the interest of Jews center mainly in the second phase of Christ's coming—His revelation to Israel.

After the world is in the Great Tribulation time it will be very simple for those who know the Bible to learn when Jesus will return. There must be seven years in Daniel's seventieth week. The Great Tribulation time itself is announced to continue 3½ years, 42 months, 1,260 days (Dan. 7:25; Rev. 11:2, 3; Rev. 12:14). The terrifying reign of the Man of Sin is definitely limited. After the first phase of Christ's second coming, the rapture, the second phase must come within a specified time. And just before Jesus returns to the earth with saints and angels to fight the Battle of Armageddon and set up His kingdom, the sign of His coming will appear in the heavens.

There is no sign of Christ's coming promised before the rapture. No preacher has a scriptural warrant for preaching that current events are signs of Christ's soon return. Mussolini was not the Antichrist, as some Bible teachers thought, and they will be as foolish if they so designate Stalin or Tito.

We are not to believe Christ is coming because of some ''signs'' but because He said so!

5. Christ's Coming Does Not Await the Preaching of the Gospel to Every Creature

A great missionary leader, a friend whom I greatly admire and love, has recently published a book in which he pictures an imaginary scene. Satan is pictured as in counsel with the princes of darkness, the leading demons who supervise his work in various countries. Some demons report proudly that the Gospel is not being preached in the countries over which they bear evil sway, and all gloat that Christ cannot now return until these people hear the Gospel.

Missionaries shot down or discouraged before they can enter Afghanistan and the failure of missionary groups to reach other isolated tribes are cited. And then Satan himself and his demons are pictured as being greatly distressed and defeated because at last there is prospect of the Gospel being preached to every creature.

Now, though they have defeated Christ's planned return so long, it appears that the Gospel will be preached to every creature and the Saviour will return.

It is here taught that Jesus cannot return to take away His saints until the Gospel is again preached to all the world.

But I believe that to be an entirely wrong interpretation of Scripture. The Gospel has already been preached to all the world in early Christian times, if not in this generation. And if Jesus could not return until the Gospel is preached to every tribe again, then His plain commands to watch, that He might come at any time, would seem out of place and misleading, if not actually dishonest. That surely we cannot concede.

The imminent coming of Christ, so clearly taught in the Scripture, means that He might have come at any moment, may come at any moment now, whether or not the Gospel is preached again to all the world.

Mistaught people sometimes think that Matthew 24:14 refers to a sign of Christ's coming: "This gospel of the kingdom shall be preached in all the world for a witness unto all nations; and then shall the end come." But the context shows that this is a message primarily for Jews who will be living in the Tribulation time and not for us today.

The next verse mentions the Abomination of Desolation, when the Antichrist will stand in the Temple in Jerusalem claiming to be God, which event must come after the rapture and which begins the Great Tribulation time. The following verse speaks of the flight of the Jews from the Man of Sin in those days, and verse 21 says, "For then shall be great tribulation, such as was not since the beginning of the world to this time, no, nor ever shall be."

So during the Great Tribulation time the Gospel of salvation will be preached to the world in view of Christ's literal return. The preaching of the Gospel to all the world mentioned in Matthew 24:14 will be after, not before, the first phase of Christ's coming.

The simple truth is that the Gospel has already been preached to all the world. Dr. R. A. Torrey called attention to two or three Scriptures which show that the Gospel has already been preached to all the world. In Acts 2:5, "There were dwelling at Jerusalem Jews, devout men, out of every nation under heaven"; and these men heard the Gospel at Pentecost. In Romans 1:8 Paul says "that your faith is spoken of throughout the whole world," and how could people have heard of the wonderful faith of the fine Christians at Rome if they had not heard the Gospel?

Colossians 1:4-6 also says that the Gospel had come to all the world in Paul's time. So Matthew 24:14 could not and does not teach that the Gospel yet is to be preached in all the world before Jesus comes.

Besides, if the preaching of the Gospel to some unknown tribe in Central America or the Amazon Valley is an event that must occur before Jesus can come, then Christ's coming could not be imminent, and the scriptural warning that we must watch since Jesus may come any day or year would be foolish.

Let us say again there are no signs that will indicate when Jesus is to come. And there is not a single prophetic event which must come before the rapture of the saints.

6. The Modern Establishment of a Nation Israel Not "the Budding of the Fig Tree," Not a Sign of Christ's Soon Return

Editor Meldau of *Christian Victory* magazine, my esteemed friend, wrote me and about a dozen well-known Bible teachers, asking us to prepare a statement for a forthcoming issue of his good magazine on a subject something like this, "Is the reestablishment of Israel as an independent nation in Palestine the budding of the fig tree mentioned in Matthew 24:32, 33, and a sign of Christ's coming?"

I was glad to give my answer, and glad indeed when the symposium came out in the good magazine that nearly all the Bible teachers agreed that the recent establishing of an independent nation of Jews in Palestine *did not* fulfill the prophecy of the budding of the fig tree as foretold in Matthew 24:32, 33, and was not especially a sign of Christ's soon return.

Since that matter has often been misunderstood, let us read the passage involved and see what the Saviour said in that Olivet discourse about the budding of the fig tree.

Matthew 24:29-34 reads as follows:

"Immediately after the tribulation of those days shall the sun be darkened, and the moon shall not give her light, and the stars shall fall from heaven, and the powers of the heavens shall be shaken: And then shall appear the sign of the Son of man in heaven: and then shall all the tribes of the earth mourn, and they shall see the Son of man coming in the clouds of heaven with power and great glory. And he shall send his angels with a great sound of a trumpet, and they shall gather together his elect from the four winds, from one end of heaven to the other. Now learn a parable of the fig tree; When his branch is yet tender, and putteth forth leaves, ye know that summer is nigh: So likewise ye,

when ye shall see all these things, know that it is near, even at the doors. Verily I say unto you, This generation shall not pass, till all these things be fulfilled."

Let us note very simply some of the things which Jesus taught in this passage:

1. The time discussed is at the close of the Great Tribulation, and some time after the rapture of the saints. It is "immediately after the tribulation of those days. . . ." So the parable of the fig tree does not apply to these days before the rapture and before the Great Tribulation, but to the days "immediately after the tribulation." Nothing before the Tribulation Period could be meant here. It is quite clear that recent developments in Palestine are not meant, since they did not happen "immediately after the tribulation of those days. . . ."

2. The meaning of the parable is explained. Certain events which will follow the Great Tribulation are like a fig tree whose branch is tender and which puts forth leaves in the spring. These events are the appearing of the sign of the Son of man in Heaven, when Christ starts to return, and the sight of the Son of man coming in the clouds of Heaven, and the sending of the angels to regather Israelites from all over the world. Then verse 33 says, "So likewise ye, when ye shall see all these things, know that it is near, even at the doors."

When converted Israelites at the close of the Great Tribulation time or other saints converted in that Tribulation time see Christ coming in the clouds of Heaven with power and great glory to set up His throne at Jerusalem and reign on the earth, and when they see the angels of God sent out miraculously around the world with the great sound of a trumpet to regather the elect, God's chosen nation Israel, from among all the lands of the earth, then these troubled people may know that Christ's coming and reign is immediately at hand.

So there would be no use speculating about the matter, since the meaning of the parable is clearly given in the words of the Saviour Himself.

And we should distinguish between the present immigration of godless Jews into Palestine, unconverted and unrepentant, and going by human means and with human purposes, from that other great gathering when every Jew left alive in the world will be gathered by the angels and brought to Palestine at Christ's return.

The present movement in Palestine is human, not particularly a subject of Bible prophecy. It has no particular significance except that the Scripture indicates that some Jews will be in Palestine and will make a treaty with the Antichrist in the Tribulation time. The present influx of Jews into Palestine is not the great regathering which will be done miraculously by the angels of God when Jesus returns in person to reign, after the rapture and after the Tribulation Period.

3. We must make sure to notice, too, that the coming of Christ here mentioned is the second phase of His coming. It is not His coming into the air invisibly to raise the Christian dead and receive them and us together and carry us away for a honeymoon in Heaven. This is not the coming of Christ *for* His saints but the coming of Christ *with* the raptured saints, after the Tribulation is over.

The rapture will come, as most reputable premillennial Bible teachers agree, before the Great Tribulation time. Then after the Great Tribulation (which will occur in Daniel's seventieth week) Christ will return with these saints and with angels to fight the Battle of Armageddon, to destroy the kingdom of the Antichrist, and to set up His throne at Jerusalem and reign on the earth for a thousand years of joy and peace.

There are two separate phases of Christ's coming. That for which we wait is His coming into the air to receive His saints. Then after the Tribulation time, those who will have been converted on the earth will long for Christ's return, with us, to set up His kingdom. It is this second phase of Christ's coming—when He shall come literally to the earth to take charge and to reign—that is discussed in this passage.

4. Jesus said in verse 34, "Verily I say unto you, This generation shall not pass, till all things be fulfilled." I rather think that "this generation" means the race of Jews, and the race will not be destroyed despite all the Hitlers and Antichrists. Dr. Scofield's notes on this verse say about *generation*:

> Gr. genea, the primary definition of which is, "race, kind, family, stock, breed." (So all lexicons.) That the word is used in this sense here is sure because none of "these things," i.e. the world-wide preaching of the kingdom, the great tribulation, the return of the Lord in visible glory, and the regathering of the elect, occurred at the destruction of Jerusalem by Titus, A. D. 70. The promise is, therefore, that the generation—nation, or family of Israel—will be preserved unto "these things"; a promise wonderfully fulfilled to this day.

But if the word *generation* here means people living in one particular life-span, it still could mean only that group living "immediately after the tribulation of those days..." as Jesus Himself places them in verse 29. The so-called "budding of the fig tree" cannot happen until after Christ comes for His saints after the Great Tribulation.

I am glad personally that there is now a land where oppressed Jews will be welcomed. But these Jews, going back in unbelief, have possession of only a very small portion of the land of Israel. They do not have even undisputed possession of Jerusalem. They have not gone back under the blessing and forgiveness of God. Blindness in part is still upon Israel. The veil is not yet taken away from their faces. The great future regathering and conversion of Israel will take place by supernatural means after the Tribulation time. And the establishment of a little state called Israel in recent months is not a sign that Christ may come soon. Christ may come very soon, but His coming needs no sign such as that to prove it. He may not come for long years. No one knows.

Let me stress with all my soul that current events do not especially affect the simple fact that we can have revival now, that God is in the saving business, and that anytime God's people meet God's requirements, they may have His glorious power and the manifestation of it in the saving of multitudes of souls, in great revivals.

Those who go by the newspapers and are greatly excited by current events may feel that the atomic bomb, the hydrogen bomb, the nuclear bomb, the upsurge of communism, the modernism in many churches, the possibility of a World War III and the establishment of the modern nation Israel mean we are in "the last days," therefore, great revivals are impossible.

But those who steadfastly depend upon the words of Christ will remember, "The grass withereth, and the flower thereof falleth away: But the word of the Lord endureth for ever" (I Pet. 1:24, 25). The harvest is still great and the laborers few. If God's people, called by His name, shall humble themselves, and pray, and seek His face, and turn from their wicked ways, God will hear from Heaven, will forgive their sin, and heal their land, as He promised in II Chronicles 7:14.

All of God's promises are still true. God's tender heart toward sinners still yearns for them to be saved. God's Holy Spirit has all the convicting and saving power He ever had. The Word of God is still quick and powerful and sharper than a twoedged sword. The blessed promise of Jesus, "He that believeth on me, the works that I do shall he do also; and greater works than these shall he do; because I go unto my Father" (John 14:12), is still true.

Do not let false teachings and heresies about these so-called "last days" keep you from believing the Word of God—that we can have revivals now!

<table>
<tr><td>

"The Last Days," a Blessed Age of Revival

</td><td>

4

</td></tr>
</table>

Many people use the term "the last days" to mean the time since World War I or the last ten or twenty-five or fifty years before Christ returns to catch away His saints. Very generally such hyper-dispensationalists mean that a certain period just before Christ will return is now upon us and that in these so-called "last days" sinners are harder, conditions more desperate, and greatest revivals not possible, or at least very unlikely.

But that use of "the last days" is unscriptural. The Bible does not use the term in that sense but in another. We ought to mean what the Bible means when we use "the last days" in speaking of Bible matters.

I should like to show you that "the last days" in Scripture really means the period from before Pentecost until Christ's return; that "the last days" is never used in the New Testament to refer to the last few years before Christ returns; and that "the last days" are intended to be a whole age of revivals—from Pentecost on until the kingdom of Christ comes.

Since on this matter there has been much misinformation and since our whole attitude toward the possibility of great revivals and soul-winning work will depend upon how we understand this question, I urge every reader to be very prayerful and careful to understand exactly what the Scriptures say on the subject.

1. "The Last Days" in Scripture Means the Period From Before Pentecost Until Christ's Return

On the day of Pentecost the mocking crowd was astonished because the apostles and other disciples preached the Gospel in their own language and in mighty power to Jews out of every nation under Heaven. Some doubted; others mocked. But Peter stood up to explain the matter, as recorded in Acts 2:15-21:

"For these are not drunken, as ye suppose, seeing it is but the third hour of the day. But this is that which was spoken by the prophet Joel; And it shall come to pass in the last days, saith God, I will pour out of my Spirit upon all flesh: and your sons and your daughters shall prophesy, and your young men shall see visions, and your old men shall dream dreams: And on my servants and on my handmaidens I will pour out in those days of my Spirit; and they shall prophesy: And I will shew wonders in heaven above, and signs in the earth beneath; blood, and fire, and vapour of smoke: The sun shall be turned into darkness, and the moon into blood, before that great and notable day of the Lord come: And it shall come to pass, that whosoever shall call on the name of the Lord shall be saved."

Joel said, as quoted by Peter, "And it shall come to pass in the last days, saith God, I will pour out of my Spirit upon all flesh.... And it shall come to pass, that whosoever shall call on the name of the Lord shall be saved." When the mighty power of God came at Pentecost and three thousand were saved in a day, Peter says, "This is it! These are the last days about which Joel spoke!"

Here we have the inspired statement that "the last days" included Pentecost. By divine inspiration Joel had in mind Pentecost when he promised that, "in the last days, saith God, I will pour out of my Spirit upon all flesh." This is a Scripture which clearly defines for us the New Testament meaning of "the last days." So let us use the term in the Bible sense.

According to this Bible use of the term, it would be utterly improper to call just the period since World War I or the last few years before Jesus comes, whenever that may be, "the last days." "The last days" includes this whole age of grace, beginning with Christ and having its first great typical manifestation at Pentecost.

Bible Christians ought to follow Bible terminology, or at least they ought not use Bible terms in a sense utterly foreign to the way they are used in the Bible. To say, "We are in the last days," is all right if you mean the gospel age including Pentecost, the whole period covered by the Great Commission. But it is not all right if you mean only the recent ten or twenty or fifty years.

No one can know how near we are to Christ's return, so it is improper to say that we are in the last days before Christ's return on that ground. And it would be improper to use the term, "the last days," if we mean the term to be a scriptural term, without including Pentecost.

At Pentecost Peter said, "This is that." Pentecost was included in the blessed prophecy of Joel, that in the last days God would pour out His Spirit and send great revivals.

Certainly "the last days," as defined in Joel, did not end at Pentecost. If we go back to the passage in Joel 2:28-32 and the following verses in chapter 3, we can see that Joel had in mind a period reaching far beyond Pentecost, to the return of Christ, the restoration of Israel, and related events. Even the part quoted by Peter in Acts 2:15-21 speaks of great catastrophes in the heavens and the sun and moon "before that great and notable day of the Lord come." And the very next verse in Joel, after those Peter quoted, beginning chapter 3, says, "For, behold, in those days, and in that time, when I shall bring again the captivity of Judah and Jerusalem...."

The period called "the last days" will continue to Israel's

restoration. The subheads of the third chapter of Joel, as given in the Scofield Reference Bible, are, "The restoration of Israel," "The judgment of the Gentile nations after Armageddon," "Retrospect: the day of the Lord," "Full kingdom blessing." I give them here to show that Joel really foretold a whole age, the revival age, the gospel age which would include Pentecost and run on to the return of Christ, the regathering of Israel and their conversion. This is the period of time called in the Scriptures, by divine authority, "the last days."

This great period of time announced by Joel as "the last days" is co-existent with the scope of the Great Commission. Jesus said in Matthew 28:19, 20:

"Go ye therefore, and teach all nations, baptizing them in the name of the Father, and of the Son, and of the Holy Ghost: Teaching them to observe all things whatsoever I have commanded you: and, lo, I am with you alway, even unto the end of the world."

The Great Commission covers a period of time beginning with Christ and ending with the "end of the world," that is, the "consummation of the age."

At once the spiritual mind sees the fitness of the great promise. God is to pour out His Spirit upon all flesh. Sons and daughters, servants and handmaids, old men and young men are to be filled with the Spirit of God and are to prophesy, that is, to witness with the supernatural power of the Holy Spirit. And during this entire age it is promised, ". . . it shall come to pass, that whosoever shall call on the name of the Lord shall be saved." During this gospel age the Gospel was to be taken to all the world, as the Great Commission had clearly outlined.

Not to Jews only was the Gospel to be preached, but literally to every creature (Mark 16:15). It is true that in Old Testament times one who sought God could find Him. It is true that Jonah preached the Gospel to the heathen at Nineveh and many were converted. It is true that there is evidence that Nebuchadnezzar, that Naaman the Syrian, that Ruth the Moabitess, that Rahab the Canaanite harlot, and many other Gentiles turned to God and were saved. But during Old Testament times the Gospel was not boldly carried to every creature.

So it was not true in this same beautiful sense then, as it is now, that "whosoever shall call upon the name of the Lord shall be saved." The "whosoever" is more prominent in this blessed gospel day.

It is also fitting that, when Jesus commands us to go to all the world, He promises power for our ministry. How sad if anyone were commanded to take the Gospel and could not have poured upon him the Holy Spirit! How sad for anybody to be commanded to preach the Gospel and get sinners saved, if he could not have a supernatural enduement of power!

You see, this great gospel age we are in now is the age of the Great Commission, the period called in the Bible "the last days." We ought not use the term in any other sense contrary to this clear Bible usage. Those who speak of "the last days," meaning these present days we are in as a separate time not like the rest of the gospel age, are wrong.

2. "The Last Days" Is Terminology Not Used in the New Testament to Refer to the Last Few Years Before Christ's Return

Several times in the New Testament, language like this is used: "these last days" (Heb. 1:2), "in the latter times" (I Tim. 4:1), "in the last days" (II Tim. 3:1), "in the last days" (II Pet. 3:3), "the last time" (I John 2:18). It is a striking fact that in none of these passages does the terminology refer to the last few years before Christ shall come.

Let us consider these Scriptures and others often used as if they marked the time we are now in, perhaps since World War I, as if it were a separate time of declension where there would be less soul winning. We will find that they do not mean the present time more than other times, and they ought not to be used in preaching that certain things now occurring are signs of the soon coming of Christ. That is a misuse of the Scriptures, since they do not refer to this time more than the whole age. As to that, you can judge for yourself after a careful examination of the Scriptures.

1. Note Hebrews 1:1, 2:

"God, who at sundry times and in divers manners spake in time past unto the fathers by the prophets, Hath in these last days spoken unto us by his Son, whom he hath appointed heir of all things, by whom also he made the worlds."

Here, "in these last days" is used of the time in which Jesus Christ brought God's revelation to earth in person, when He walked on earth. In the ministry of Jesus Christ, then, began the period of time called "these last days." The period properly means the whole age, we suppose, as defined by Joel, and the period certainly began with Jesus Christ.

2. Consider I Timothy 4:1-3:

"Now the Spirit speaketh expressly, that in the latter times some shall depart from the faith, giving heed to seducing spirits, and doctrines of devils; Speaking lies in hypocrisy; having their conscience seared with a hot iron; Forbidding to marry, and commanding to abstain from meats, which God hath created to be received with thanksgiving of them which believe and know the truth."

"In the latter times," this Scripture says, "some shall depart from the faith, giving heed to seducing spirits, and doctrines of devils; Speaking lies in hypocrisy; having their conscience seared with a hot iron." But verse 3 tells us that this departure from the Faith, under the influence of seducing spirits and doctrines of devils, with seared conscience and lying tongue, will result in certain heresies. First, those who depart from the Faith will forbid people to marry; second, they will command to abstain from meats.

Does anyone suppose that these are recent heresies? We know that for centuries the Catholic church has forbidden priests and nuns to marry. In medieval times more stress was laid upon this than today. There were countless thousands of monks of every kind, and monasteries and convents on every hand. Here "in the latter times" could not refer to the last few years.

We also know that the Catholic church has commanded its members not to eat meat on Friday or during lent, etc. These commands are not of God. But this heresy has come down for centuries. And "the latter times" certainly does not mean, in recent years. It must mean that in this gospel age, at various times, such heresies will again arise as they have already arisen.

3. Consider II Timothy 3:1-5:

"This know also, that in the last days perilous times shall come. For men shall be lovers of their own selves, covetous, boasters, proud, blasphemers, disobedient to parents, unthankful, unholy, Without natural affection, truce-breakers, false accusers, incontinent, fierce, despisers of those that are good, Traitors, heady, highminded, lovers of pleasures more than lovers of God; Having a form of godliness, but denying the power thereof: from such turn away."

What does "in the last days" mean in this Scripture? Verse 6 says: "For of this sort are they which creep into houses, and lead captive silly women laden with sins, led away with divers lusts." Some of that sort were living even when Paul wrote the letter to Timothy.

And in verse 8 Paul says, "Now as Jannes and Jambres withstood Moses, so do these also resist the truth: men of corrupt minds, reprobate concerning the faith." Again Paul is writing in the present tense. Paul himself knew some of these wicked people in the last days and said, ". . . so do these also resist the truth: men of corrupt minds, reprobate concerning the faith." And he uses Jannes and Jambres in the time of Moses as an example. So we know this is not a new kind of heresy.

Modernism is not new. Falling away from the truth is not new. For people to have a form of godliness but to deny the power thereof, as prophesied in verse 5, is not new. All the Pharisees in the time of Christ were guilty of that sin. We certainly could not say that Paul meant, by divine inspiration, to here picture the last few days or years of this age, just before Christ would come. He was talking about the course of the whole age, and the things mentioned here have been manifested throughout the age. Some of it was manifested in Paul's time, and he refers to definite men then alive who were guilty of the things mentioned.

It is perfectly all right for a preacher to preach on II Timothy 3:1-5, but it is wrong for him to leave the impression that the sins here mentioned are marks of the last few years and not of the whole age, the whole period of "the last days" as defined by Joel.

4. Consider II Peter 3:3, 4:

"Knowing this first, that there shall come in the last days scoffers, walking after their own lusts, And saying, Where is the promise of his coming? for since the fathers fell asleep, all things continue as they were from the beginning of the creation."

In the last days there shall come scoffers who will walk after their own lusts and doubt the second coming of Christ. Now consider honestly: Is this a mark only of the last few years?

I was converted at nine years of age, joined a sound Baptist church when I was twelve, was baptized, then heard fine preaching all my life. There was never a doubt about the inspiration of the Bible, the deity of Christ, the need for the new birth. My teachers and preachers were not modernists. Yet I never heard any clear teaching on the second coming of Christ all these days. I did not hear it when I attended Decatur Baptist College nor when I attended Baylor University, where I got my degree. I did not hear it in the good Southwestern Baptist Theological Seminary which I attended. Not until I had been out of the seminary some years was the matter forcibly brought to my mind and I began a careful study.

Until I was about thirty, I was always among good Christian people, good Bible preachers, but I never heard anything taught about the second coming of Christ! Forty years ago most Christians in America knew nothing about the second coming of Christ. But a hundred years ago they knew even less. The truth is, premillennial truth and teaching about the second coming of Christ became prominent in America largely through the ministry of D. L. Moody, R. A. Torrey, and the teachers and preachers whom they called together and helped to establish in this matter. The truth was spread widely through Bible institutes and Bible conferences which grew out of the ministry of D. L. Moody, R. A. Torrey, and their associates. For hundreds of years there had been little teaching about the second coming of Christ. In England the Plymouth Brethren spread widely the teaching about Christ's coming.

Commentaries written long ago scoff at the "Chiliasts," that is, those who believe in a millennial reign of Christ on earth. Those who believed in Christ's personal, premillennial return and reign were counted literalists and fanatics. There is more teaching right now about the second coming of Christ than the world has heard for three hundred or four hundred years!

So this heresy of men walking after their own lusts and scoffing at the second coming of Christ is not a new heresy. We cannot say that it is peculiar to the last few years since World War I, and it certainly will not be peculiar to the few years before the Lord Jesus returns, whenever that may be.

So "in the last days" evidently means during this gospel age, as defined by Joel. It certainly does not mean some particular short period in the last part of this age when, according to some, there can be no more great revivals!

5. Consider I John 2:18:

"Little children, it is the last time: and as ye have heard that antichrist shall come, even now are there many antichrists; whereby we know that it is the last time."

Here twice is the clause, "it is the last time," but it is obvious that John meant the time then present. And that verse expressly says that, though one great Antichrist is to come after the rapture of the saints, antichrists were present then.

All those who cry that great apostasy is on, that there are hearts which are hardened against God, that this age is a wicked age with the spirit of Antichrist, should notice that it has been so in every age!

These are the last days, beginning before Pentecost, really beginning with Christ. These are the last days before Christ will come to personally take over the world and destroy the wicked Gentile world powers. But it was "the last time" when John the apostle wrote his first epistle. The great falling away had already begun then, as it has begun in every age.

So the term, "the last time," is meant to fit the whole age and not any last few years of the age. It does not fit the 1950s or 1960s any better than it fit the year A. D. 90. A man who preaches on this text must preach that the whole age is alike, with the falling away of people, with hatred and opposition to the Gospel, and with wicked, anti-Christian people, infidels, atheists and haters of God occurring all through the age.

From a consideration of all the passages which speak about the last days in the New Testament, it is quite clear that the term in the Bible never means just the few years preceding Christ's coming. And it is quite clear that God has not set off the last few years before Christ's coming to be different from the rest of the age. God has not even intimated in the Scriptures that before Christ comes there will be a special period of time when men will be harder, when revivals will be impossible or more difficult. All that is the manufactured excuse of those who do not pay God's price for revival and for soul winning.

It is the subconscious rationalization of people who do not feel that God is able to meet this age, do not feel that the Gospel is sufficient, do not feel that God's power and God's promises are sufficient. It is the excuse of those who are defeated, backslidden and unbelieving. Or it is the cry of those who have been misled in doctrine by the ultradispensationalists who have taught a false doctrine about a period of "last days" at the close of the age—in which it is not supposed that there can be great revivals and when it is supposed men are more wicked, that God's Word does not work the same, and that revivals are much more difficult, if not impossible.

The Scriptures teach the exact opposite—that the whole age alike is the age of revival.

3. "The Last Days" Are This Whole Age of Great Revival

To many, any thought of the last days is a thought of defeat, of sadness about the futility of Christian work. It ought not so to be. The term, "the last days," ought to bring real joy to the heart; for it means this age of grace, this age when the Great

Commission is given to us, this age in which Christ has promised, "And, lo, I am with you alway, even unto the end of the world." It means this age which is to be marked by great revivals, and those revivals are to mark the end of the age as well as the beginning of it—at Pentecost.

Consider again Joel's prophecy quoted by Peter at Pentecost, and let us see some of the blessed features which mark this whole age, features which make soul winning comparatively easier than in other ages, and make great revivals always possible.

First, the whole age is to be characterized by the pouring out of the Holy Spirit upon Christian workers. In Acts 2:17, 18 Peter said:

"And it shall come to pass in the last days, saith God, I will pour out of my Spirit upon all flesh: and your sons and your daughters shall prophesy, and your young men shall see visions, and your old men shall dream dreams: And on my servants and on my handmaidens I will pour out in those days of my Spirit; and they shall prophesy."

"I will pour out of my Spirit upon all flesh," on all kinds of people, on all races. The Holy Spirit is not to be poured out upon a prophet here and there, but upon Christians everywhere who are willing to pay God's price for soul winning.

Sons and daughters shall prophesy (which means to speak and witness in the power of the Holy Spirit). Young men shall see visions, old men shall dream dreams. Even on servants and handmaidens God will pour out in those days of His Spirit, and they shall witness for Christ in the supernatural power of the Holy Spirit.

We cannot emphasize too strongly that these blessed promises are for the whole age. This mighty pouring out of the Holy Spirit came upon John the Baptist, the forerunner of Christ (Luke 1:15). It came upon Christ Himself before He started His public ministry (Luke 3:21, 22). The mighty power of the Holy Spirit came upon the apostles after they had waited at Pentecost. That mighty revival at Pentecost was "a specimen revival," as D. L. Moody loved to say.

Oh, how we need to learn that it is the pouring out of the Holy Spirit which enables people to speak for God with power! The Spirit-filled testimony, the Spirit-empowered prophesying of Christians, whether sons and daughters, servants and hand-maidens, old men or young men, is what is needed to win souls. Without a supernatural enabling, a supernatural enduement of power, it is impossible to win souls, impossible to have great revivals.

But, thank God, this pouring out of the Holy Spirit is characteristic of this age. D. L. Moody had it, just as did Peter at Pentecost. R. A. Torrey, Billy Sunday, and every other soul winner have had it. We, too, may be filled with the Holy Spirit, mightily endued with power from on High for soul winning. It is the heritage of this age! It is the first mark clearly promised for these last days, which began with Christ's ministry and had its great, typical, sample manifestation at Pentecost.

If we may have the fullness of the Holy Spirit, then we may have revivals! We can have God's best, God's all, if we but have the mighty power of His Spirit! Thank God that all through this age, even to the end, the Lord has promised this power to those who seek His face and pay His price! We can have revival now because we can have the floodtides of the Holy Spirit, just as they had at Pentecost. It is the divinely given mark of this age!

And again, let us take courage from this blessed Scripture passage which Peter quoted from Joel at Pentecost: "And it shall come to pass, that whosoever shall call on the name of the Lord shall be saved" (Acts 2:21). This is said of the whole period of time, including Pentecost and all the time down until the coming of Christ to reign, and His kingdom, on earth.

We have called attention already to the fact that the great revival in the Tribulation Period will be wrought by the same fullness of the Spirit as the great revival at Pentecost. The beginning and ending of the age, and all in between, are to be marked not only by the pouring out of the Holy Spirit upon God's people for witnessing and soul winning, but by the wonderful ease with which anyone who will may be saved! "Whosoever shall call on the name of the Lord shall be saved."

Every honest heart who wants salvation may have it. Only those who will not come to Christ miss salvation. Those who are willing to trust in Christ and receive Him are never cast out! What a simple, wonderful, beautiful offer of salvation: "Whosoever shall call on the name of the Lord shall be saved." Every sinner who honestly asks for mercy may have it. And this is a mark of the whole age.

Note the "whosoever." This is a Gospel not just for Jews but for Gentiles, too—all races, in every clime, in every circumstance. It is a Gospel for the rescue mission and the slums of the cities, a Gospel for little children as well as reprobates and derelicts. It is a Gospel for mature, upright, moral religionists like Nicodemus. Whether up-and-out, whether down-and-out, this "whosoever" includes all—heathen people in every race, darkest Africa and poor enslaved China. And this "whosoever" is, in a particular way, the mark of this whole age.

And this verse indicates that the aim of the Gospel throughout the age is the same—to get people saved. The expectation of the church ought to be that people will be saved. Every preacher should aim his preaching at this, which is the aim and intention of the Gospel and a great mark of this gospel age.

People should be saved under our preaching! Our Sunday schools, our preaching services, and all the work of the church auxiliaries should head up in this one thing—getting people to call on Christ for mercy and be saved.

The salvation of multitudes of sinners is a characteristic of this whole age, as it was the striking characteristic of the services at Pentecost when Peter spoke these immortal words quoted from Joel: "And it shall come to pass, that whosoever shall call on the name of the Lord shall be saved."

How wonderful that the age should have near its beginning this mighty outpouring of the Holy Spirit, this mighty revival at Pentecost! It seems quite clear to any careful student that Pentecost was intended to be a great sample of what the Gospel would do. The Gospel was preached there to Jews, devout men out of every nation under Heaven, as if to remind us that the whole age would be marked by the spread of the Gospel to every race everywhere. In other words, Pentecost was intended to be the first fulfillment of obedience to the command to take the Gospel to every creature.

The disciples had been commanded, along with the Great Commission, to tarry at Jerusalem until they should be endued with power from on High. It was impossible, they were told, to do the work they were ordered to do without supernatural enduement. They waited; and when the mighty power of God came, the revival at Pentecost resulted.

The revival at Pentecost is intended to be a sample revival, a pattern for the whole age.

Were there miracles there? Yes. And that is as if the Lord Jesus would say that we may have His power in any measure necessary. There would be no situation, no age, no civilization, no hardness of human hearts, no combination of circumstances of which the Christian, filled with the Holy Spirit, might not be the master, might not be enabled to win souls in those circumstances.

It is true that Christians may be persecuted and may sometimes die for Christ. But the course of the Gospel through this age is intended to be a triumphant course. The promise of Psalm

126:6 is, "He that goeth forth and weepeth, bearing precious seed, shall doubtless come again with rejoicing, bringing his sheaves with him." It is a triumphant and certain end that a Christian faces when he goes in the power of the Holy Spirit, preaching and witnessing the Word of God to lost sinners! Pentecost is a sample of what Christians ought to have throughout this wonderful age of grace, these "last days" prophesied by Joel and Peter.

They spoke in tongues at Pentecost, but mark you, only in the natural languages of people then present who heard the Gospel. This is evidently intended to be a sample and model case here. The gift of tongues was not a gift in some strange jabber, given only for the ecstasy and private and selfish joy of the Christian. The gift of tongues means that we can have help for any genuine need in getting out the Gospel. If I must get the Gospel to a Chinese man who cannot understand English, and if I have no time or cannot learn the languge, then God can, when He wills, give me the power to speak to the man in his own language.

We ought to take Pentecost as a sample of what God planned to give Christians during this age, the power we should have and the results we should have.

Perhaps one of the reasons D. L. Moody had such mighty power and won a million souls to Christ and shook two continents was that D. L. Moody believed that God would give him this same power, these same kinds of revivals; and, praise God, He did!

I hope that every honest reader will shake out of his mind the wicked defeatism which often accompanies the thought of "the last days." "The last days" means this whole gospel age. It is an age of the pouring out of the Holy Ghost. It is an age of the conversion of multitudes. It is an age when "whosoever shall call on the name of the Lord shall be saved."

The fullness of the Spirit, the power to win souls, is for all flesh—servants and handmaidens, old men and young men, sons and daughters—all who will pay God's price for fullness of power.

What a wonderful gospel age in which we live! How our unbelief, our defeatism, our selfish alibis for our powerlessness and fruitlessness have grieved God! These "last days" are the blessed days of revival, the one period in all the world when revival is easiest, when the power of God is promised in the greatest fullness, when the Gospel is offered most freely to every creature! Let us take advantage of our heritage, and enter into the power promised and the fruitage promised!

Fainthearted Christians, who watch the clouds so much they do not sow and observe the wind until they do not reap, are defeated by the manifest wickedness on every side and do not believe that God can give revival now.

Many cite coldness of Christians, modernism and infidelity in many pulpits and denominational leadership, the widespread appeal of pleasure, the outrageous wickedness on every hand as evidence that God cannot or will not give great revivals as He once did.

But if fainthearted Christians should make a study of the great revivals in Bible times, they would find that these revivals came in most cases in the midst of wickedness as great and apostasy and false religions as prevalent as those we face today. It is a most heartening study to observe some of the great revivals in the Bible and see how, against amazing odds, God used one person or a few, to turn a whole nation or a strategic city back to God.

There are innumerable examples.

Among captive Israelites in far-off Babylon, Nehemiah had his heart warmed and stirred and was used in a revival that took a remnant back to Jerusalem and reestablished the nation Israel in Palestine, with walls and gates rebuilt, and eventually the Temple, so that Christ could be born in a Jewish Beth-

lehem and preach in Jerusalem and there be crucified according to prophecy.

There was the revival under the mighty preaching of John the
Baptist when for four hundred years the heavens had been shut
up, without a prophet, without a divine revelation—and when
unregenerate, formal Pharisees on the one hand and rational-
istic, unbelieving Sadducees on the other had made of the Jewish
religion a powerless thing of dead letter and no heart, no contact with God. That was a mighty revival, under the most unlikely circumstances, when all Jerusalem and Judaea went out to
hear John preach by the Jordan and were baptized, confessing
their sins.

But I pass these and other examples of great Bible revivals
to mention only four. These include the great revival led by Elijah on Mount Carmel, the revival at Nineveh led by Jonah, both
in the Old Testament; the revival at Sychar in Samaria where
the Saviour won the woman at the well, and the revival at
Pentecost, both in the New Testament.

These show, beyond any shadow of doubt, that the God of the
Bible can give revivals in the most distressing situations of
declension, apostasy, idolatry and sin, provided He has one or
a few who can lay hold on God's mighty power by obedient faith
and prevailing prayer and will give God's witness to sinners.

1. God Could Have a Revival in Decadent, Idolatrous Israel at Mount Carmel

One of the most remarkable revivals this world ever saw was
led by the Prophet Elijah at Mount Carmel, among the Northern
tribes, when Ahab was king, described in I Kings 18, which
seemed to save the nation from utter and immediate ruin. At
least it helped to postpone the captivity and destruction of Israel;
and it must have resulted in multitudes truly turning to God.

Consider, first, how wicked the times were, how apostate the people, when this revival occurred. Ahab, the son of Omri, was king. Read how wicked Ahab was:

"And in the thirty and eighth year of Asa king of Judah began Ahab the son of Omri to reign over Israel: and Ahab the son of Omri reigned over Israel in Samaria twenty and two years. And Ahab the son of Omri did evil in the sight of the Lord above all that were before him. And it came to pass, as if it had been a light thing for him to walk in the sins of Jeroboam the son of Nebat, that he took to wife Jezebel the daughter of Ethbaal king of the Zidonians, and went and served Baal, and worshipped him. And he reared up an altar for Baal in the house of Baal, which he had built in Samaria. And Ahab made a grove; and Ahab did more to provoke the Lord God of Israel to anger than all the kings of Israel that were before him."—I Kings 16:29-33.

Later it was said of Ahab, "But there was none like unto Ahab, which did sell himself to work wickedness in the sight of the Lord, whom Jezebel his wife stirred up" (I Kings 21:25).

Notice that Ahab walked in all the sins of Jeroboam. He "went and served Baal and worshipped him." He built an altar to Baal in a temple of Baal which he built in Samaria, the capital city. He made a grove for idolatrous and lewd ceremonies unspeakable. He married Jezebel, a wicked heathen woman, a murderess and idolater. And "Ahab did more to provoke the Lord God of Israel to anger than all the kings of Israel that were before him." What a blight upon the nation! It would appear difficult to have a revival in Israel under such conditions.

Later we are told that Jezebel killed all the prophets of the Lord except one hundred whom Obadiah hid (I Kings 18:13).

The whole nation seems to have turned to Baal worship. And, as far as we know, no prophets were active nor anyone else outspoken for God in the whole nation, except Elijah.

Obadiah, the governor of the palace, was a man of God but

a secret disciple, a timorous soul who dared not speak out for the right and who would not risk his place and income by boldly coming out for God. Secretly he hid prophets of God in a cave and fed them on bread and water, but he had no power with God, no influence with men for God. The whole nation would have gone to Hell for all that Obadiah could do about it, without paying a new price for power.

So great was the sin in the land that God had turned His face away. He had revealed to Elijah that there would be no rain, nor even dew, for years, as His curse. So Elijah told Ahab, "As the Lord God of Israel liveth, before whom I stand, there shall not be dew nor rain these years, but according to my word" (I Kings 17:1).

After three and one-half years of drought, Elijah came to show himself to Ahab, urging him to call the people of Israel to Mount Carmel, with the 450 prophets of Baal and the 400 prophets of the groves, all of which ate at Jezebel's table. These 850 wicked, idolatrous prophets came, along with the multitudes, to Mount Carmel. There the one man of God challenged Baal and the prophets of Baal, insisting that they ask for a miraculous manifestation from God or from Baal. "And the God that answereth by fire, let him be God," said Elijah.

The people were unmoved by Elijah's exhortation. "How long halt ye between two opinions? if the Lord be God, follow him: but if Baal, then follow him." The people answered him not a word.

It is a time when preaching falls on deaf ears.

It is a time when the rulership of the nation is idolatrous and murderous.

It is a time when society is sold out to false cults and evil religions. It is a time when God has turned His face away.

It is a time when what few believers there are in the whole nation keep themselves hidden.

Now, if God can give a revival in those circumstances, He can give one today!

You know the thrilling story told in I Kings 18. Elijah asked that the prophets of Baal put a bullock on their altar, with wood under it but no fire. He asked them to pray for their god to answer by fire.

Throughout the day, until the time for the evening sacrifice, the prophets of Baal prayed, "O Baal, hear us."

Nobody answered! Nobody ever did answer the heart that depended on any god but our God. No heathen religion ever did show a single example of answered prayer, such as is commonplace with Christians. Demons show themselves, but the hand of a great God has never appeared when men called on any god but the true God.

These prophets leaped on the altar, cut themselves with knives and lancets till the blood gushed out, but—no answer. Perhaps they did not expect one. At least they put on as good a show as anybody could, they must have thought.

Then Elijah called the people to come near. It was time for the Lord God of Israel to show His power. Elijah rebuilt the altar that was broken down, using twelve stones. He put wood upon the altar, but no fire. They killed the bullock and placed the sacrifice on the wood. Then Elijah asked for four barrels of water. It was poured over the sacrifice. The wood was now soaking wet. Then four barrels more, then four barrels more; then Elijah had them fill a trench round about the altar with water.

Let everybody know that, when the fire of God falls now, it is a miracle, not human and natural, but supernatural and extraordinary. A God who cannot have a revival in hard times, a God who cannot start a fire with wet wood would not be sufficient for this wicked world.

Then Elijah prayed:

"Lord God of Abraham, Isaac, and of Israel, let it be known

this day that thou art God in Israel, and that I am thy servant, and that I have done all these things at thy word. Hear me, O Lord, hear me, that this people may know that thou art the Lord God, and that thou hast turned their heart back again." —I Kings 18:36, 37.

Then, marvel of marvels, God answered!

"Then the fire of the Lord fell and consumed the burnt-sacrifice, and the wood, and the stones, and the dust, and licked up the water that was in the trench. And when all the people saw it, they fell on their faces: and they said, The Lord, he is the God; the Lord, he is the God." —Vss. 38, 39.

Oh, to see multitudes on their faces convinced and surrendered to the Lord God! Oh, to see the idolaters, the unbelievers, the atheists, the drunkards, the harlots, the worldlings on their faces bowing to Jesus Christ as Saviour and Lord, like Elijah saw them that day, trusting and confessing Him!

Well, the God who brought revival to Mount Carmel can do it again!

Our own nation is no further gone into sin than was Israel under the leadership of Ahab and murderous Jezebel. The modern infidels in the pulpit, the false cults, the atheists in our colleges are not more arrogant nor more powerful than the prophets of Baal and the lewd prophets of the groves in Elijah's time. Preachers these days who stand true to the Bible and to God have far more company than Elijah did, who stood alone.

In your community, in your own heart, in your own meager talents, in your own sin-cursed nation, do you have only wet wood with which God may build a revival fire? Are the circumstances all apparently against God, against revival?

If so, then remember that the God of Elijah can set a fire to wet wood. He can give a revival in the face of Ahab and Jezebel and 450 prophets of Baal and 400 prophets of the groves and an arrogant, thoughtless, rebellious, apostate people. The God who could give a revival at Mount Carmel can give one now! How wicked, how unbelieving we are when we do not depend on such a God for revival!

2. God Could Have a Revival Even in Violent, Heathen, Fish-Worshiping Nineveh

A second example is that of the revival in Nineveh under Jonah. However unwilling was the evangelist until God worked him over, the revival at Nineveh was one of the greatest in the history of the world. And it is a good example to prove to us that in any circumstance of wickedness, of idolatry, of false religion, of the impending doom and wrath of God, revivals are possible if only God can have workers who will pay His price for revival.

Nineveh was not a city of the Jews but a heathen city. We suppose that it was one which had never heard the Gospel. We suppose that the only worship there was idolatry. We read that they worshiped the fish god, and this may be one reason why God prepared a great fish to swallow Jonah and then to vomit him out on dry land. Be that as it may, here is a city so idolatrous, so violent, so wicked, that God said to Jonah, "Arise, go to Nineveh, that great city, and cry against it; for their wickedness is come up before me" (1:2). And the message that God had for Nineveh was, "Yet forty days, and Nineveh shall be overthrown" (3:4).

The city was large and mighty. "Now Nineveh was an exceeding great city of three days' journey" (3:3). and Jonah went one day's journey into it before he began preaching.

We understand from archeologists that Nineveh included several settlements, all under one king, and one outer wall, perhaps. The population was so great that it contained "sixscore thousand persons that cannot discern between their right hand and their left hand; and also much cattle," as God told Jonah (4:11).

The presence of cattle indicates that the city contained pastureland and suburbs, besides settlements. The suburbs were included, and that makes reasonable the size indicated by three days' journey. If there were 120,000 children and babes who did not know their right hand from their left, there may have been 600,000 population in the city.

The king, the nobles, the people were wicked. God's wrath was aroused against the city. He had determined to destroy it, so sent Jonah to announce its destruction. The city seemed almost past hope of redemption.

Yet when God got one man ready to preach to the city, the king, the nobles and the people repented in sackcloth and ashes and pleaded for God's mercy, until the dear Lord repented of His plan and would not destroy it.

It is significant here that Jonah did not want to go to Nineveh and preach. I dare say that this is simply an illustration of the thing the Saviour so often said, "The harvest truly is plenteous, but the labourers are few" (Matt. 9:37), and "The harvest truly is great, but the labourers are few" (Luke 10:2), and, "Say not ye, There are yet four months, and then cometh harvest? behold, I say unto you, Lift up your eyes, and look on the fields; for they are white already to harvest. And he that reapeth receiveth wages, and gathereth fruit unto life eternal" (John 4:35, 36).

The trouble is not with the harvest but with the laborers! God's trouble about revival is not with the world but with the church. And His trouble is not with the sinners but with the saints. Anywhere God can get Christians who will pay God's price, He can give a revival.

So God could and did have a mighty revival in Nineveh as soon as He could get Jonah ready.

Consider the message of Jonah. It was what modernists and many weaklings would today call "a negative sermon." He preached, "Yet forty days, and Nineveh shall be overthrown."

It was a message that appealed to fear, a message of judgment. It proclaimed the wrath of God, not His mercy. Yet God used that message to bring revival.

That ought to remind us that, if men are willing to preach as God tells them to do—preaching His righteousness, His hatred of sin, His solemn warning, His judgments, the certain eternal destruction of Christ-rejecting sinners—God can use that kind of preaching to bring a revival in the most distressing, wicked and unpromising situations.

If God could give a mighty revival in Nineveh, with no better worker than Jonah and with no more Gospel than he preached, God can have a revival in any wicked city in America, with proper prayer, power, testimony and preaching of the Word in the power of the Holy Spirit. We can have revival now, surely, since God could have a revival in Nineveh.

3. Christ Could Have a Revival in Half-Breed, Prejudiced Samaria

Another good example of revival under difficulties is that in the little Samaritan town of Sychar. John, chapter 4, tells how Jesus departed into Galilee, "And he must needs go through Samaria." At Sychar He sat on the curbing of Jacob's well, tired after a half day's walk. At noon a woman came to draw water. She was a woman of shabby character, one often married and now living with a man to whom she was not married. Despite her own hostility, the indifference of the disciples, and the enormous prejudice that separated Jews and Samaritans, Jesus led her to see what a sinner she was and how she needed a Saviour, and then revealed Himself.

She was wonderfully saved and ran to the city, leaving her waterpot, to say to the men, "Come, see a man, which told me all things that ever I did: is not this the Christ?" Then the multitude came out to see Jesus.

Many were saved at the woman's testimony before they ever saw Him. Others believed when they saw Him and heard Him speak, and said to the woman, "Now we believe, not because of thy saying: for we have heard him ourselves, and know that this is indeed the Christ, the Saviour of the world" (vs. 42).

The difficulties which would seem to prevent a revival were almost insuperable. The Samaritans hated the Jews, and with some reason. In Luke 9:51-54 we read how the Samaritans in one village would not even give Jesus a room and bed when they learned that He was going to Jerusalem. Sense their hostility:

"And it came to pass, when the time was come that he should be received up, he stedfastly set his face to go to Jerusalem, And sent messengers before his face: and they went, and entered into a village of the Samaritans, to make ready for him. And they did not receive him, because his face was as though he would go to Jerusalem. And when his disciples James and John saw this, they said, Lord, wilt thou that we command fire to come down from heaven, and consume them, even as Elias did?"

Jesus rebuked His disciples. He came to save, not to destroy. But one would think that the same Jesus and the same disciples would have difficulty bringing a Heaven-sent revival to a city of such prejudices, ignorance and hate.

Even the woman to whom Jesus talked was full of suspicion. When He asked for a drink, she said, "How is it that thou, being a Jew, askest drink of me, which am a woman of Samaria? for the Jews have no dealings with the Samaritans." As the talk proceeded she insisted that Samaritans had the well that their father Jacob had given, so they needed no help from any Jew!

There was also the difficulty of the woman's sad past and her sinful present. She had been married five times; now she lived with a man to whom she was not married.

Would she confess her sins? Would she renounce her present

wicked alliance? Gently, Jesus pressed the matter of her sin and told her that He knew all about it. When she saw her need of the Messiah, Jesus said, "I that speak unto thee am he." And the woman was won.

But consider also the hostility or indifference of the disciples, which was nearly as bad as the prejudice of the woman! They had been into the city to buy food and said not a word to those they met of the Son of God, the Saviour of the world who sat on the curbing of the well outside the city! They marveled that Jesus talked to the woman. Why should He waste time on a Samaritan, particularly on a shabby, castaway woman such as this one appeared to be? When Jesus was dealing with her soul, they thought only of their stomachs! They could hardly see the point when Jesus said, "I have meat to eat that ye know not of."

Here are twelve disciples to whom Jesus will give the Great Commission to take the Gospel to every creature, and a poor, sinful woman whom they ignore and despise! And when Jesus wins her to repentance and faith and salvation under their very noses, they take no notice of what goes on, being absorbed only with food for their bodies.

If any pastor today feels that a revival is hindered by the indifference in his own church, let him remember that a part of the work of revival is to revive the saints, to give them a burden for sinners, to get them on a praying basis, and to arouse in them a burden for souls! Part of the work of every revival effort is to get Christians ready for revival.

There would be little credit to an evangelist who could have people converted only when the church was right to start with, and when all the Christians were on fire, burdened, praying and working.

Note that in this revival effort there was no building, no advertising, but the glad testimony of a converted soul! There were none of the outward conveniences that we often think necessary to revival. Yet in the midst of this suspicion and hate, despite the indifference, even the callousness and prejudice of His disciples, Jesus got the woman saved; then she helped to bring the whole town to Jesus!

Does some earnest soul winner face the fact that the people with whom he would labor are self-satisfied religionists? Are they well content because they were christened when babies and confirmed in the church when they learned the catechism? Are they jealous of the forms of their own cult and satisfied with the externals of religion?

Well, their case is not so bad as these Samaritans who said, "Our fathers worshipped in this mountain; and ye say, that in Jerusalem is the place where men ought to worship" (John 4:20). They had their own well, dug by their ancestor Jacob. They knew the true religion as well as anybody. Weren't they descended from Abraham, Isaac and Jacob? And for many, many years their fathers had worshiped in this mountain, and here came some narrow-minded Jews who thought you should worship in Jerusalem! That was about their attitude.

But God could give revival there, and He can give revival now, if God finds some people anywhere who will pay His price.

Deep in the heart of this sinful woman there was a need, a longing. She may have been a sinner, but she had a conscience, as does every other sinful woman, every other depraved man! She was a sinner, and she had lived in outrageous sin, but she feared death. Something in her heart cried out for forgiveness, cleansing and peace, which she could not find, however many men she lived with. That hunger was not immediately apparent, but it was there. The harvest really was white.

And the people in the city were probably as prejudiced and as unlikely as she to be friendly toward a Jewish preacher. Yet when they saw a woman really transformed, a shabby, sinful woman forgiven, cleansed and happy, and found that the Lord

Jesus knew all about her heart and therefore about their hearts and their sins, they were glad to turn to Him. Some were so eager to be saved that they trusted in the Saviour on the woman's word. Others went to see Him and hear Him first, then were gladly saved.

The Saviour was right when He said:

"Say not ye, There are yet four months, and then cometh harvest? behold, I say unto you, Lift up your eyes, and look on the fields; for they are white already to harvest. And he that reapeth receiveth wages, and gathereth fruit unto life eternal: that both he that soweth and he that reapeth may rejoice together." — John 4:35, 36.

The harvest was ripe then; it is ripe now. It did not appear to be ripe to the eye of unbelieving and indifferent disciples. To the cold in heart, the backslidden, the worldly-minded, the self-satisfied, the harvest does not appear to be ripe now. The harvest does not appear to be ripe now to preachers who have no passion, who do not have the mighty moving of the Spirit of God upon them. But, oh, if you who hear and you who read will be filled with the Spirit of God, you will find that God has hungry hearts everywhere, and the revival will come when you pay God's price.

Isn't it blessed how God can use the most unlikely instruments in revival! That poor Samaritan would seem to be a very unlikely instrument in revival. But her glad testimony had this to recommend it: she really meant business! She had no time to carry water now, so she left her waterpot at the well. She had a message to tell. Her heart overflowed with it! She ran, she did not walk! And she exaggerated the matter a little, as a woman might be forgiven for doing under the circumstances, when she said, "Come, see a man, which told me all things that ever I did." Jesus did not really tell her everything that she ever did. But He gave her enough as a sample that she knew that He knew everything that she ever did.

Oh, God can use anybody as a soul winner, provided he is thoroughly, with all his heart, committed to the soul-winning business and sets out to work at it with all his heart. The Holy Spirit can come upon such weak Christians and give mighty power to what they say and what they do.

You see, there is no complaint about the harvest. It is white. Many could be won. God's trouble is with the laborers! He had to bypass Peter, James, John, Bartholomew, Andrew, Matthew, James the less, and others, and had to save this poor Samaritan woman before He could get anybody to win souls in Sychar.

The harvest truly is plenteous, but the laborers are few. Anywhere God can get some Christians ready to pay His price, He can have a revival. He had a revival at Sychar; He can have one in your city, or in any city, where a few people will pay God's price to be used in soul winning.

4. God Could Give a Revival in the Hardest City— Jerusalem—Fifty Days After the Crucifixion!

If ever there was a gospel-hardened city, it was Jerusalem after the crucifixion of Christ. Here John the Baptist had preached like a flaming fire! Spirit-filled John, mighty in the Scriptures, had called men to repentance and had baptized multitudes in the River Jordan. Many of the Pharisees and Sadducees had rejected John's preaching, but they had felt the impact of it.

Then the Saviour Himself was announced and began His public ministry. He had preached and baptized (through His disciples) more disciples than John. He had worked mighty miracles. He had raised Lazarus from the dead in Bethany just outside Jerusalem, and everybody in the city knew it. He had opened blind eyes, cleansed the lepers, stilled storms, saved a maniac, wrought all kinds of miracles.

He had ridden into Jerusalem, according to the prophecy of Zechariah 9:9, "upon a colt the foal of an ass," and the multitudes had thrown their garments before Him and littered the road with palm branches as He made His triumphal entry.

He had boldly claimed to be the Messiah. He had driven the moneychangers from the Temple. He had warned of the coming destruction of Jerusalem.

Many were saved, but the Jewish leaders were not. They hated Jesus with an unreasoning hatred and set out to kill Him.

At last they had their way. At the Passover season the high priest and the Sanhedrin, with scribes and Pharisees, planned to take Jesus. They bribed one of His followers, Judas, the only unsaved one of the twelve, to lead them to Jesus in the night. He was tried in an illegal season of the Sanhedrin at night, then condemned in Pilate's judgment hall, but only by political pressure on the governor.

Then with suborned witnesses and with an incited mob, the people were moved to deny their King, to choose for release Barabbas instead of Jesus. And Jesus, despised and officially rejected by His nation, was scourged with a Roman scourge, mocked, blindfolded and crowned with thorns, then made to bear His cross out to Golgotha. And there, amid the jeers of the multitudes, Jesus hung six hours and died.

Was there ever a city so steeped in religion of a formal kind, a Christ-rejecting kind? They knew more about Passover lambs and atoning blood in Jerusalem than any city in the world now knows. They knew more about tithes and offerings and public prayers and forms and ceremonies of religion than any other group in the world did. They were insanely proud of their circumcision, of their descent from Abraham, of their prophets and their Mosaic law. They had hated John the Baptist, and John had gotten his head cut off. They hated the Lord Jesus Himself and killed Him, murdered the Son of God! What chance would there be here in Jerusalem for a revival now?

And consider the shameful state of His disciples. When Jesus was arrested, the disciples all deserted Him and fled (Matt. 26:56). Judas had betrayed Him for thirty pieces of silver, the price of a common slave. Then this treasurer of the little band had hanged himself. The frayed rope later broke, and his body fell and burst open, his bowels gushed out. It was a scandalous bit of gossip all over Jerusalem!

And worse still, the main spokesman for His disciples, Simon Peter, at the trial had consorted with the soldiers who were to crucify Jesus, and then had openly denied that he was a disciple of Jesus, even cursed and swore that he did not know Jesus!

So betrayed, denied and deserted by His friends, the Lord Jesus came to trial. And He died with only three or four Christians near the cross: Mary, the mother of Jesus; Mary Magdalene, John, and perhaps one or two more.

Let that defeated, unreliable, immature bunch of disciples reassemble and try to have a revival now in Jerusalem! Let Peter, who cursed so loudly a few weeks ago and denied that he even knew Jesus, now try to preach Christ to these multitudes! What chance have they for a revival in Jerusalem?

But they had it nevertheless! They waited in an upper room for ten days. "These all continued with one accord in prayer and supplication, with the women, and Mary the mother of Jesus, and with his brethren" (Acts 1:14). And when the day of Pentecost was fully come, the power of God came upon them. They were filled with the Holy Spirit, as John had been filled and as Jesus had been filled at His baptism. Being filled with the Spirit, they spoke the Word of God with boldness and power.

God stretched out His hand to give miraculous confirmation of their message. Sinners were cut to the heart, there was a great repenting, and three thousand were saved in one day and added to the church! Then multitudes of others were saved day after day in the mighty initial revival, the sample revival which God gave early in the age for all of us to know what He could do and wanted to do in revivals.

If God could give a revival in Jerusalem at Pentecost, He can give one anywhere. Never a city, never a country in the world where people have hated Christ more than they hated Him at Jerusalem. Never a city or country in the world where they have rejected more pure Gospel and have despised more the manifestation of God's grace, than at Jerusalem. Nowhere in the world is there a place where God's disciples have failed Him so signally as that little band of disciples seemed to have failed Christ in the hours of His arrest, trial and death.

They did not even believe that He had risen from the dead. They had thrown away all their hopes. Peter had quit the ministry and had gone back to fishing. Thomas would not believe in His resurrection for a week after others had been convinced of it. But the Lord Jesus met and empowered those disciples and used them in a mighty, mighty revival!

Oh, then, weak, discouraged Christians, you who have made a shabby failure of your lives, take heart! The Lord Jesus can empower and use you mightily if you will but wait upon Him with holy abandon and seek and find the fulness of the Spirit for soul-winning power!

We know God can give us a revival now because He gave one at Jerusalem, at Pentecost. How foolish to suppose that times are getting too hard for God, or hearts are getting too hard for God, or the circumstances are too difficult for God to deal with! Oh, rather how we ought to say that our great God, with the power of the Word of God and the power of the Spirit of God and in answer to the prayers of His believing people, can give a revival anywhere, when we meet His requirements and pay His price!

If we are willing to wait upon God and plead His promises and stay before Him in humility and seek until we find the mighty power of the Holy Spirit, we too can have Pentecostal revivals.

We have taken these four examples of revivals in Bible times to show that God can give revivals in the most difficult times. We could have taken many other examples, all of them proving the same thing—that our mighty God has grace greater than all the sin in the world; that the Gospel is the power of God unto salvation; that the Holy Spirit can reach the hardest and most wicked hearts.

And I have shown that God has one great need—a need for Spirit-filled, empowered workers, those with a holy abandon and a deep, moving compassion that puts soul winning above everything else!

It took God longer to get Jonah ready to preach the Gospel than it took to get all Nineveh on their faces repenting.

It took the Lord Jesus longer to get one shabby Samaritan woman saved and ready to witness than it took to get many others saved.

At Mount Carmel, God could turn the hearts of all the people back to Him; He could put them on their faces crying out, "The Lord, he is the God; the Lord, he is the God!" just as soon as He had one man who could pray down the fire of God from Heaven!

And at Pentecost God could change hard hearts and save multitudes as soon as He had a group who were willing to wait before Him long enough and with singleness of mind to be mightily filled with the Spirit of God.

You see, it is the old, old story that Jesus often told: "The harvest truly is great, but the labourers are few" (Luke 10:2); and again, "The harvest truly is plenteous, but the labourers are few" (Matt. 9:37); and, "Say not ye, There are yet four months, and then cometh harvest? behold, I say unto you, Lift up your eyes, and look on the fields; for they are white already to harvest" (John 4:35).

God's great lack is not power enough to save sinners, not sinners enough who can be saved, not circumstances that are favorable. No. God suffers for lack of workers, and He earnestly pleads with us, "Pray ye therefore the Lord of the harvest, that he will send forth labourers into his harvest" (Luke 10:2; Matt. 9:37).

The trouble is not with the world, but with the church. The trouble is not with the sinners, but with the saints. The revival problem is a Christian problem. We can have revival now if we want it enough to do God's will.

We Can Have Revival Now Because of God's Infinite Resources, Freely Available for Soul Winning

6

Peter, walking on the water to come to Jesus at His command, saw the boisterous wind and waves and was afraid. He lost his faith and began to sink. His trouble was that he looked at the circumstances instead of the Lord Jesus, the Creator of all the winds and waves.

When Jesus wanted to feed the five thousand, Andrew said, "There is a lad here, which hath five barley loaves, and two small fishes: but what are they among so many?" (John 6:9). Andrew looked at the one boy's lunch of barley biscuits and sardines, looked at the great multitude of five thousand men, besides women and children, and knew that the boy's lunch was inadequate. But he was looking at the conditions instead of Jesus Christ.

So all who say that the apostasy on the part of Christian people is too great to have a revival, that the voice of atheism among scholars and infidelity in the pulpits is too loud and convincing for us to ever have a revival; those who say that the shrill voice that calls to pleasure with all the competition of radio, television, sports, luxuries, leisure, the theater, the dance, and enticing sin is too clamorous and loud for us to have a revival—such people are looking at conditions instead of at God. They forget the infinite resources which have always made revival possible, the resources abundantly available to all who would win souls according to the will of God.

Hear how Paul had mighty confidence in the resources of God, the spiritual weapons of our warfare!

"For though we walk in the flesh, we do not war after the flesh: (For the weapons of our warfare are not carnal, but mighty through God to the pulling down of strong holds;) Casting down imaginations, and every high thing that exalteth itself against the knowledge of God, and bringing into captivity every thought to the obedience of Christ."—II Cor. 10:3-5.

Oh, these mighty "weapons of our warfare"! Through God they are mighty "to the pulling down of strong holds."

Paul had wonderful success in his spiritual warfare, his conquest of men with the Gospel. His confidence was not based on any thought that men were easier to reach then than they might be in a later generation nor in any thought that the circumstances made the Gospel powerful. No, no! Paul had the infinite resources of an Almighty God at his command, and the weapons of his warfare were mighty to the pulling down of strongholds, and casting down imaginations, and bringing men to obedience to Christ.

When Paul contemplated going to Rome, the center of the world, to preach the Gospel, he wrote ahead to Christians in this city, "And I am sure that, when I come unto you, I shall come in the fulness of the blessing of the gospel of Christ" (Rom. 15:29). There was no failure to Paul. Whether at Corinth or Ephesus or at Rome, it was all the same. He could write to Corinth: "Now thanks be unto God, which always causeth us to triumph in Christ, and maketh manifest the savour of his knowledge by us in every place" (II Cor. 2:14).

What are these mighty spiritual weapons of our warfare? What are these infinite resources of God available to the soul winner, which load the scales always in favor of those who would have revival and are willing to pay the price for it?

I maintain that the infinite grace of God, always loving sinners, grace greater than all their sin; the mighty power of the Word of God when preached and witnessed in the Spirit, "the power of God unto salvation"; the miracle-working energy of the Holy Spirit when He fills and endues Christians; and the power of persistent, prevailing, heart-broken, believing prayer are resources that are absolutely irresistible and make revival possible now or anytime and anyplace in the world where people with holy abandon use these resources!

I. God's Inexhaustible Grace and Boundless Love for Sinners Make Revival Always Possible

If anyone here doubts whether we can now have as great revivals as were ever given to bless humanity and keep souls out of Hell, let him simply turn in his Bible and see if John 3:16 is still there! God loves this world! Let me say it again, because our hearts are so callous to the blessed truth that it makes little impression upon us—God loves this world and every sinner in it. The extent of His love is beyond human comprehension. He gave His own perfect Son to be a man, to be tempted as a man, to live a perfect life, to minister among men, then to die a shameful death of agony that men might be saved.

Do you believe that, if God had it to do over, He still loves lost men enough to let Jesus die? If it were to be, not the generation in Palestine nineteen hundred years ago but in this generation and in our modern world and civilization, with all its wickedness, its pride, its arrogance, its lewdness, its unbelief, its hatred of God and goodness—if it were to be in this generation, would God still give His Son to die? Does the heart of God beat with the same compassion and yearning over lost sinners as it ever did?

Do you believe it is still true, just as true as it ever was, that God loves the world with an infinite, boundless love that would pay *any* price that is proper and good to keep people out of Hell?

Remember that, when God gave His Son, He gave everything with Him. "He that spared not his own Son, but delivered him up for us all, how shall he not with him also freely give us all things?" (Rom. 8:32). Is that still the extent, measure and indication of the yearning, compassionate, weeping heart of God who will not stop until He has paid every price that infinite mercy can pay to save sinners and keep them from ruin?

I know that it is true! I know that the infinite grace of God is still on the side of revival, on the side of soul winning, on the side of mass evangelism. And the grace of God means that revival is possible.

I believe that part of our trouble is that we do not enter into this loving compassion, into this sacrificial giving of God and of Christ; and so, since we do not love men as Moody and Billy Sunday and Wesley and Spurgeon and Finney did, we do not believe that we can have the revivals they had. Oh, for some understanding and some holy union with God and Christ in compassionate love and grace that would save sinners!

Men talk to me about the sin of this world, about the wickedness of mankind, about all the strident clamor that would turn men's minds away from God. Men talk to me about the lawlessness of the age, the pre-occupation with pleasure, the strife between capital and labor, the warring between nations, the increase of divorce and the breakdown in the home, the lack of any authority in the home, and the breakdown of authority everywhere, whether in the laws of the nation or in parental supervision, even the authority of the Word of God over men's hearts.

But do you talk to me of sin? I know something greater than all the sin in the world! "But where sin abounded, grace did much more abound: That as sin hath reigned unto death, even so might grace reign through righteousness unto eternal life by Jesus Christ our Lord" (Rom. 5:20, 21).

I am conscious of the all-pervading rot and stench and bent and chaos and suction and lure and malevolence of sin! I find it in all the world about me. I find men depraved, degenerate, fallen, ruined and needing new hearts for the old wicked hearts. They need cleansing, forgiveness, new life for the deadness that is in men. I preach against sin and weep over it. I am ever conscious of it. Yea, I find it even in my own heart and nature. But, thank God, 'where sin did abound, grace did much more abound'!

Do you talk to me about apostasy, about a falling away in the churches, about the invasion of infidels coming in as wolves in sheep's clothing, claiming to be Christians when they are children of Hell, unregenerate, not believing the Bible, the enemies of historic Christianity who would tear the crown of deity with impious hands from the brow of Jesus Christ? Apostasy? Yes!

But where there is such sin, there is the grace of God, greater than all the sin in the hearts of impostors and infidels. It is greater than all the sin in the hearts of drunkards and harlots. It is greater than all the sin in unbelieving Jews, in rite- and priest-ridden Catholics. The grace of God is enough for sinners everywhere. And then it is more, much more, *infinitely* more than man's sin can ever require.

Oh, the boundless grace and love of God! Where there is such grace, such an outpouring of love and mercy and yearning and atonement, we can have revival!

This is just another way of saying that the cross of Jesus Christ, that Calvary, is so far-reaching, so colossal, such an outpouring of the heart of God for the saving of sinners, that revival is possible, that there is always an answer to sin that is more than enough. How we sin against the love of God and the grace of God when we give sinners up! How we sin against the love and grace of God and the price paid for sin when we give communities and nations up to sin!

Men who think the days of great revival are over have simply forgotten the infinite adequacy of the death of Christ, and the grace of God!

One may feel that all this is true, that God's love, God's grace, the atoning death of Christ, the intent and purpose of God is sufficient for revival, but may feel that he himself is totally inadequate to be used. Many Christians feel that they cannot win souls. Many preachers feel that they cannot be used as instruments in revivals, cannot be used to win hundreds, yea, thousands of sinners. Many feel inadequate to deal with drunkards and harlots, infidels and criminals, hardened old sinners and members of false cults. But again the grace of God is the answer.

Are you weak? Are you encumbered with care and temptation? Is there a sense of utter insufficiency and inadequacy? Does Satan himself send many a messenger of Satan to buffet you? Then let Paul tell you how he solved that problem.

Once when he begged God again and again that the thorn in the flesh might be removed so that he could have more power, so that he could be adequate for the burden and ministry laid upon him, God gave him the answer, "My grace is sufficient for thee: for my strength is made perfect in weakness." Paul then gladly accepted the grace needed: "Most gladly therefore will I rather glory in my infirmities, that the power of Christ may rest upon me. Therefore I take pleasure in infirmities, in reproaches, in necessities, in persecutions, in distresses for Christ's sake: for when I am weak, then am I strong" (II Cor. 12:9, 10).

God's grace is sufficient for you, dear Christian, to do all you ought to do, to be all you ought to be, to be a channel of the infinite grace of God to the hearts of sinners.

Never will I forget when early in my first full-time pastorate we came to a seeming impasse. I had started revival services.

I had, in my own heart, made this a condition: if the church would ask me to lead in revival services so that I would have a chance to get acquainted with the people and God would have a chance to use me in winning souls and in building up a poor, discouraged, divided congregation, I would accept the pastorate.

When they had agreed that I should lead in revival services, we were besieged by days of rain and storm. The pitiful handful of people who came were not expectant but impassive, though kindly. Many had vowed never to again attend the little church where there had been bickering, strife and barrenness. It seemed that even God had turned His face away. The church building had been struck by lightning and burned to the ground. Now we were meeting in a little board tabernacle. And I had come to the end of my strength.

That morning I walked up the railroad track, anywhere to be alone. I sat disconsolately upon a rock and cried out to God not to let me go back and face my problems and burdens in the ministry without some assurance that He was with me and would give victory.

I found this blessed passage where Paul learned the secret of grace sufficient for all the weakness, for all the thorns of Satan, all the infirmities, all the persecutions and distresses. God said to me, as He had said to Paul, "My grace is sufficient for thee: for my strength is made perfect in weakness."

I rose from there determined to have the strength of God in my weakness. A marvelous revival followed. And, thank God, for many long years I have found that always the grace of God, the marvelous, infinite, matchless grace of God is enough for revival, enough for soul-winning power.

Oh, do not go on defeated! Do not go on without power! Do not go on without the fruit of souls saved. God's grace is sufficient!

As long as the infinite grace of God is poured out upon mankind, we can have revival. Christians may have His power, may carry His message to sinners, may see men born again and lives changed, homes changed, communities changed by the grace and power of God!

Oh, it is a wonderful Gospel that I preach to you today! Grace for the drunkard! Grace for the harlot! Grace for the profane! Grace for the infidel! I have seen it work. How many drunkards I have seen made sober, whoremongers and harlots made pure. I have seen Catholics, Jews and members of other false cults and isms turn to God. I have seen the murderer made into a godly and humble and devoted child of God. I can bear witness that the grace of God is enough for every kind of sin and sinner. And that means that we can have revival now.

II. The All-Powerful Word of God Makes Revival Possible Now

"I am not ashamed of the gospel of Christ," Paul said by divine inspiration, "for it is the power of God unto salvation to every one that believeth; to the Jew first, and also to the Greek" (Rom. 1:16). The word *power* here is the Greek word *dunamis*, from which we get our word *dynamite*. So the Gospel Paul preached was the dynamite of God. He said it was not only good for Jews but for Greeks. God's mighty Word, as Paul preached it, was as powerful with the learned Greeks as it was with the religious Hebrews.

Let us thereby learn a lesson. What this modern, educated race needs is the same old Gospel. With all our gadgets, machinery, inventions; with all our luxuries, our proud independence and arrogant unbelief, the Gospel of Jesus Christ, preached in the power of the Holy Spirit, is still the answer for man's sin.

In Jeremiah 23:28, 29 is this plain word from God:

"The prophet that hath a dream, let him tell a dream; and he that hath my word, let him speak my word faithfully. What is the chaff to the wheat? saith the Lord. Is not my word like as a

fire? saith the Lord; and like a hammer that breaketh the rock in pieces?"

What is the chaff to the wheat? Not moral essays, not human argument, not personality and magnetic influence; but the mighty Word of God is the preacher's weapon. If a dream is all you have, then tell your dream, though it will not make black hearts white. But if you have the Word of God, then speak it faithfully. "Is not my word like as a fire? saith the Lord; and like a hammer that breaketh the rock in pieces?" Oh, the living, burning Word of God! Oh, the mighty hammer to break hearts of stone and crush resistance to God!

Heed what the Lord says to us in Hebrews 4:12, 13:

"For the word of God is quick, and powerful, and sharper than any twoedged sword, piercing even to the dividing asunder of soul and spirit, and of the joints and marrow, and is a discerner of the thoughts and intents of the heart. Neither is there any creature that is not manifest in his sight: but all things are naked and opened unto the eyes of him with whom we have to do."

He who preaches the Word of God faithfully and in the power of the Spirit finds it a living and powerful weapon, sharper than any twoedged sword. He finds that the Word of God, preached or witnessed with the power of the Spirit, pierces even to the dividing asunder of soul and spirit. That is, it is a revealer and discerner of the thoughts and intents of the heart. When a man preaches the Word of God in the power of God, every creature who hears finds his soul under the gaze of Almighty God. He finds that his conscience, his motives, his nature are all naked and open before the eyes of the Lord with whom one has to do. Oh, that God would give us a heart to preach the Word of God and believe in that!

I find that the people who do not believe we can have revival now have always a tendency away from absolute faith in the

Bible. To Spurgeon, the Bible was word-for-word, in original manuscripts, given of God. He believed in verbal inspiration. So did Moody and Torrey and Finney. So did all the great evangelists. They preached not merely good things, with the thought from God. They preached, as they were assured, *the very words of God*! They could say with Paul:

"But we received, not the spirit of the world, but the spirit which is from God; that we might know the things that were freely given to us of God. Which things also we speak, not in words which man's wisdom teacheth, but which the Spirit teacheth; combining spiritual things with spiritual words."—I Cor. 2:12, 13, R.V.

God gave the content of the message. He also gave the very words in which they were couched, in the original manuscripts. And preachers who preach the Word as burning words which themselves came from God and preach such Scripture in the power of the Holy Spirit have seen the mighty working of God's Spirit in the saving of multitudes.

A few years ago when Evangelist Billy Graham was in England and being greatly blessed of God in revivals, with many being saved, I had a letter from him. He told me that he had gotten away from the short messages, gotten away from the light approach and the entertainment, and had begun to speak often for an hour or more on sin, Hell, judgment and Christ's second coming. He had begun to learn the mighty power that is in the Word of God itself, when it is preached with boldness.

I have before me now an account from Billy Graham of the blessed revival in Los Angeles where some three thousand people came to Christ late in 1949. Evangelist Graham says:

> How foolish I have been so many times. I have worked so hard to build a message, replete with illustrations, with perhaps an experience or two of my own thrown in. True, God blessed those messages in the past.
>
> But, oh, how He blessed the plain and simple Word of God in this campaign!

The Scriptures say . . . The Bible says . . . The Scriptures say . . . The Bible says . . .

I got to the place where I could not preach any of my old sermons. Studying from six to eight hours a day, I received new sermons, burned into my heart by God. I did away with all illustrations. I used from twenty-five to one hundred passages of Scripture each evening. People, I found, cannot stand under the impact of the Word of God. Even the hardest sinner will capitulate.

I am sure that God often wants men to use illustrations to throw light on the Word of God. I am sure that God wants every gift dedicated to Him in the preaching of the Word. But, oh, may God help us to know that the dynamite of God is in the message itself, from the Word of God. "Is not my word like as a fire, saith the Lord, and like a hammer that breaketh the rock in pieces?" "The word of God is quick, and powerful, and sharper than any twoedged sword, piercing even to the dividing asunder of soul and spirit, and of the joints and marrow, and is a discerner of the thoughts and intents of the heart" (Heb. 4:12).

What a divine resource! The Bible, the Word of God, is as strong as ever it was, and it can cut to the hardest hearts.

I was in revival services in Washington, D. C. One morning I preached to a great crowd. A Catholic woman was present and was disturbed at my preaching on "Ye Must Be Born Again." She had never before been in a Protestant service. That morning after the service she apologized to me for thinking that this could not be the house of God, that I could not be a messenger of God nor these people the people of God. She expected God to manifest Himself only in a Catholic church. But she was so disturbed that she asked for audience with me.

To get around any question of her church and any argument about differences, I simply had her answer to me question after question from II Timothy 2:5, 6. She, looking on the Scriptures, answered that there was only one God, that there was only one Mediator between God and men, that this Mediator was not a preacher, not a priest, not the saints, not the Virgin Mary. She looked again to verify it, and tears started in her eyes and her lips trembled as she said, "No! It is not the blessed virgin."

Then I asked her, "Who, then, is the one Mediator, the one Go-between, the one Peacemaker between God and man?"

She read the answer from the Scripture again, "The man Christ Jesus, who gave himself a ransom for all. . . ."

She was weeping and soon trusted the Saviour. As she wiped her eyes, she said, "I never would have believed that if you had not showed it to me in the Bible!"

Oh, if we would only believe what the Word of God will do, when preached in faith and power of the Holy Spirit!

Remember the blessed promise of Psalm 126:5, 6: "They that sow in tears shall reap in joy. He that goeth forth and weepeth, bearing precious seed, shall doubtless come again with rejoicing, bringing his sheaves with him." Here is the plain promise of God, never repealed. One who takes the Word of God to sinners and sows that Word with tears, with a contrite, broken heart, is certain to see results. He will return with joy, bringing his sheaves with him.

Then sow the Word of God. Sow it broadcast. Sow it here and yonder. In every way possible get out the Gospel. "Blessed are they that sow beside all waters, that send forth thither the feet of the ox and the ass" (Isa. 32:20).

We often think of Galatians 6:7, 8 as a solemn warning to sinners, and so it is: "Be not deceived; God is not mocked: for whatsoever a man soweth, that shall he also reap. For he that soweth to his flesh shall of the flesh reap corruption; but he that soweth to the Spirit shall of the Spirit reap life everlasting." But God adds in the next verse the emphasis that He mainly wants us to see: "And let us not be weary in well doing: for in due season we shall reap, if we faint not."

How can one who believes this blessed principle of the law of sowing and reaping the Gospel say we cannot have great mass revivals again? If we sow, we shall reap. If we plant the precious seed of the Word of God and water it with our tears, the blessed Spirit of God will make it sprout in many a heart.

We can have revival now because we have the infinite resource, always available, of the all-powerful Word of God. If the Word of God ever comes to its own in our lives, we will have mighty revivals.

III. The Miracle-Working Holy Spirit, Who Empowers Christians and Convicts and Regenerates Sinners, Makes Revivals Always Possible

That sad and terrible night when Jesus was talking to His disciples the last time before His crucifixion, one thing burdened Him so that He returned to the subject again and again. In John 14:12 He tells the disciples, "He that believeth on me, the works that I do shall he do also; and greater works than these shall he do...." He gives them the wonderful promise of answered prayer, that whatsoever they shall ask in His name, He will do it (vss. 13, 14). Then He gives them the secret of the Holy Spirit, the Comforter who is to come and abide with them forever. "...the Spirit of truth" whom the world cannot receive is to dwell in them (vs. 17), is to teach them all things and bring all things to their remembrance. They are to have perfect peace because of the Holy Spirit's dwelling within.

Jesus emphasized the importance of the work of the Holy Spirit in a Christian. And in John 15 it says this work of the Holy Spirit in Christians shall bring much fruit.

Jesus was crucified, and the third day He rose again and talked often to His disciples. But when He was going away to Heaven, one thing He laid on their hearts more than all others: they were to be His witnesses, they were to carry the Gospel to every creature, beginning at Jerusalem. "And, behold, I send the promise of my Father upon you," He said: "but tarry ye in the city of Jerusalem, until ye be endued with power from on high" (Luke 24:49). All would be vain unless they should have a mighty enduement of power from on high. They were not ready to start revival services, not ready for house-to-house visitation, not ready for personal contacts, until they received this supernatural enduement of power.

Again in Acts 1 the command of the Saviour is repeated, that they should "wait for the promise of the Father," the enduement of power from on high. They should "be baptized with the Holy Ghost not many days hence." That did not mean Christ's return, nor the coming of the kingdom or restoration of Israel. "But ye shall receive power, after that the Holy Ghost is come upon you: and ye shall be witnesses unto me both in Jerusalem, and in all Judaea, and in Samaria, and unto the uttermost part of the earth." Those were the last words that Jesus spoke while on earth. Then, "while they beheld, he was taken up; and a cloud received him out of their sight" (Acts 1:8, 9).

The disciples "continued with one accord in prayer and supplication" till the mighty power of God came on the day of Pentecost. They won three thousand souls that day, then continued in the mighty power of God.

Throughout the book of Act the fullness of the Spirit is the one great equipment mentioned for Christian workers.

The disciples were filled with the Holy Spirit in Acts 2:4.

The same crowd was filled with the Spirit again in Acts 4:31, after they had again prayed.

Stephen and other deacons were filled with the Holy Ghost.

When Paul was converted and had fasted and prayed three days, Ananias came to him "that thou mightest receive thy sight, and be filled with the Holy Ghost" (Acts 9:17).

Barnabas "was a good man, and full of the Holy Ghost and of faith: and much people was added unto the Lord" (Acts 11:24).

When Philip went and preached the Gospel in Samaria and multitudes were saved, then the apostles sent Peter and John there "who, when they were come down, prayed for them, that they might receive the Holy Ghost" (Acts 8:15).

Paul, Barnabas and others fasted and prayed until "the Holy Ghost said, Separate me Barnabas and Saul for the work whereunto I have called them. . . . So they, being sent forth by the Holy Ghost, departed. . ." (Acts 13:2, 4).

At the first opposition, "Saul, filled with the Holy Ghost," rebuked the sin of Elymas the sorcerer publicly, and Sergius Paulus was wonderfully converted.

Oh, those thrilling, thrilling days and years when men did not pretend to preach the Gospel nor try to win souls except they were endued with the mighty power of God!

This is the lost note in our music, the lost chord that leaves unsatisfying all our efforts at service.

The Darbyites have come along and taught us that we need not wait on God for power, that it is fanaticism to ask to be baptized with the Holy Ghost. They have told us that we already have all of the Holy Spirit we may have; so men have ceased to wait on God and seek the mighty power of God as did Moody, Spurgeon, Finney and Torrey. And, ceasing to depend on the mighty power of God, they have ceased to have it. And everywhere we have bland, self-assured "Bible teachers" preaching to little groups of saints, but having no drunkards made sober, no harlots made pure, no lives and homes and cities transformed.

We cannot have revival without the mighty power of the Holy Spirit. But, thank God, His power is available for those who wait on Him and give themselves wholly to His will.

It is the plain command of God, "Be not drunk with wine, wherein is excess; but be filled with the Spirit" (Eph. 5:18). We, too, need exactly what Bible Christians needed. We, too, can have the mighty enduement of power from on high.

We have retreated from fanaticism. We are afraid of "wild fire." The truth is, fearing what men would say, we have not thought enough about what God would say. We have gone in human wisdom, gone with educated sermons, with entertaining sermons, with doctrinally sound sermons—but gone without the holy anointing, without the miracle-working, supernatural power of the Holy Spirit!

I do not wonder that the Darbyites say that we are in the last days, that we cannot have any more great revivals. After people are taught that they need not wait on God, that the wonderful events in the book of Acts were given only temporarily, in a transition period, and that such power and manifestations can never be repeated again, I do not wonder that they think we can have no more great revivals. But they are wrong! His Spirit and His power are still available.

Some people preach the Word and forget that it is "the sword of the Spirit." They cannot wield the sword; but the Spirit of God must do so, if the wonder-working results are to follow. Oh, for holy anointing! Oh, for a supernatural enduement of power! Oh, that men may speak for God as prophets; then our prophecy will be supernatural revelation, a miracle-working message from God!

We can have revival if sinners still tremble under the Word, if the Word of God can make men see their nakedness of soul, their wickedness before God, the impending doom that hunts them down! Men can be saved if they can but be wooed with the entrancing pathos, devotion and love of Christ, revealed by the Holy Spirit.

Yes, we can have revival. The enduement of the Holy Spirit of God makes revival possible for anyone who will pay the price for that power.

What set Moody apart? The power of the Holy Spirit!

What made Billy Sunday powerful? If you think it was

baseball slang, enthusiastic, dramatic gesture and activity in the pulpit, you have missed the whole point of his ministry. Billy Sunday's message was made powerful by a special anointing of the Holy Spirit. Every time he preached, he opened his Bible at Isaiah 61:1 and placed his manuscript upon that Scripture: "The Spirit of the Lord God is upon me; because the Lord hath anointed me to preach good tidings unto the meek; he hath sent me to bind up the brokenhearted, to proclaim liberty to the captives, and the opening of the prison to them that are bound." Billy Sunday knew that he had a covenant with God. He preached in the mighty power of God.

If it was a sober, rather matter-of-fact, inexorable logic of R. A. Torrey or the pungent slang of Billy Sunday or the tender pathos and vivid illustrations of D. L. Moody, the fundamental power was the same—the mighty power of the Spirit of God. They had revival because they were anointed to preach.

We can have revival, too, if we are anointed. We can have revival because the Spirit of God is the Miracle-worker who is always available for the soul-winner's power.

IV. Resource of Persistent, Heart-Broken, Prevailing, Believing Prayer Makes Revival Always Possible

I trust that all who read this lecture are beginning to see that fundamental Christianity naturally provides for blessed, powerful revivals and the winning of multitudes.

One who does not win souls is not even a normal Christian. A church that does not have revival is not a normal New Testament church. A preacher who does not have the mighty enduement of power upon him to the saving of sinners is backslidden, disobedient and unfaithful, because New Testament Christianity inevitably involves the power of God upon His people and the fruitful preaching of His Gospel.

For example, here is a fundamental of the Christian faith: God answers prayer! Prayer changes things. Prayer moves the hand that moves the world.

Nothing is clearer in the Bible than the fact that certain things happen because people pray, which would not happen if they did not pray.

Hezekiah, for example, was "sick unto death." God sent Isaiah to tell him frankly, "Set thine house in order: for thou shalt die, and not live" (Isa. 38:1). But Hezekiah turned his face to the wall and prayed, and God sent back the prophet to say, "I have heard thy prayer, I have seen thy tears: behold, I will add unto thy days fifteen years" (vs. 5).

James 4:2 says, "Ye lust, and have not: ye kill, and desire to have, and cannot obtain: ye fight and war, yet ye have not, because ye ask not." Infidel Harry Emerson Fosdick says that God is not a Santa Claus, that one of the first things we must learn about prayer is that God does not give things.

I know better. The Bible clearly says the opposite of that. God is better than any Santa Claus; and while He does not give on any wicked whim, God does answer prayer. He has sent money in answer to prayer, the exact sum needed in literally dozens of cases.

I know from never-to-be forgotten, holy experience that He brought rain in answer to prayer in drought-stricken West Texas when there was no likelihood of rain. The surrounding country remained arid; and when we asked God to send rain within twenty-four hours, He sent it in a five-mile radius in the little town where I preached and where we agreed to pray.

I know that God raised up a woman with T. B., sent home from a state sanitorium to die, after years of wasting away. She was healed at once, as far as all of us could see, and in two weeks she was up doing her own housework. She still lives after eighteen years.

I say that I can testify that God changes things in answer to prayer. God does things when we pray aright which He would not do if we did not pray aright.

But does not this fundamental doctrine, that God has committed Himself to answer a certain kind of prayer, mean necessarily that we can have a revival if we seek God for it properly? Here prayer is divinely given as a resource for every Christian, a resource that makes revival always possible.

Are conditions wrong for revival? Then prayer can change conditions. Are people wrong for revival? Then prayer can change people. "The king's heart is in the hand of the Lord" (Prov. 21:1).

God can change newspaper editors and writers if He wants to, to give the Gospel publicity. God can change hearts of public officials, to make great auditoriums available for rental. God can make Christians concerned when they are unconcerned, if a few keep on praying. God can restore the backslider, if people mean business and keep on praying. God can change people in answer to prayer.

Is the preaching powerless? But God answers prayer! Let preacher and people wait on God until power is given. Prayer changes things, changes people, changes the weather. Prayer can change self. The weak can be made strong.

It is true that one of the conditions of proper prayer is that it should be in Christ's name. "And whatsoever ye shall ask in my name, that will I do, that the Father may be glorified in the Son. If ye shall ask any thing in my name, I will do it," said Jesus in John 14:13, 14.

But this condition is fulfilled more easily about soul winning and revival than about anything else! It may be that a man will want a new car and cannot honestly say that it is just for Jesus' sake. It may be that one will wish to be raised from a bed of sickness, and his own desire may be the real reason back of the request. All right, friend, pray on, even in such cases. There are other promises that encourage you to pray.

But on this matter of keeping people out of Hell, of saving souls for whom Christ has died, we can more easily come to pray in Jesus' name than about anything else!

If there is anything in the world that I know about God, it is that He loves sinners. Do I know what Jesus Christ thinks? Do I know what His dear heart desires and craves? Do I know the thing that is most often in His thought? I do know! The dear Lord Jesus wants sinners saved.

We learn from I Timothy 1:15, "This is a faithful saying, and worthy of all acceptation, that Christ Jesus came into the world to save sinners; of whom I am chief." Jesus said, when He saved Zacchaeus, "For the Son of man is come to seek and to save that which was lost" (Luke 19:10).

This is what Jesus came into the world for. This is what He died for. If you seek the meaning of His lonely long years away from Heaven and His Father and the angels, then His love for sinners is the answer. If you seek to know why He endured the shameful traitor's kiss on His cheek, the spittle in His face, the scourging of the Roman lash, and the indignities and torture of the cross, then I can tell you. His heart was broken over lost sinners. Even in His dying, He could not forbear praying, "Father, forgive them, for they know not what they do."

Now that He is seated on the right hand of God, I know what is in His heart. "I say unto you, that likewise joy shall be in heaven over one sinner that repenteth, more than over ninety and nine just persons, which need no repentance" (Luke 15:7). I know what lights up the face of the Saviour and makes His heart glad even now. Oh, how He rejoices to see souls saved!

How bold I ought to be, then, when I come to pray in Jesus' name about souls being saved! I sometimes, in my prayers, need to say, "If it be Thy will." But I never need to say that when I pray for God, in His own way, to bring a blessed revival, to endue Christians with power and save sinners. That I know is the will of God and the will of Christ.

Prayer is a mighty weapon that makes revival inevitable for all who seek God's face as they ought to seek it.

Faith is often mentioned as a condition of proper prayer. "Without faith it is impossible to please him: for he that cometh to God must believe that he is, and that he is a rewarder of them that diligently seek him" (Heb. 11:6). It ought not be hard for Christians who know God's loving care to believe that He will give them daily bread, raiment and shelter. How tender are His mercies, and how bountiful His provision!

But faith surely ought to come easily when we read all the Scripture has to say about the love of God for sinners and His pleading that we go to win them. "Faith cometh by hearing, and hearing by the word of God," says Romans 10:17. And if you go to the Bible to build your faith, you will surely find it easy to believe that God wants to save sinners, wants to give revival.

Do you want to pray for power? Then how encouraged we are when we find how Jesus insisted that the disciples tarry in Jerusalem until they be endued with power from on high. How it ought to strengthen our faith!

This is why all the great evangelists were mighty men of prayer.

Charles G. Finney would frequently feel some lack of power and blessing and would set apart a day of fasting and prayer "for a new baptism of the Holy Ghost," as he was wont to say.

Moody sought God unceasingly for two years, until he was mightily endued with power. R. A. Torrey started the prayer meeting in Moody Church in Chicago and there prayed for two years that God would send a great revival. Then suddenly a committee from Australia came and sought out Torrey, the Bible teacher who had never been much thought of as an evangelist; and Torrey began the mighty campaigns in Australia that led him finally around the world, with hundreds of thousands of souls saved under his great ministry. Torrey learned to pray, so he learned to have revivals. If you want to know the simplicity of Torrey's prayer life and his teaching on prayer, read the little book, *How to Pray* (Moody Colportage Library) or *The Power of Prayer and the Prayer of Power* (Fleming H. Revell).

I do not wonder that we have seen so few revivals, when we have such little praying. May God send again upon His people the spirit of supplication, the spirit of prayer.

Is not this His promise in II Chronicles 7:14, "If my people, which are called by my name, shall humble themselves, and pray, and seek my face, and turn from their wicked ways; then will I hear from heaven, and will forgive their sin, and will heal their land"?

Prayer is one of those mighty weapons of God which are not carnal but mighty to the pulling down of strongholds. If people pray aright, they can have revival. May the dear Lord Jesus teach us anew to pray.

Let us remind you again, in summary, of these four infinite resources of God which make revival always possible.

There is, first, the infinite grace of God, the love of God, the tenderhearted tendency toward forgiveness and mercy that is greater than all sin.

Second, there is the Word of God, living and powerful and sharper than any two-edged sword, like a fire and like a hammer that breaks the rock in pieces, a mighty weapon that makes revival always possible.

Third, there is the miracle-working Spirit of God who is always available to endue and empower Christians and preachers, to convict and regenerate sinners, to stir, convict and change hearts and homes, cities and nations.

And fourth, there is the mighty power of persistent, prevailing, brokenhearted, believing prayer.

We would be overwhelmed with revival, if we would make full

use of these mighty resources. God can yet save millions in nation-sweeping revivals, if His people will enter into their holy heritage and use their resources, so richly given by a loving God who is disappointed that we do not claim His blessings.

Present-Day Wickedness, Apostasy and Modern Civilization Cannot Prevent Revival

7

The God whom some people worship is old and tired. The present-day civilization is entirely too much for Him! Maybe He could one time give great revivals, but He cannot anymore. Mankind has simply gotten to be worse than that old-fashioned God can handle—the God of some people's faith.

The only thing that God and the people of little faith and little passion who serve Him can do is to retreat from the world. Such people can read only the newspaper reports of atomic bombs, hydrogen bombs, nuclear bombs, the spread of communism, modernism among church leaders, and say, "Jesus is bound to come very, very soon!"

These Christians and their Gospel are not adequate to face and meet the conditions in this world; so they, in defeat and despair, do not "watch" in the scriptural sense, do not "occupy till I come," as Jesus commanded, but rather they study technical details and speculate upon the Antichrist, and whether Russia is now forming the great northern confederacy (Gog and Magog of Ezekiel).

Christians with belief in that kind of a defeated God can have no great revivals. They are like the remnant of the British army at Dunkirk, surrounded, hounded and cut to pieces by the German Blitzkreig, and waiting only to be taken from the beaches by British boats, to escape annihilation!

So many Christians look for the rapture as a last resort of a God who cannot cope with the present world, in a Christianity which is more or less out of date, very nice for the few who have it but inadequate to reach multitudes, to shake and change cities and nations and save millions!

Can you see the wickedness, the near-blasphemy of that kind of an attitude toward God and the Gospel? How God must be grieved by our defeated unbelief about revivals!

I look for the Saviour's coming because He said for me to look for Him, not because I read about the destroying bombs in the newspapers! My heart will leap with unmeasured joy to see His face. But I know what rejoices His heart, and I am trying to do that. He wants sinners saved, and left me to do this task while I await His coming. I long to be pleasing Him, should He come today! And if He does not come for another thousand years, I will serve Him gladly till I die, winning all the souls I can. Then I will rejoice with Him in the blessed revivals that will continue in this age until the Saviour does come.

Dr. Hyman Appelman, Jewish evangelist, told how in San Angelo, Texas, in a hotel room he, as a state evangelist under the employ of the Baptist State Convention, discussed revivals with his superior. That godly man tried to comfort Dr. Appelman, saying that he must not expect such great revivals as had occurred in other ages, since now people were distracted by television and other worldliness, by a pleasure-mad society. Dr. Appelman should go on and do the best he could but not hope for a return of the revivals of D. L. Moody, said the good man.

Dr. Appelman told how he bowed his head upon the bed and wept uncontrollably. Then he told his distressed superior that, if the Lord Jesus Christ and His Gospel and the power of the Holy Spirit were not adequate for this wicked age, as well as all other ages, then the Gospel was truly out of date and Christ was not all He had claimed to be. Dr. Appelman was not willing to make that concession; nor am I.

The simple truth is, mankind is insatiably wicked, but no more wicked than he has been since the Fall. The truth is, there is everywhere a great tendency toward spiritual decline and unbelief. But this is not essentially different from what it has always been. In Bible times it was so. It was so in all the ages of great revival. The wickedness, apostasy and all the distractions in all ages have never been enough to prevent great revivals when God's people paid God's price; and they cannot prevent revival now.

If I seem bold in this matter, then let me thank God that I have such a Saviour, such a Gospel, such divine resources available for revival, that I know we have the answer to the world's need. This world has not gotten beyond God's power. The hydrogen bomb, the nuclear bomb have not fazed God. The present civilization is not more complex than the Lord anticipated. Man's wickedness and unbelief have not surprised Him, nor reached a stage for which He made no provision.

In this lecture I want to show that present-day wickedness and unbelief is not worse than in Bible times when God gave great revivals; that all great revivals since were not prevented by the failures of Christianity in Bible times; that the awful Dark Ages could not prevent the Reformation and its marvelous revival; that wickedness and depravity everywhere could not prevent the greatest revivals in modern times. Christ, the Gospel, the Holy Spirit, the promises which were adequate in other days, are adequate now. All of modern wickedness, apostasy and distraction cannot prevent revival.

I. Mankind's Spiritual Conditions and Apostasy No Worse Than in Bible Times When God Gave Great Revivals

Those who believe that men are more wicked and the days more desperate now than in New Testament times have failed to see the picture clearly given in the New Testament of human wickedness and failure, and have underestimated the power of the New Testament Gospel and Spirit-filled New Testament Christians.

First, consider that man was then the unregenerate, depraved sinner—as alien from God then as now. It was to a leading Pharisee that Jesus insisted, "Ye must be born again."

He taught Nicodemus that that which is born of the flesh is only flesh, and cannot see the kingdom of God; that the new birth was the only chance to avoid Hell.

He told the nicest church people of their time—tithers, praying, law-abiding, religious people—"Ye are of your father the devil, and the lusts of your father ye will do" (John 8:44). To them He said, "Ye serpents, ye generation of vipers, how can ye escape the damnation of hell?" (Matt. 23:33). He said that all the civilization, all the religious forms and ceremonies they observed were only the whitewash on sepulchres filled with dead men's bones and all uncleanness. He likened the hearts of these outwardly righteous Pharisees to decaying, stinking bodies.

The hearts of men in Bible times were as wicked as the hearts of men today.

Paul wrote to the converts at Ephesus, "And you hath he quickened, who were dead in trespasses and sins." Lost sinners then were not only wicked but spiritually dead. They had in them no power to be good or to do good, though they might put on the outward appearance of goodness.

It is hard to see how a race that is totally bad can get any worse, or how a man who is dead can get any deader. The Bible pictures that men by nature, in Bible times as now, are utterly incapable of saving themselves or of doing good. It takes a miracle of God's grace to make men into the children of God. If you believe the foolish chatter of the Christ-rejecting modernists that all men are by nature the children of God, then you do not believe the Bible, and your conception is fundamentally unchristian and anti-Christian. Men, according to the Bible, are a fallen race, alien from God and enemies of God by nature, in Bible times as now.

Don't you see that, if the Gospel could reach and save such men in Bible times, it can reach them now? There is nothing in the nature of wicked men that can prevent great revivals. The Gospel of Jesus Christ is enough for the hardest sinners now as it was when some of those who crucified Jesus Christ were converted and when Paul the persecutor found Christ on the road to Damascus. The Gospel that could save Mary Magdalene, possessed of seven devils, and chief priests who mocked Jesus while He died, is today the Gospel which can reach the hardest human heart, if it is preached in the power of the Holy Spirit by men who will pay God's price for revival.

Consider how in New Testament times floodtides of persecution rose everywhere the Gospel was preached in power. If you think that opposition to the Gospel is stronger now than in Bible times, you have very carelessly read your New Testament.

The inhabitants of Christ's own home village in Galilee knew and honored Jesus for years, until He was filled with the Spirit and began His public ministry. Then the first day He spoke in the power of God in their synagogue they "rose up, and thrust him out of the city, and led him unto the brow of the hill whereon their city was built, that they might cast him down headlong" (Luke 4:29).

John the Baptist had his head cut off.

The Lord Jesus Himself was crucified.

Stephen, one of the first seven deacons, was martyred for the faith.

Right in the midst of the blessed revival which began at Pentecost was much persecution, and Peter and John were arrested and thrown in jail.

Early church traditions say that every one of the twelve

apostles save John the beloved died a martyr's death.

We know that Paul barely escaped from Damascus with his life, that he was stoned at Lystra and left for dead, that he spent some years in jail and finally was taken in chains to Rome. After years as a prisoner, Paul seems to have been released for a little while, then arrested again and finally was beheaded under Nero.

Do you think there is opposition today to the Gospel? It was customary for Paul and his companions to be run out of town!

In Acts 13:50 we are told, "But the Jews stirred up the devout and honourable women, and the chief men of the city, and raised persecution against Paul and Barnabas, and expelled them out of their coasts." That was after the Jews were filled with envy and there was much contradiction and blaspheming, and Paul had said to them, "Lo, we turn to the Gentiles" (Acts 13:45, 46).

At Philippi, Paul and Silas had their clothes ˈrn off, were beaten and placed in jail in stocks. In answer to prayer, God shook the jail, doors opened, and the jailer was wonderfully saved. But the officers and people "besought them, and brought them out, and desired them to depart out of the city" (Acts 16:39).

Paul and Silas had to slip out of Thessalonica by night to save their skins; then when the tumult reached Berea, Paul had to slip away, pretending to go to the sea.

At cultured Athens they mocked Paul.

In the synagogue at Corinth they opposed and blasphemed, and Paul said, "From henceforth I will go unto the Gentiles" (Acts 18:6).

Paul was seized by a mob in a riot, and another riot filled Ephesus with confusion when Paul went there!

Yes, we can have revival today if we are willing to preach the Gospel as they did and suffer persecution as they did. If there were a few willing to be martyrs for Christ, then the blood of the martyrs would be the seed of the church now, as it has always been.

We hear on every hand foolish statements as, "The foreign mission fields are closing." People mean that there are some nations where the government will not protect a missionary, so someone may hit him in the head with a stone. There are some nations where soul winners may be persecuted. Then, the whole world was a closed mission field when Paul began his missionary journeys.

If men will not be missionaries unless they can have their entire family with them, have every comfort of life, have regular support of a certain amount of money, have a guarantee that no one will ever stone them or burn down their houses, then of course there will be some places where men cannot preach the Gospel with such ease and protection.

But in Bible times men expected to suffer for Christ when they went out to have a revival. We should expect the same kind of opposition.

Opposition in Bible times did not stop revivals. Neither does opposition today stop revivals. What hinders revival is that God's people are not willing to pay God's price to win souls. We have the same Great Commission. We meet the same kind of sinners. We would have the same kind of opposition if we pressed the battle to the gates for the Lord as they did. But we could have the same kind of results.

Consider, thirdly, that the tendency of backsliding and spiritual decline in Bible times did not prevent revival then, and cannot prevent revival now.

There is one sad fact that all of us must recognize when we consider this matter of revivals: even born-again people have still the old nature and have a tendency to wander, to grow spiritually cold, to lose soul-winning power and Christian joy. This tendency to backsliding and to spiritual decline was exactly the same in Bible times as it is now. Those who are Christians have a tendency to grow less spiritual. All parents bring children into the world who are unsaved, and even Christian parents have a tendency to let them grow up unconverted. The tendency in churches everywhere is to grow more formal and less spiritual. The preaching tends to degenerate from clear, plain reproof of sin and a demand for repentance, to comforting messages to the saved, and moral essays.

The first chapter of Romans tells us how a race of men who once knew God, a race descended from Noah and his sons and spared from the Flood, became heathen and idolatrous. That chapter tells us how the ancestors of heathen people, "when they knew God, they glorified him not as God, neither were thankful; but became vain in their imaginations, and their foolish heart was darkened" (vs. 21). They began to make images in worship; "wherefore God also gave them up to uncleanness" (vs. 24), and ". . . God gave them up unto vile affections" (vs. 26). Then, "even as they did not like to retain God in their knowledge, God gave them over to a reprobate mind . . . " (vs. 28).

The foolish idea that man descended from brute ancestry and that man has climbed up from an animal-like state through savagery, barbarism and civilization to enlightenment is a theory made in the imagination of men. It is neither taught in the Bible, nor verified by history. The idea that man came through an old stone age, a new stone age, an age of metals, and so forth, to the present civilization is belied by facts uncovered by archeologists and ethnologists everywhere. Heathens did not reach their present state by ascending from brute beasts but by apostasy and declension, going away from a knowledge of God and light and truth. That is the constant tendency of the human heart everywhere, a tendency toward straying from God, turning away from the light. God said, "My people are bent to backsliding from me" (Hos. 11:7).

What became of all the converts of John the Baptist? We remember that, when John was preaching by Jordan, "then went out to him Jerusalem, and all Judaea, and all the region round about Jordan, And were baptized of him in Jordan, confessing their sins" (Matt. 3:5, 6). Some would lightly smile at John the Baptist's revival and scoff at his converts. But I remind you that he preached exactly the same Gospel as Jesus did, as we see from John 3:36 which quotes His words; that Jesus Himself said there was never a greater prophet born of woman; and that the impact of his ministry was so powerful that multitudes thought he was the Messiah.

Not only Jesus but all of the twelve apostles were baptized by John the Baptist, it is inferred. The revival under John the Baptist was powerful. John the Baptist was great in the sight of the Lord, was filled with the Holy Ghost even from his mother's womb and 'turned many of the children of Israel to the Lord their God,' as the angel plainly revealed to Zacharias before his birth (Luke 1:15, 16).

But what had happened to these many converts of John the Baptist when Jesus was crucified some three or four years later? Doubtless many of them were truly converted people, but they did not have much faith in the resurrection of Christ; they did not stand by Him when He was arrested and crucified. The frailty of the best Christians in the world is here illustrated. Yet a mighty revival could be had at Pentecost despite their failure and the failure of the disciples whom Jesus Himself had won.

If you think that revivals are not possible when Christian people grow cold or fall into false doctrine or bicker and divide and sin, then you should remember what Paul said to the elders of the church at Ephesus, gathered to meet him at Miletus:

"Take heed therefore unto yourselves, and to all the flock, over the which the Holy Ghost hath made you overseers, to feed the church of God, which he hath purchased with his own blood. For I know this, that after my departing shall grievous wolves enter in among you, not sparing the flock. Also of your own selves shall

men arise, speaking perverse things, to draw away disciples after them." —Acts 20:28-30.

Paul had a mighty revival among fickle, immature Christians, and he knew that after his departure some of these very same elders would arise to speak perverse things and draw away disciples, and grievous wolves would enter the flock. Christians then were the same kind of frail creatures that they are today. Backsliding and apostasy were the constant tendency.

In deadly urgency Paul wrote to Timothy about this very thing.

"I charge thee therefore before God, and the Lord Jesus Christ, who shall judge the quick and the dead at his appearing and his kingdom; Preach the word; be instant in season, out of season; reprove, rebuke, exhort with all longsuffering and doctrine. For the time will come when they will not endure sound doctrine; but after their own lusts shall they heap to themselves teachers, having itching ears; And they shall turn away their ears from the truth, and shall be turned unto fables. But watch thou in all things, endure afflictions, do the work of an evangelist, make full proof of thy ministry." —II Tim. 4:1-5.

Paul was ready to be offered. He knew that the apostasy prevailed everywhere, then as now. Yet Timothy was enjoined to watch, to endure afflictions, to do the work of an evangelist. Then good Christians might have sung that old hymn which says:

> **Prone to wander, Lord, I feel it,**
> **Prone to leave the God I love.**

But that did not prevent revivals. God can have revivals with poor, frail, human instruments. He can revive His saints. He can use them in soul winning. The declension and backsliding are so natural to men that they never surprise God, and we may be sure they never make powerless His Gospel, if a few Christians will pay God's price for the revival.

II. Failures in New Testament Times Could Not Prevent All Great Revivals Since

We had as well admit that Christians often failed God in New Testament times. Critics might well have said then, as they sometimes say now, "Christianity has failed."

After Paul warned Timothy, "For the time will come when they will not endure sound doctrine; but after their own lusts shall they heap to themselves teachers, having itching ears; And they shall turn away their ears from the truth, and shall be turned unto fables," then Paul spoke to Timothy about his own strait.

He was in jail at Rome, about to be executed. Rather sadly he said:

"Do thy diligence to come shortly unto me: For Demas hath forsaken me, having loved this present world, and is departed unto Thessalonica; Crescens to Galatia, Titus unto Dalmatia. Only Luke is with me. . . . "—II Tim. 4:9-11.

He said:

"Alexander the coppersmith did me much evil: the Lord reward him according to his works: Of whom be thou ware also; for he hath greatly withstood our words. At my first answer no man stood with me, but all men forsook me: I pray God that it may not be laid to their charge. Notwithstanding the Lord stood with me, and strengthened me; that by me the preaching might be fully known, and that all the Gentiles might hear: and I was delivered out of the mouth of the lion."—II Tim. 4:14-17.

We might suppose that Paul was writing in our day. Alexander the coppersmith hated Paul and opposed him, just as people turn against evangelists today. When Paul was tried for his life and stood to answer for himself, there was not a single witness who would stand up and risk his life for Paul! All men forsook him!

Alone he gave his testimony and was delivered temporarily. But a little later he was taken out to the executioner's block, and his head was chopped off.

The worldliness and unspiritual state of Christians became so bad that even the beloved disciple John, the only apostle left alive, was not allowed to speak in some of the churches. He writes in the third epistle of John:

"I wrote unto the church: but Diotrephes, who loveth to have the preeminence among them, receiveth us not. Wherefore, if I come, I will remember his deeds which he doeth, prating against us with malicious words: and not content therewith, neither doth he himself receive the brethren, and forbiddeth them that would, and casteth them out of the church."

Does not that sound much like some churches and Christians today, where godly soul-winning evangelists are kept out and where there are divisions and strife? Does not that remind you of worldly-minded church officers who hound the pastors in some churches today and limit the power of God? The decline in spirituality, the increase of worldliness and selfishness among Christians, happened in all ages.

Does someone tell me that churches are failing in these days? Consider that every single church that was known to New Testament times also utterly disappeared! Where is the church at Jerusalem, filled with Spirit-filled disciples, at the birthplace of Christianity? It is gone! Long centuries ago, longer than even history has any record of, that church disappeared. Likely it happened in A.D. 70 when Jerusalem was taken by Titus and much of it destroyed.

Where are the seven churches of Asia? Even the church of Philadelphia, so greatly commended, has disappeared, as well as all the other churches in Asia Minor.

Where are the churches established in Paul's ministry? Where is the mighty church of Ephesus? Where is the church at Corinth? Where is the Christianity which flamed so brightly all around the Mediterranean Sea, established by Paul's journeys? Gone! All gone!

Paul wrote to the Christians at Rome, "Your faith is spoken of throughout the whole world." And at Rome the Christianity so greatly favored of God drifted more and more into formalism and ritualism, and became what is now Roman Catholic apostasy. Roman Catholicism with the papacy, with worship of Mary, with prayers to saints, with the idolatry of images, with purchased masses, with confession to priests instead of to God, offering at best a dubious purgatory instead of outright regeneration and assurance of salvation, is a constant witness to the frailty of human nature, the constant tendency to spiritual decline and false doctrine, unbelief and worldliness.

Don't you see that, if cold churches, formal churches, modernistic churches, if unbelief in pulpit and pew in these modern days could prevent revival, they would have prevented all the great revivals since New Testament times! For in all Bible ages Christ has not failed, but the church. Christianity has not failed, but the preachers, the Christians, the teachers.

Thank God, He is able to revive backslidden saints! Thank God, He is able to save cold, formalistic, unconverted church members! Thank God, all the wickedness, the false cults, the worldliness, the sin of these days cannot prevent revival if a few of God's people pay God's price for power and blessing!

III. The Dark Ages Could Not Prevent the Reformation Revival

Few people realize how black was the midnight of spiritual darkness in the Dark Ages. Never in the world was the "failure of Christianity" so obvious to unbelievers as in the Dark Ages when Rome had stifled opposition, when there was a famine of the Word of God, when in all the world there were only a little handful of spiritually intelligent believers. Here and there, like a tiny candle gleaming in the dark, was a group of "heretics" who still read the Scriptures copied by hand, who believed in individual regeneration by faith in Christ and who could be called New Testament Christians.

Practically every town in America today of ten thousand or twenty thousand people has more gospel preaching true to the Word of God than a nation of millions had during the Dark Ages. Sunday school scholars usually know more Bible than priests and monks usually knew in those days.

What chance was there for revival when indulgences to sin were openly sold; when salvation was not put on the basis of faith in Christ, but on confession to a Roman priest and payment for masses in the church? What chance was there for revival when not only kings but often the popes themselves were licentious and immoral?

Yet out of the welter of those Dark Ages God gave, in the Reformation, one of the greatest revivals the world has ever seen. He raised up Luther, Calvin and others and literally turned millions to personal faith in Christ and to a knowledge of salvation by faith—in Germany, the Scandinavian countries, Scotland, England, and parts of many other countries. There was really a counter-Reformation in the Catholic church that profoundly moved the whole corrupt organization. Protestantism as we know it in the main, particularly with reference to Lutheran, Reformed, Presbyterian and Anglican churches, came out of the mighty revival of the Reformation.

Thank God that no such spiritual darkness as that of the Middle Ages is on the world today, not in America, not in England, not in any English-speaking country! If world conditions, if spiritual decline, if false doctrine could not prevent revival in the Dark Ages, surely world conditions today cannot stop the power of God, the progress of the Gospel, and the salvation of multitudes of sinners, if some of God's people will pay God's price for soul-winning power.

IV. Wickedness and Unbelief Could Not Prevent the Great Modern Revivals

All through recorded history one truth stands out forever the same: God has given revivals in spite of man's wickedness, man's unworthiness, unbelief and unfaithfulness.

Consider England in Wesley's day. In the book, *This Freedom Whence*, by John Wesley Brady, we read of the alarming state of England when Wesley began preaching. The complete breakdown of government and morals which took place in France and brought about the French Revolution bade fair to bring a similar convulsion in England.

The established church, the Anglican church, was unutterably corrupt. The church was, of course, supported by taxation and church leaders appointed as something like political patronage, by government leaders. Bishops had estates with enormous incomes, had them by appointment of political leaders and kept them by subservience to political ends. The clergy were everywhere simply political appointees, without any reference to spiritual fitness, and generally did not even profess to be converted, born-again men.

Gambling was everywhere prevalent among the clergy. Drinking, even drunkenness, was very common. Most of the clergy were Deists. They believed in a Supreme Being but did not believe the Bible nor in the deity of Christ nor in the new birth. Church ceremonies were simply a stiff form. People in the parish were sprinkled as babies, "christened," and were counted members of the church.

We have no record of anybody in the Anglican church at the time doing revival preaching—preaching the new birth or calling sinners to repentance. Puritan pastors had been barred from preaching in principal towns and had often been fined and jailed and worse, for simply preaching the Gospel. We remember that John Bunyan was kept twelve years in Bedford jail to keep him from preaching.

English vessels carried on the slave trade for most of the world. Armed thugs would land in Africa, raid villages, murder those who opposed them and carry off slaves. Herded in pens and holds like animals, the slaves were carried to the West Indies, to the American colonies, to England and elsewhere. Many died and were pitched overboard en route.

Smuggling, gambling, thieving, licentiousness were everywhere common. The Shakespeare plays give an idea of how common was adultery. A man was jailed or hanged for catching a wild rabbit on an earl's estate. Little children slaved in mines and mills as much as twelve or fourteen hours a day.

There were no Sunday schools of any kind, no free day schools. Most people could not read nor write.

Wesley was often assaulted physically just for preaching the Gospel. Mobs were raised again and again against him and his fellow preachers. Occasionally a Methodist meetinghouse would be utterly destroyed, and the officers often favored the culprits.

England was as unlikely a place for a great revival as one could imagine. The Puritan revival had been suppressed with great violence. Independent-minded and Bible-believing preachers were everywhere abused, jailed, run out of the country, or their property confiscated. England was hardly civilized, utterly foreign to what we now know as England.

Yet God breathed upon John and Charles Wesley, on Whitefield and the preachers whom He raised up with them, and a mighty revival transformed England. Besides leading to the salvation of millions of souls, the Wesleyan revival indirectly started a Sunday school movement, caused prison reforms, stopped the slave trade, caused immense reforms in government, and largely created what we know as traditional English character, justice and society.

The unbelief, the lewdness, the immorality and dishonesty among the people and among church and government leaders when the Wesleyan revival began were far more discouraging than is true in America today. In view of the mighty revival God gave in Wesley's day, it is foolish and faithless to believe that God could not now stir America, England and anywhere else where men shake God and pay His price for revival, as mightily as He did in Wesley's day. The trouble is not with the hardness of world conditions and wicked hearts. The trouble is with the laborers. "The harvest truly is great, but the labourers are few."

The Wesleyan revival came to America through Whitefield, Coke, Asbury and others. But you will remember that in America, Tom Paine, one of the leaders of the American Revolution, was at the height of his popularity. He wrote *The Age of Reason* in which he set out to prove the Bible false. Multitudes read his books and pamphlets with enthusiasm. At one time his popularity rivaled that of Washington, Jefferson and Franklin.

Leaders of thought in early America were also Deists, denying the inspiration of the Bible, the deity of Christ, and the need for regeneration. Yet Benjamin Franklin heard Whitefield preach and was profoundly moved. He did not make a public profession of faith, but Franklin's *Autobiography* shows that in his later years Franklin believed in the God of the Bible, that he earnestly urged people to pray and to read the Bible. George Washington himself became an earnest man of prayer and was, it seems, a believing Christian.

God brought revival in early America in spite of infidelity and flagrant wickedness. Why would the Almighty God be hindered by human conditions now if His people meet His requirements for revival?

Consider the revival from 1857-1859, which began outwardly in the Fulton Street prayer meeting in New York City only three years before the Civil War. The flames of hate, strife and every wicked passion were rising high. That marvelous revival came in the midst of all the agitation for and against war, and it did not prevent the mighty Civil War.

Consider the state of America in the days of D. L. Moody. Robert Ingersoll, an infidel, was at the height of his popularity following the Civil War in which he had a distinguished military record. He came near being governor of Indiana, and many think he would have been president but for his position as an outspoken infidel. All over America he lectured to great crowds against the Bible and the Christian religion. Infidel clubs were formed. Unbelief has never been more arrogant, more outspoken than it was in America when D. L. Moody began his great ministry.

Moody worked among soldiers during the Civil War. He did not become widely known until after the war. All the aftermath of the war, with its hatred, its economic dislocation, with the oppression of southern states and flaming sectional hatred, did not prevent a revival. American frontiers were pushed westward with lawlessness and bloodshed, crimes against Indians, and whole communities were often kept in terror by murdering outlaws.

When Moody went to England, infidels, openly scoffing at the Bible and God and Christ, were so bold that infidel clubs were more popular and active than lodges are today. In fact, Mr. Soltau, in *The Sword Book of Treasures* (Sword of the Lord Publishers), tells how Moody preached one night to five thousand infidels in a service advertised especially for them. And they came, on order of their infidel leader, as a joke and to put Evangelists Moody and Sankey to shame. They knew no gospel hymns. Aside from a few Christian workers, no one was invited but infidels. Yet God's mighty power came upon them, and some five hundred turned to the Lord, and the infidel clubs were broken.

Those who imagine that revivals are simply the product of certain happy circumstances are foolish. They ignore the teaching of the Word of God and ignore the facts back of all great revivals. The moral and spiritual conditions when the D. L. Moody revival came to America and England were tremendously bad, even in many ways worse than conditions today. Conditions did not deter the power of God then, and cannot prevent His blessing now, if His people pay the price for revival.

God must feel it as an insult to His power and grace that people think revivals can only be had in propitious circumstances!

On the verge of the destruction of Jerusalem and the captivity of Judah, about which Jeremiah had been forewarned and which he had faithfully preached, God instructed Jeremiah to buy a field and do it openly and officially as an evidence that "houses and fields and vineyards shall be possessed again in this land" (Jer. 32:15). In view of the wasting and the utter destruction which was even then taking place, when the Temple would be destroyed, the gates of the city burned with fire, the walls torn down, the people slaughtered or dispersed to Babylon, revival of the nation seemed impossible.

But Jeremiah said, "Ah Lord God! behold, thou hast made the heaven and the earth by thy great power and stretched out arm, and there is nothing too hard for thee." God answered back, "Behold, I am the Lord, the God of all flesh: is there any thing too hard for me?" (Jer. 32:17, 27).

Elijah had people pour twelve barrels of water over the sacrifice on Mount Carmel before he called on God to send a fire from Heaven. He knew that God could start a fire with wet wood as well as with dry. He knew that God could give a revival in the midst of the awful depravity, idolatry and sin of Samaria.

And God's believing people know that God can do the same today.

What kind of a God is this we worship? Can puny men block the power of God when His people trust Him? Are sinners so strong and impervious to God's call that the Spirit of God cannot bring conviction, cannot pale the sinner's cheek, cannot put tears in the sinner's eye, cannot set a burning in the sinner's conscience?

What kind of a God is this we preach and serve? Is He so weak that the weather, the competition of radio, sports, television, business and vacationing has left Him helpless? Can God not compete in this brave modern world of which we boast? Shame on us for the thought! Down through the centuries God has proved Himself the God over all the circumstances, over all the people. He is the God above all human rulers. "Where sin abounded, grace did much more abound" (Rom. 5:20). Man proposes, but God disposes. Man's extremity is God's opportunity.

If I had a God who could not save a drunkard, I would never preach Him to little children. If I had a God who could not cleanse the harlot, I would never preach Him to a chaste wife and mother. If Jesus Christ cannot save Catholics and Jews, criminals and infidels, then I would never risk my own soul into His hand. If God cannot give great citywide revivals with mighty results with thousands saved from the public preaching of the Word in mass evangelism, I would never preach Him in a class in child evangelism, or a class of junior boys and girls!

What sin, what reproach upon God, what a mark of our unbelief, when we indicate that conditions are too hard for God, that conditions prevent a revival! History down through all the ages cries that it is a lie! All the revivals in Bible times, the great Reformation revival with Luther, Calvin and others, the Wesleyan revival that saved England from its French Revolution and made English and American civilization and freedom what it is today, the Moody revivals and more—these were all brought about in the face of horrible, widespread and flagrant sin, in the face of spiritual decline and unbelief in the churches and out.

Are you impressed with all the power, might, wickedness and the bent away from God of this present modern world? Then listen to the words of Jesus Christ: "In the world ye shall have tribulation: but be of good cheer; I have overcome the world" (John 16:33). The world? Remember that "this is the victory that overcometh the world, even our faith" (I John 5:4).

World conditions have never yet stopped a revival when God's people met God's requirements and had His mighty power for soul winning. World conditions cannot stop a revival now. "The harvest truly is great, but the labourers are few: pray ye therefore the Lord of the harvest, that he would send forth labourers into his harvest" (Luke 10:2).

Throughout these lectures we have felt constrained to return repeatedly to the Scripture given in Matthew 9:35-38, where Jesus gave us this law that the harvest is plenteous but the laborers are few—that the trouble is not with the circumstances, the sinners, the world, but with the church, the people of God. Let us read that Scripture again with the thought in mind that sinners themselves are ripe for the harvest, in the sight of the dear Saviour.

"And Jesus went about all the cities and villages, teaching in their synagogues, and preaching the gospel of the kingdom, and healing every sickness and every disease among the people. But when he saw the multitudes, he was moved with compassion on them, because they fainted, and were scattered abroad, as sheep having no shepherd. Then saith he unto his disciples, The harvest truly is plenteous, but the labourers are few; Pray ye therefore the Lord of the harvest, that he will send forth labourers into his harvest."

This passage centers about the work Jesus did among the people. He taught them in their synagogues, knowing how hungry their hearts were. He preached the Gospel of the kingdom, and the word "*Gospel*" means good news; so the people must have felt very hungry for it and surely heard it gladly. He healed every sickness and disease among the people; so here He calls attention to the ravages of sin, the unrest, the want and need which are felt everywhere in a world of sin.

We are told that Jesus "saw the multitudes" fainting. (The term is plural; not a single multitude, but "multitudes.") That indicates that the people were not only needy but felt their need. They followed Christ, hung onto His words and sought His help.

And the great heart of the Lord Jesus was moved with compassion on these people. He saw how weary and faint, how discouraged and whipped they were. He saw how they "were scattered abroad, as sheep having no shepherd." They had no one to whom they could go, no leader to follow, no fold for refuge.

All this was in the mind of the Saviour when He said to the disciples, "The harvest truly is plenteous, but the labourers are few; Pray ye therefore the Lord of the harvest, that he will send forth labourers into his harvest."

Not only do sinners need the Gospel, but they will hear the Gospel. Many of them are hungry for the Gospel and eager to accept it, if it is preached clearly and with boldness, love and tears, and in the power of the Holy Spirit.

Jesus evidently had in mind the same truth, that multitudes of sinners are ripe for the harvest, when He sat on the curbing of the well at Sychar in Samaria and said to His disciples:

"Say not ye, There are yet four months, and then cometh harvest? behold, I say unto you, Lift up your eyes, and look on the fields; for they are white already to harvest. And he that reapeth receiveth wages, and gathereth fruit unto life eternal: that both he that soweth and he that reapeth may rejoice together." — John 4:35, 36.

Here Jesus had in mind particularly this city of Sychar. He had won a wayward woman. She had left her waterpot and had run to the city to tell the men, "Come, see a man, which told me all things that ever I did: is not this the Christ?" They would be coming in a few minutes to see for themselves and to hear His words. Some were so eager for peace and forgiveness, so eager to know the Saviour that they trusted Him, unseen, on the testimony of the woman. Others would come and beseech Him to stay. He would stay in that town two days, and many more would believe because of His preaching.

So Jesus told these disciples that they should not feel that the harvest would later be ripe, after four months—it was ripe already.

And what Jesus said about Sychar, He said in principle about the whole world.

Everywhere there is such unrest on the part of sinners, such disillusionment over unfulfilled promises, over the wages of sin, over burning consciences, over lost loved ones, over the fear of death, that sinners can be won. Unnumbered millions—lost people who need saving—are today ripe for the harvest. That is what Bible examples prove. And by God's grace I shall try to give some of the fundamental reasons why there are always sinners who can be won to Christ and why revival is always possible.

I. Bible Illustrations of Hungry Sinners Who Longed for Peace, Forgiveness and Salvation

Again and again in the New Testament we find hungry-hearted sinners, like ripe fruit on a tree, waiting to be won. Not all knew exactly what they needed, but they had some deep need that left their hearts open to the Gospel and made them quick to trust the Saviour when the good news was presented to them.

1. Cornelius, the Roman Centurion at Caesarea

In Acts 10 we find the remarkable story:

"There was a certain man in Caesarea called Cornelius, a centurion of the band called the Italian band, A devout man, and one that feared God with all his house, which gave much alms

to the people, and prayed to God alway. He saw in a vision evident-
ly about the ninth hour of the day an angel of God coming in
to him, and saying unto him, Cornelius. And when he looked on
him, he was afraid, and said, What is it, Lord? And he said unto
him, Thy prayers and thine alms are come up for a memorial
before God. And now send men to Joppa, and call for one Simon,
whose surname is Peter: He lodgeth with one Simon a tanner,
whose house is by the sea side: he shall tell thee what thou
oughtest to do.''—Vss. 1-6.

Or, as repeated in Acts 11:13, 14 in Peter's words,

"And he shewed us how he had seen an angel in his house,
which stood and said unto him, Send men to Joppa, and call for
Simon, whose surname is Peter; Who shall tell thee words,
whereby thou and all thy house shall be saved."

The Lord had to show Peter a thrice-repeated vision before He
could break down his Jewish prejudice enough to get Peter to
go to a Gentile's house to preach the Gospel! But at last when
two servants and a soldier sent from Cornelius came to urge
Peter to come to tell Cornelius and his whole household how to
be saved, Peter was convinced, so on the morrow they went.

It is interesting to note that Peter seems to have prepared a
great sermon. No doubt he thought this ignorant Gentile would
know so little that it would take a great deal of teaching. But
if he had intended to preach a long sermon, he did not get to
finish it. In a brief introduction, Peter told the plan of salvation
in these words, "To him [Jesus] give all the prophets witness,
that through his name whosoever believeth in him shall receive
remission of sins" (Acts 10:43). And he never got to preach the
rest of his sermon! Cornelius and his whole household were converted at once. Peter, telling of it later, said, "And as I began
to speak, the Holy Ghost fell on them, as on us at the beginning."

So the new converts were baptized, and Peter went on his way

back to try to explain to critical Jewish Christians why he had
gone to the house of a Gentile to preach the Gospel!

In this charming story from the Scriptures it becomes apparent
that God often has more trouble getting a soul winner ready to
work for Him than He has in getting sinners ready to hear the
Gospel! It took signs and wonders to get Peter ready to preach
to that poor unsaved man, a man of prayer, a man who gave
alms, a man who fasted and waited on God, trying to find how
to be saved. Just so God had more trouble in getting Jonah ready
to preach than He had in getting the Ninevites to repent. Cornelius is a good example of hungry-hearted people who in almost
every community would be easy to reach with the Gospel.

2. The Ethiopian Eunuch Whom Philip Led to Christ

This treasurer of Candace, queen of the Ethiopians, had been
to Jerusalem to worship and, returning, sat in his chariot and
read the Prophet Isaiah.

*"Then the Spirit said unto Philip, Go near, and join thyself
to this chariot. And Philip ran thither to him, and heard him
read the prophet Esaias, and said, Understandest thou what thou
readest? And he said, How can I, except some man should guide
me? And he desired Philip that he would come up and sit with
him. The place of the scripture which he read was this, He was
led as a sheep to the slaughter; and like a lamb dumb before his
shearer, so opened he not his mouth: In his humiliation his judgment was taken away: and who shall declare his generation? for
his life is taken from the earth. And the eunuch answered Philip,
and said, I pray thee, of whom speaketh the prophet this? of
himself, or of some other man? Then Philip opened his mouth,
and began at the same scripture, and preached unto him Jesus.
And as they went on their way, they came unto a certain water:
and the eunuch said, See, here is water; what doth hinder me
to be baptized? And Philip said, If thou believest with all thine*

heart, thou mayest. And he answered and said, I believe that Jesus Christ is the Son of God. And he commanded the chariot to stand still: and they went down both into the water, both Philip and the eunuch; and he baptized him. And when they were come up out of the water, the Spirit of the Lord caught away Philip, that the eunuch saw him no more: and he went on his way rejoicing."—Acts 8:29-39.

It is to Philip's credit that he went without protest, leaving the great revival in Samaria to meet the unknown man with a hungry heart! This man had already been to Jerusalem to worship. He was already seeking in the Word of God for peace.

Notice that the unsaved man took the initiative all the way through this meeting. He begged Philip to sit with him in the chariot and explain the Scriptures. The eunuch asked Philip to explain "of whom speaketh the prophet this? of himself, or of some other man?" So Philip deserves little credit that he "opened his mouth, and began at the same scripture, and preached unto him Jesus" (Isa. 53). It was the eunuch himself who begged to be baptized, though doubtless Philip had told of this rite and what it meant.

About men like this the Scripture says that "the harvest truly is plenteous."

3. Zacchaeus the Publican Who Climbed
a Tree to See Jesus

Let us read the beautiful story from Luke 19:1-10.

"And Jesus entered and passed through Jericho. And, behold, there was a man named Zacchaeus, which was the chief among the publicans, and he was rich. And he sought to see Jesus who he was; and could not for the press, because he was little of stature. And he ran before, and climbed up into a sycamore tree to see him: for he was to pass that way. And when Jesus came to the

place, he looked up, and saw him, and said unto him, Zacchaeus,
make haste, and come down; for to day I must abide at thy house.
And he made haste, and came down, and received him joyfully.
And when they saw it, they all murmured, saying, That he was
gone to be guest with a man that is a sinner. And Zacchaeus stood,
and said unto the Lord; Behold, Lord, the half of my goods I give
to the poor; and if I have taken any thing from any man by false
accusation, I restore him fourfold. And Jesus said unto him, This
day is salvation come to this house, forsomuch as he also is a
son of Abraham. For the Son of man is come to seek and to save
that which was lost."

There are many reasons why one would suppose that Zacchaeus would be hard to reach. For one thing, he was rich, and
rich people do not always feel their need for help. They are not
always humble. For another, he was a publican, a crooked tax-
collector, hated by many and despised by all. But his heart was
hungry.

He was a short man, and when a big crowd gathered around
Jesus as He walked down the road and taught, Zacchaeus could
not see Him. So he ran ahead and climbed a sycamore tree so
that when Jesus came along he should see Him well.

Oh, how different the dear Saviour is from us, His blind and
unbelieving disciples! Jesus saw the man, read the signs of his
hungry heart, and said, "Zacchaeus, make haste, and come
down; for to day I must abide at thy house."

Would you think that this man would be so easily won? As
soon as he knew that the Saviour loved him and would forgive,
he slid down that tree and hit the ground a saved and happy
man! As evidence of his salvation, he immediately resolved to
give half of his goods to the poor and to restore fourfold to any
man from whom he had taken money by false accusation, so common among publicans. And Jesus said, "This day is salvation
come to this house."

Zacchaeus is an illustration of the verse of the old song:

> **Down in the human heart, Crushed by the tempter,**
> **Feelings lie buried that grace can restore;**
> **Touched by a loving heart, Wakened by kindness,**
> **Chords that are broken will vibrate once more.**

Zacchaeus is a type of many another sinful man who needs forgiveness and knows it and whose heart would delight to see Jesus!

4. The Sinful Woman Who Anointed Jesus' Feet at the House of Simon the Pharisee

Jesus went to the home of Simon the Pharisee and ate at a low table in the cool, stone-paved plaza, within the horseshoe-shaped house. As they reclined on couches to eat, each leaning on his elbow in Oriental fashion, a strange thing occurred:

"And, behold, a woman in the city, which was a sinner, when she knew that Jesus sat at meat in the Pharisee's house, brought an alabaster box of ointment, And stood at his feet behind him weeping, and began to wash his feet with tears, and did wipe them with the hairs of her head, and kissed his feet, and anointed them with the ointment. Now when the Pharisee which had bidden him saw it, he spake within himself, saying, This man, if he were a prophet, would have known who and what manner of woman this is that toucheth him: for she is a sinner."—Luke 7:37-39.

But Jesus loved the woman whom the Pharisee despised. He told the parable of the two debtors and rebuked the Pharisee who had not loved the Lord Jesus enough to wash His feet or anoint His head—but this woman had washed the Saviour's feet with tears and wiped them with her hair and had anointed His feet with precious ointment, a token of love and worship. Hear, then, the wonderful words of Jesus about how this woman's sins were forgiven:

"Wherefore I say unto thee, Her sins, which are many, are forgiven; for she loved much: but to whom little is forgiven, the same loveth little. And he said unto her, Thy sins are forgiven. And they that sat at meat with him began to say within themselves, Who is this that forgiveth sins also? And he said to the woman, Thy faith hath saved thee; go in peace."—Vss. 47-50.

People often do not look for converts among sinful women such as this woman, probably a harlot. It may be that you who say we cannot have revival now are more concerned with the Pharisees than with the sinful women. But wherever sin has done its worst work, often there is the deepest hunger for Christ.

This poor woman, so gloriously forgiven and saved, is typical of many, many others who are ripe for revival, if God only had some Spirit-filled workers to go with boldness, tears and holy abandon to win them.

5. The Woman With an Issue of Blood Twelve Years, Healed When She Touched the Hem of His Garment

As Jesus went to the home of Jairus, ruler of the synagogue, to raise his little daughter,

". . . a woman having an issue of blood twelve years, which had spent all her living upon physicians, neither could be healed of any, Came behind him, and touched the border of his garment: and immediately her issue of blood stanched. And Jesus said, Who touched me? When all denied, Peter and they that were with him said, Master, the multitude throng thee and press thee, and sayest thou, Who touched me? And Jesus said, Somebody hath touched me: for I perceive that virtue is gone out of me. And when the woman saw that she was not hid, she came trembling, and falling down before him, she declared unto him before all the people for what cause she had touched him, and how she was healed immediately. And he said unto her, Daughter, be of good

comfort: thy faith hath made thee whole; go in peace."—Luke
8:43-48.

This woman had tried everybody else, and probably from absolute necessity or despair, she was ready to come to Jesus. She
touched the hem of His garment. The Saviour tells us that it
was genuine faith she had. "Thy faith hath made thee whole;
go in peace." So we must be sure that the Lord forgave her sins
and that she gladly loved and trusted Him for salvation as well
as for healing.

Do you know anyone who has reached the end of human help?
Do you know anybody who, with broken health or with wayward
children or with burdens more than human shoulders can possibly bear, would turn to Jesus? There are countless thousands
of them, if we would go to them with the Gospel in love and
power. The harvest truly is plenteous.

6. The Woman of Samaria, at Sychar

I have called your attention more than once to the woman of
Samaria to whom Jesus spoke in chapter 4 of John and who was
so wonderfully saved. Here I take time only to call your attention to the fact that her heart was hungry. It is true she was
prejudiced, that she had lived a careless and worldly life. It is
true that she was ready to argue. But when Jesus pressed upon
her the fact of her sin and showed her that He knew all about
her life, she immediately believed that He was the Messiah. She
trusted Him and set out to serve Him and to bring others to Him
that very day.

Jesus had known by some divine wisdom about this woman
in Samaria, for instead of going down to Jericho and following
the usual river route up the Jordan, "he must needs go through
Samaria."

The Saviour never got away from the sense of hungry hearts
about Him, the multitudes like sheep without shepherds. God

forgive us that we do not sense the need of people, the hunger of people and their readiness to hear the Gospel! Surely that woman had grieved over her shabby reputation and wished she might be as acceptable as those more virtuous. No doubt she had even grieved that Jews had no dealings with Samaritans, a half-breed people with a half-breed religion and despised by the Jews. No doubt she had longed for a peace and satisfaction that the world had failed to give her, despite all her marriages and efforts at pleasure. This was a typical case of sinners ready for revival.

We can have revival now because all over the world are sinners with hungry hearts, those who could be won if we went to them in the mighty power of God.

II. Fundamental Reasons Why There Are Always Sinners Who Can Be Won

There are certain deeply felt needs in human hearts that tend to turn men toward God when they hear the Gospel in love and power. Often men may feel these needs very indefinitely. Sometimes these needs are very intangible. Nevertheless they are real; and every man and woman who seeks to win souls, every evangelist who seeks to lead in revival, ought to rejoice that there are certain deeply seated, fundamental causes which work on the side of the Gospel and revival.

1. There Is Among Men a Universal, Subconscious Realization of God.

Someone has said, "Man is incurably religious." Heathen races whose ancestors long centuries ago turned their backs on God, races that have had no Gospel for many centuries, yet have a doctrine about God, a tradition, a race consciousness of God.

As Wordsworth teaches in his *Ode: On Intimations of Immortality From Recollections of Early Childhood*, children do not come in entire forgetfulness from the hand of God into this world, but rather come with an inborn sense that there is a Creator, a God, a Judge to whom man must give an account.

A world without a Creator is unthinkable to sensible men. No wonder the Bible calls a fool an atheist who says in his heart, "There is no God" (Ps. 53:1). In the conscience, men have evidence of a God. In the sun, moon and stars, in the seasons, the tides, in God's provisions for man on this earth are abundant evidences to the heart that there is a God.

And men are made for God. How depraved is the savage race that does not believe in a hereafter! Man subconsciously feels that there is a place where wrongs are made right, where men get their just dues.

Man, made in the image of God, finds the image now greatly marred by sin. And yet it is there! It is there so that it may well be said, "Our souls, O God, are restless, until they find their rest in Thee!"

This means that most men are not hard to convince that there is a God, a hereafter, that God punishes sin, that men need a Saviour. Deep in the consciousness of men is an ally of the Gospel; and that helps to make the harvest always white, a harvest of sinners for the gospel reaper.

2. The Failure of This World to Satisfy Leaves Disillusioned People Ripe for the Gospel.

Sometimes Christians talk about all the pleasures of the wicked. I have sometimes sensed envy in Christians who talk about the way sinners drink and carouse and live for wealth or pleasure. If the world could satisfy the human heart, it might indeed be difficult to reach men with the Gospel. But one who preaches Jesus Christ, forgiveness, a need for a new heart, the comfort of the Holy Ghost, and a home in Heaven, has so much more to offer than the world ever gives its devotees that the scales are weighted in favor of the soul winner!

Do you think that the man who pursues wealth and finds it is happy? Well, if he does not have peace and joy of the Lord, his money certainly cannot give him peace and joy. Proverbs 15:6 says, "In the house of the righteous is much treasure: but in the revenues of the wicked is trouble." How many men have found that in the revenues of the wicked is trouble! That is, to an unsaved man, money—whether gotten by fair means or foul—cannot satisfy. Money is not what the heart needs, not the stuff out of which happiness is made.

After a blessed citywide revival campaign in Buffalo, New York, the pastors asked me to return for a week of services in the interest of Buffalo Bible Institute. They had procured a mansion, a very expensive property on half a city block in an expensive section of Buffalo. The three-story mansion had bedrooms large enough for classrooms. The flooring was of hardwood parquet. The bathroom by each bedroom had silver-mounted hardware. The interior doors were of three-inch thick solid mahogany, imported from Honduras. There was a private elevator. The dean lived in what had been the servant's quarters. He said it was like a seven-room mansion. The walls of this beautiful building were covered with tapestry.

I understand that the big home itself cost a quarter of a million dollars, besides the cost of the one-half city block in downtown Buffalo.

I asked one of the committee who had helped to obtain the new property, "Where in the world did you get $300,000 or so to buy such a property as this?"

"It did not cost us $300,000," he said; "only a tenth of that amount!" Then he told me about the rich man's wife, for whom he built the beautiful home. When she had been afflicted with heart trouble, he had put in the expensive private elevator; but one day she died. Then his only daughter ran off and married against her father's will. The hungry-hearted man, left alone, found his wealth no better than dust and ashes. He told his agents to dispose of the property, to sell it at any necessary price at once and get the matter off his hands. He never wanted to see the place again!

Oh, there are no pleasures in the revenues of the wicked! Men who do not know Christ can never find themselves satisfied with the husks of this world, no matter what money can buy.

Never envy those who go the merry rounds of pleasure! Proverbs 14:12, 13 says, "There is a way which seemeth right unto a man, but the end thereof are the ways of death. Even in laughter the heart is sorrowful; and the end of that mirth is heaviness." I remember a ballad of my boyhood, "After the Ball," which had the sad refrain,

> After the ball is over, after the break of morn,
> After the dancers are leaving, after the stars are gone;
> Many the hearts that are aching, could we but read them all,
> Many are the hopes that have vanished, after the ball.

Don't think that wine, women and song, the theater, travel and music can give any permanent satisfaction to the heart. Among the most unhappy people I have ever met are those who had nothing to do but have "a good time."

In Shamrock, Texas, I was pastor of the First Baptist Church. A young woman, an earnest Christian, told me of a friend who threatened to commit suicide. Would I talk to the girl and try to help her? Of course I would. She was brought to my home to visit us. I discovered, to my shocked surprise, that she was beautiful, that she was of a good family, that she had a college education.

"Miss Irene tells me," I began, "that you have been sad and unhappy, and I have asked her to bring you to me that I might see if I could help you."

"Yes," she said, "I am unhappy. I had a good chance to try everything that would bring happiness, and it has all failed me.

I wanted to go to college, and my father was glad to send me. He has bought me the nicest clothes. I have traveled in Europe. I was interested in art and in literature, and I have had time and money to travel. I have gone into society, have enjoyed all the pleasures that other decent young people enjoy. But I have found that life is not worth living! If I go to a party or a dance, I may seem lighthearted enough; but by the time I am home again I know it is all empty, hollow and vain. There is nothing to satisfy the heart, and life is a cheat. I wish I were dead! I would have killed myself before now but for the grief to my mother and father."

"Oh, no!" I said. "Life *is* fit to live. Life is good. And you ought to find happiness and have great joy and peace."

She turned her face to me and said with sharpness, yet with sadness, "If you know how to be happy, how to have peace, I wish you would tell me how!"

I answered her, "I can certainly do that. Just get down on your knees here and tell the Lord what you have told me. Tell Him that you have tried all the other things in the world. Tell Him that what all the world promises is a cheat, that it never delivers. Tell the Lord Jesus that your heart is heavy and you want Him to come in and fill it and make life worth living. Turn yourself over to Him now, in your failure, in your emptiness, your sin and sadness. I promise He will come in and make your life happy and worth living."

She uttered not a word of argument. She dropped on her knees and began to weep. I asked the Lord to forgive, to help her to trust Jesus, to heal her broken heart. I asked Him to supply all that the hollow tinsel of this world had failed to give a hungry heart.

She trusted Him, took my hand on it gladly, then rose with a light in her face, and wiped away her tears! She found that the world cannot satisfy. She was only an example of the truth that everywhere there are hearts that are hungry and so ripe for revival.

If you think that success and fame bring happiness, then remember that "the paths of glory lead but to the grave." Woodrow Wilson was at one time on the peak of world fame and honor; a few months later he was a disillusioned sick man on S Street in Washington, betrayed by his friends, attacked by his enemies and bypassed by his subordinates.

President Calvin Coolidge, urged to run again for the presidency, said, "I do not choose to run." He resisted all urging and would not have the nomination that would have meant almost certainly a third term as president of the greatest nation in the world.

But later, writing in *The Saturday Evening Post*, he reminded us of his beloved, fine and fair son who had blistered his heel playing tennis; then the blister became infected and killed him. Coolidge said, "When my son died, the glory of the presidency faded away."

Being in the White House does not make the heart happy. The fame of this world cannot satisfy the longings of a broken heart.

Had Hitler happiness? Was Mussolini a shining example of joy? You may be sure that all the promises of this world are as vain to others as they proved to be to those men.

When men have tried all that this world can give and find still a heart unsatisfied, they are ripe harvest for the Gospel. Sinners everywhere have in their bosom the unrest and the disillusionment that make them hunger for what can be found only in Christ. They may not know what they need, but they know instinctively that they need something. You and I know that Christ is the answer, the Balm in Gilead, the ease for every heartache, the satisfaction for every void in the human heart. Such a hunger by sinners proves that we can have revival.

3. The Wages of Sin Are Often the Incentive to Salvation.

Satan often overreaches himself. When he wanted to plague

Job by the destruction of his property, God permitted it. When he wanted to kill Job's sons and daughters, God allowed that. Still Job trusted and honored God. And Satan, in a rage of jealousy, said that, if he could but touch Job's body, Job would curse God. God allowed the experiment. And instead of Satan getting honor, the Lord showed how wonderfully He can give patience to a Christian in trouble and how wonderfully He comes to the help of His own afflicted. Millions have been comforted by Job's example. Satan meant it for evil, but God overruled.

The brothers of Joseph sold him into slavery; and he went to Egypt, they thought, to be forever out of their lives. But God used Joseph to save a nation, even his own family, from starvation during the famine. And Joseph said to his brothers, "Ye thought evil against me; but God meant it unto good" (Gen. 50:20).

Of course God hates sin. Sin is wicked rebellion against God. And Satan, who leads people on to sin, intends the damnation of their souls and the ruin of all happiness. But in this matter God often allows Satan to prepare the way for a revival. Where sin has done its normal work, there are broken hearts that can never be healed but by the Gospel of Jesus Christ and the saving touch of His salvation!

John 8:1-11 tells of a woman taken in adultery, in the very act, and brought before Jesus with the hope that He would condemn her to stoning or that Jesus could be accused of being the enemy of the law. You remember how Jesus stooped down and wrote with His finger on the ground, as though He heard them not, and then said to them, "He that is without sin among you, let him first cast a stone at her." And when He stooped again and wrote on the ground, these men, convicted by their own consciences, stole away one by one and left the woman alone with Jesus. And when Jesus looked up and saw no one but the woman, He said, "Woman, where are those thine accusers? hath no man condemned thee?'' She answered, "No man, Lord." And Jesus said unto her, "Neither do I condemn thee: go, and sin no more."

All these, the woman's captors and enemies, had stolen away. Why did she not leave, too? Jesus had obviously turned His back to leave the responsibility wholly upon His hearers. He did not detain the accusers, and He did not detain the accused. Yet she stayed! She did not want to leave. And I think we can see that clearly when she called Jesus, "Lord."

The adultery had brought no peace to her heart, only public shame and exposure, only the accusation of her neighbors. It made her a public spectacle. And it showed her, no doubt, that she needed something far more than any pleasure of this world.

When she saw Jesus, she knew that He was the One whom she wanted, that He could give what she needed. She trusted Him. She took Him as her Lord.

We cannot doubt but that this woman honestly turned to Jesus for mercy, and that He gave to the surrendered and believing heart the salvation she wanted.

Oh, in that case, sin overreached itself and prepared a woman's heart for God!

I know a beloved Christian worker, a professional musician who lived fast and loose in sin until suddenly he discovered that he was about to lose his wife, his home, and all the things that seemed most dear. He had never valued them before; now when he found that sin was about to rob him of home, love and happiness, he immediately turned to Christ. After long crying and many tears, he won his wife to Christ.

Sin overreached itself there, and the wages of sin simply prepared a heart for the Gospel.

We lament the sin everywhere about us. The wickedness of men, the drunkenness, divorce, adultery, unbelief in the Bible, lack of parental respect, lack of discipline of children, lack of reverence for the Bible—do you think that these things indicate that God cannot have revival? If so, you are dead wrong! For these things guarantee that there are broken hearts that need the Gospel, hearts that cannot be satisfied without the Gospel. Sin itself paves the way, with its wages, for revival.

When I was in the seminary, I drove a bus of Christian workers from the seminary to the jail every Sunday morning for services —one Sunday with men, the next with women. One morning when we had service in the women's chapel, I spoke on the woman taken in adultery and the forgiveness of Jesus.

A number of the women confined in the jail turned to Christ. Among them was one of the most striking conversions I have ever known. This woman trusted Christ and claimed Him openly. She seemed greatly assured about it. Then she praised God aloud. Walking back and forth, clapping her hands as the tears of joy ran down her face, she kept saying, "Thank God I got in jail! I wouldn't go to church, wouldn't listen to a preacher on the radio, wouldn't read a gospel tract, wouldn't allow anybody to talk with me about the Lord. I went on in sin with no sense of my need for God. But I went too far, and I got in jail. I thought I would rot in that lonely cell with no one to talk to, with no way to pass my time but to think about the ruin of my life. I came out here to the chapel only for a change, but, thank God, He spoke to my heart and saved me! Thank God I got in jail! God let me get in jail to keep me out of Hell!"

I believe she was exactly right—that God let her reap the wages of her sin to bring her to her senses and show her her need for God.

Do you know that many a man turns to God when the only alternative is suicide? Did you know that many a man has turned to God when he otherwise had determined to kill his estranged wife? Do you know that many a man has turned to God when he lost his job and was driven from his home and had become a bum? I have preached in city rescue missions all over

America and I have found that many, many of the men who turn
to Christ are brought to a readiness for the Gospel by the wages
of sin.

The more saloons we have, the more certain we can have
revival. The more divorces we have, the more hungry and broken
hearts there are that need God. The more men turn to infidelity and reap the barrenness of it, the heartbreak of it, the despair
of it, the more room there is for the Gospel.

How foolish and wicked to suppose that sin can keep down
revivals. The wages of sin makes men fit subjects for the Gospel,
makes the harvest ripe.

4. The Loss of Loved Ones Prepares
People to Hear the Gospel.

God has many ways to plow the hard ground of a sinner's
heart and get it ready for the gospel seed. One way is the loss
of loved ones.

While in revival services at Hastings, Minnesota, I went to
visit a family out on an island in the Mississippi River. The man
was notoriously hard and bitter. He had been nominally a Catholic. Now he seemed to hate God, the Bible and preachers, they
told me.

I was friendly with him and paid attention to his family,
learned the names of his children, talked and prayed with them.
Then I said to him, "Are these all of your children?"

There was a hushed silence. Then with choked voice he told
me of his three-year-old baby girl who had fallen into the
Mississippi River and drowned.

I was grieved for the man. But I told him about David's baby
and how David said, "I shall go to him, but he shall not return
to me" (II Sam. 12:23). I told him how little babies are kept by
the power of God, how that "as in Adam all die, even so in Christ
shall all be made alive." I told him how that whatever taint of

sin had been left by the baby's human inheritance, all of that had been paid by the blood of Christ and she was kept safe and so had gone to meet the Saviour. And I told him that, if he would trust the Saviour, he could see her, too.

Suddenly the man was utterly changed. He leaned against me and wept. I found that a Catholic priest had told him that, since the baby had not been sprinkled, she was lost. He had thought that the Christian religion taught that his beloved little girl was in Hell. If his baby was in Hell, he hardly wanted to go to Heaven. But now, since he had Bible assurance that the little one had gone to be with God, suddenly his heart was hungry for God and for Heaven. He had confidence in this poor preacher who had brought him the Gospel, and so wept on my shoulder. When I told him how to be saved, he instantly accepted the Saviour with glad heart.

I went away with this thought in my heart: multitudes whom we think are hard and impossible cases are really very near to the kingdom of God, if only we knew. In many a heart that seems hard, God has had His breaking plow and His stump puller at work. And the death of a loved one has prepared the soil to hear the Gospel.

Don't suppose that, because a woman is a Catholic or a Jew or because she is a professed unbeliever in the Bible, she does not miss the little one who is torn from her arms by death. Many women, when the breakfast dishes are washed and the men of the household have gone to their work and the children to school, get out of the dresser drawer or from a nearby table a baby book and look over the momentos of the little one who is gone.

There is the little footprint for identification, taken at the hospital. There is the little bit of blond baby hair, slightly curled, tied with a blue baby ribbon! There is the snapshot of the little one taking its first toddling steps. And there, it may be, is a picture of the grave and the flowers when the little one was put in the casket and carried out to the Silent City of the Dead and buried, along with the mother's heart.

I say, do not believe that such mothers cannot be reached with the Gospel. These mothers, whose arms are so empty, whose hearts are so hungry, who wonder if they will ever meet their little ones again—don't think they cannot be reached for Christ. God has in thousands, yea, in hundreds of thousands of cases, beckoning hands on the heavenly shore who are doing more than others of us could do, to woo these to Heaven, if we but take the Gospel in the power of God.

I remember the good deacon, "Daddy" Hickman, who died in Dallas, Texas. He had cancer of the liver. I, his pastor, was called to his bedside at three o'clock in the morning. For two hours I sat there beside him. We talked of heavenly things. He knew he was going to Heaven. He said to me, "Brother Pastor, I have carried the burden of prayer for these boys of mine these years. Now I am going. I must leave the burden on you. I ask you to never give up my boys. They must be saved!"

Those fine grown sons were gathered beside their father in these last hours. The Grim Reaper was only a few hours or minutes ahead, we knew. So we brought these grown sons one by one to tell their father good-by. He would grip their hands, look in their faces, call each by name and say, "Are you going to meet me in Heaven? You can't lie to your father on his death-bed. And I must know. Tell me, may I expect to meet you there?"

One by one these men broke down. Those who were unsaved would bury their faces in the pillow and weep, then promise their father to meet him in Heaven. Then I would take the Scriptures, and we would have the matter assured from the Word of God while he dealt with another son.

Thank God, when he went away at 5:00 a.m., already the whole family was depending upon the Saviour! Some had trusted the Lord before; some in that holy hour found Christ because their father was going to Heaven.

You see, the harvest is white, and God has ways of preparing it all the time in the hearts of sinners.

People mocked at Charles Alexander because he had people sing, "Tell Mother I'll Be There." But that is a proper and Christian sentiment. If God deals with people's hearts by the home-going of a mother, it is right to sing about it and preach about it. The song says,

> **I promised her, before she died,**
> **For Heaven to prepare:**
> **O Saviour, tell my mother I'll be there!**

You and I would be foolish not to thank God that He has dealt with many a heart and fixed there a longing that can never be satisfied but in Jesus and salvation.

5. *The Burning of Conscience Prepares*
Men to Hear the Gospel.

Thank God for that spark of celestial fire called conscience! Thank God that when I preach to a wicked man I know that he has within his own breast a voice that is on my side and on the side of God.

John the Baptist had preached to Herod, and Herod had imprisoned him; then at the request of a dancing girl and his adulterous wife, Herod had cut off the head of John the Baptist. Then he heard of the preaching of Jesus. And Matthew 14:1, 2 tells us:

"At that time Herod the tetrarch heard of the fame of Jesus, And said unto his servants, This is John the Baptist; he is risen from the dead; and therefore mighty works do shew forth themselves in him."

Oh, John the Baptist! Herod would never get away from him!

Herod would forever hear the warnings of that good man. He would dream about him. Now that Jesus was preaching and doing miracles, Herod's heart smote him, and he said, "This is John the Baptist; he is risen from the dead." I will tell you that one could preach to Herod more easily, knowing that God had a silent minister in his own breast reminding him of his sin.

Joseph's brothers sold him into slavery in Egypt. One would suppose that these hardhearted men were glad to be rid of the young sprout who had such dreams of his dominance over them. When they came to Egypt and saw Joseph but did not know him, and when their brother Benjamin was to be retained because of the money found in their sacks and Joseph's cup, they did not know that anybody else in the world knew about their sin. Yet they said one to another,

"We are verily guilty concerning our brother, in that we saw the anguish of his soul, when he besought us, and we would not hear; therefore is this distress come upon us. And Reuben answered them, saying, Spake I not unto you, saying, Do not sin against the child; and ye would not hear? therefore, behold, also his blood is required."—Gen. 42:21, 22.

I would not mind preaching to those brothers about their sins and their need of forgiveness. Their own consciences, at everything I might have said, would have risen up to brand them as the sinners they knew themselves to be.

Thank God, He has a witness in the heart of every man and woman in the world!

In Seattle, Washington, in a citywide campaign, I preached in one of the early services on restitution. I pleaded with Christians to go to offended brothers and be reconciled, make right their wrongs, to pay their debts, to see that there was nothing to hinder their prayers and their influence.

After the service, a despairing man met me in the back of the auditorium and asked me for help. "You have talked about making good the wrongs we have done," he said. "But how can I do it! I can never undo my sins. And I don't see how I can ever have peace with God."

He told me that he had been for years a panderer, that he had procured girls for the white slave trade. He would first win a girl's confidence and love, then lead her into sin, then reveal his purposes and leave her in a house of shame. He told me that for a year he had been haunted by the faces of the girls he had led into sin and ruin. "Many of those girls are already in Hell," he said. "How can I make any restitution for things like that! And how can God ever forgive me?"

He told me how that very day as he had ridden a ferry across Puget Sound he had looked down into the dark waters and longed for peace and wondered if he might slip over the rail and into the waters at the bottom of the Sound and there someway forget the tortured memories of the wrongs he had done!

Oh, you may be sure it was easy for me to tell him of the blood of Christ which washes away the vilest sin. It was easy for me to tell him, though it seemed almost too good for him to believe, that, "though your sins be as scarlet, they shall be as white as snow." I told him that a Christian should try to be reconciled with other Christians, but that a lost sinner could never pay God for his sins, could never undo most of them.

And I assure you that there was no difficulty for a brokenhearted preacher, with some blessed anointing upon him, to win that man to Christ that night. God had already cut him down with the sword of conscience.

And I say to you that God has put that candle of the Lord, that little spark of celestial fire—conscience—in the hearts of sinners to work with the Gospel for revival and soul winning. In every lost man's heart God has some voices crying out to him to repent.

6. *The Fear of Death on Every Hand Is a Powerful*
Influence to Aid the Gospel and Give Power
to Plain Bible Preaching.

In that Spirit-filled and exalting bit of praise which Zacharias, the father of John the Baptist, uttered after his son was born and named, he says that Christ came "the dayspring from on high," and He came "to give light to them that sit in darkness and in the shadow of death." The shadow of death coming, surely coming, whether soon or late, is over every thoughtful man and woman in the world.

I know that many will say that the fear of death is an unworthy motive. I know that many people foolishly urge preachers never to use the fear motive in preaching the Gospel. But they ignore the teaching and the example of Bible preachers.

Nineveh repented when Jonah preached, "Forty days, and Nineveh shall be overthrown." The fear of death turned men to repentance.

Jesus used this motive when He said, ". . . those eighteen, upon whom the tower in Siloam fell, and slew them, think ye that they were sinners above all men that dwelt in Jerusalem? I tell you, Nay: but, except ye repent, ye shall all likewise perish."

And we are told very sensibly that "Noah . . . moved with fear, prepared an ark to the saving of his house." Noah was moved with fear, and God intended that the preaching of the Gospel should use the fear of death which God has implanted in the human heart.

Wherever men hear the verdict of the doctor, "Cancer"; wherever the doctor says, "Active tuberculosis"; wherever men feel the infirmities of age and are reminded that they, too, must die, there is ground broken up, ready for the gospel seed.

But young people as well as old die. And young as well as old fear death. A girl, thirteen, came to Christ in one of my services in Texas. Then after she had trusted the Saviour and had assurance of forgiveness, she dried her eyes, smiled and said, "Now I will never be afraid to go to sleep anymore!"

Let us honestly face this truth taught in the Bible, that everywhere, even among sinners, the harvest is white. Let us admit that God has people ready to hear the Gospel if He only has people ready to go, people with the power of God on them, and ready to pay any price to win sinners.

The harvest is white!

Throughout these lectures we have insisted that we can have revival now. The Bible prophesies great revivals yet to come. This age is the age of revival, the age of the pouring out of the Holy Spirit for soul winning, the age when "whosoever shall call upon the name of the Lord shall be saved." We have insisted that God's mighty resources are sufficient for revival today. And we have tried to show that in all ages the circumstances were more or less inconsequential and could not prevent mighty revivals when the people of God paid His price for His power and were willing and fit to be used in winning souls. I trust we have showed that among lost sinners the ravages of sin, the disappointments of this world, the loss of loved ones, the burning of conscience, and the fear of death make sinners always ripe for revival. We can have revival now.

How, then, may we have revival? What are God's requirements, that He may pour out upon us His mighty, conquering, soul-winning power to win the hardest sinners, to change hearts, lives, homes and cities?

What must men do to have the revival God wants to give?

1. Revival Always Waits on God's People

In Matthew 9:37, 38, Jesus said to His disciples, "The harvest truly is plenteous, but the labourers are few; Pray ye therefore the Lord of the harvest, that he will send forth labourers into his harvest." God is not limited in the nature of the harvest but in the laborers.

On sending the seventy by twos into cities and places where He Himself would later come, Jesus told them, "The harvest truly is great, but the labourers are few: pray ye therefore the Lord of the harvest, that he would send forth labourers into his harvest" (Luke 10:2). To the twelve He said, "The harvest truly is plenteous." To the seventy He said, "The harvest truly is great." To both alike He said that the laborers are few and that they should pray the Lord of the harvest to send forth laborers. God has a manpower shortage in the matter of soul winning.

Jesus emphasized the same thing when the twelve disciples sat eating their lunch beside the well of Sychar in Samaria: "Say not ye, There are yet four months, and then cometh harvest?" Jesus told them, "Behold, I say unto you, Lift up your eyes, and look on the fields; for they are white already to harvest." Then He assured them that the reapers would receive wages and would gather fruit unto life eternal (John 4:34-36).

Please do not think the repetition of these three passages of Scripture either thoughtless or unnecessary. God does not wait for conditions to get right; He waits for men to get right! The harvest is not waiting because it is not ripe, but because the laborers are few. Jesus sent the seventy, new converts whom He could not call mature sheep but only lambs, because He had no one else to send. And as they went they were to pray that God would send forth laborers into the ripe harvest.

This teaching that revival waits on men and is postponed only for lack of adequate workers is often found in the Bible. In II Chronicles 7:14 is the promise, "If my people, which are called by my name, shall humble themselves, and pray, and seek my face, and turn from their wicked ways; then will I hear from heaven, and will forgive their sin, and will heal their land."

It is God's own people, those called by His name, who must pay the price for revival. Bartenders cannot have a revival. Modernists cannot have a revival. Atheists and infidels cannot have a revival. But, thank God, they cannot stop one either! Conditions, including the hearts of sinful men, are already ripe for revival. And when God's people meet His requirements, revival always comes.

When the disciples asked Jesus, "Lord, teach us to pray," He said we need to come like a man who pounded on his neighbor's door at midnight and said, "Friend, lend me three loaves; For a friend of mine in his journey is come to me, and I have nothing to set before him" (Luke 11:5, 6).

The trouble is not that there are no sinners who are hungry, but that we do not have the bread. Most of us would rather blame sinners for not eating than blame ourselves for not providing the bread; but Jesus said that the blame is with us!

In these lectures we have mentioned particularly certain great Bible revivals. In these revivals one easily sees that God did not give the revival until He found a man or men willing and fit to be used in the revival.

At Mount Carmel God could turn the whole nation back to Himself, causing them to forsake their Baal worship and return to the Lord, when Elijah was ready to challenge the people and pray down the fire of God.

It appears that it took God longer to get Jonah ready to preach in the great revival at Nineveh than it took to turn nearly the whole city to Him in sincere repentance.

Jesus came to Sychar, a city of the Samaritans, and there He knew that the field was ripe to harvest. The twelve apostles were with Him, but not one of them seemed to have had the slightest interest in getting anybody in the town saved. Just as Jesus had finally revealed to the woman that He was the Messiah, the attitude of the disciples is revealed as follows: "And upon this came his disciples, and marvelled that he talked with the woman: yet no man said, What seekest thou? or, Why talkest thou with her?"

The disciples really "marvelled" that Jesus would even talk to the woman. They did not dare say so, but each one would have liked to have asked Jesus, "Why talkest Thou with her?" Here was a ripe harvest and nobody to reap it.

But when Jesus got the woman saved, she left her waterpot and ran to the city. Her testimony was that of a new convert; yet God used it to bring all the people of the city out to see Jesus. He stayed there two days, and many were saved. Here is another striking example that God waits on Christians to have a revival. He waits on laborers to reap His harvest.

Before Pentecost the apostles and other disciples faced an almost impossible task. But Jesus plainly told them that they should tarry in Jerusalem until they were endued with power from on high. They—the twelve and some of the women and other disciples—continued steadfastly in prayer and supplication; and the mighty power of God came upon the disciples and a blessed revival, with about three thousand people saved.

Here again the problem was workers with the power of God on them. As soon as these Christians waited on God and were mightily filled with the power of the Holy Spirit, multitudes were converted in the hardest city in the world! It was another example that God waits on workers for revival.

2. For Great Revivals, We Must Have Evangelists

God had an Elijah for Mount Carmel, a Jonah for Nineveh. The Lord Jesus Himself was the evangelist at Sychar in Samaria, but a saved and Spirit-filled convert helped to collect the crowd and do personal work. At Pentecost God had Peter standing up with the eleven to preach, and others of the disciples, no doubt, preached. In the great revival by the River Jordan where such multitudes went to hear John the Baptist condemn sin and announce the Saviour who would save all who would repent and trust Him, we cannot ignore the preacher himself, the Spirit-filled evangelist, John the Baptist.

God has always used evangelists, men who are especially anointed and dedicated leaders, in great revivals.

It has been so in modern times. You cannot have a Reformation without a Luther or a Calvin. You could never have had the great Wesleyan revival without a John and Charles Wesley and Whitefield. We would never have had Charles G. Finney revivals except for Finney himself, the Spirit-filled, mighty prophet of God who did the work of an evangelist. The Moody revivals are inseparable from Moody himself. And the Billy Sunday revivals cannot be imagined without Billy Sunday. Other great revivals have been led by mighty evangelists. They had their weaknesses, but they were called of God to the work of evangelism, and dedicated and anointed for that work.

God has given to the church men for different purposes. "And he gave some, apostles; and some, prophets; and some, evangelists; and some, pastors and teachers" (Eph. 4:11). After apostles and prophets, and before pastors and teachers in importance, God gave evangelists.

There are some who would like to do without evangelists, some who would scorn them, curb them, berate them. But all such sin against God and against His holy Word. He has set the work of an evangelist in the body of Christ. These evangelists are not only called to give a gospel message to the unsaved, but according to the Scripture, they are "for the perfecting of the saints, for the work of the ministry," to the end that the body shall make increase (Eph. 4:12-16).

The church is a sick church that does not have evangelists. People will not be taught personal soul winning, will not be edified and built up for the ministry of God without the work of Spirit-filled, full-time, called and anointed evangelists.

Churches will lose their revival flavor if they do not have evangelists.

It is true that some pastors will win souls, but they will be fewer and fewer as we have fewer evangelists to set the pace. Without evangelists, we may not expect the great revivals God wants us to have. All the efforts to put evangelists into a minor place, to rob them of influence, circumscribe their preaching and keep them out of the churches, is working against God's harvest and great revivals.

A widely-known prophetic teacher was called to a principal city, the capital of a state, to lead in a citywide "revival campaign." His sermons on "The Mark of a Beast," on "The Coming Antichrist," "The Tribulation Period," etc., did not bring about a revival but division and strife among pastors. The result not only failed to be a revival, but it greatly hindered any future effort to get Christians united for a citywide revival effort in that city.

A blessed preacher and Bible teacher recently was invited to hold a citywide revival campaign. In recent years America has seen a number of great revivals. It was my privilege to lead in one such campaign where many hundreds were converted and the city profoundly moved. The preacher selected, a friend of mine, is not an evangelist, nor has he ever claimed to be. That is not his calling, not his anointing. He will preach good messages, but he will not see a great revival unless his ministry is entirely transformed. God does not give great revivals without evangelists.

In another city, good pastors got together to have a "revival campaign." So there would be no hard preaching against sin, no issue raised about movies, dances, lodges and other worldliness, they asked a good pastor to lead in the "revival campaign."

He preached good sermons, but he did not take the time for preparation of Christians by preaching against sin, by getting them to pray and win souls, as Moody and Torrey and Billy

Sunday and other blessed evangelists have always done. He preached sermons to the unsaved; but not many unsaved attended the services, there was a notable lack of real conviction, and pastors were disappointed because there was no genuine revival.

A lot of good preachers, sound preachers, devoted preachers are not called, not anointed, to be evangelists.

Don't suppose that a group of men could select a man more to their liking than D. L. Moody, put him in Moody's place in the Moody revivals and still have the same results. God chooses evangelists and anoints them. The best of them have learned by much waiting on God and by long experience how to promote a revival, how to get Christians to forsake their sins, pray and win souls, how to get sinners to the meeting, then how to get them convicted and saved.

It would be as foolish to set out to change the whole plan of Christian churches and say that we would do away with the local congregations called churches and the office of a pastor, as it is to try to do away with the office of an evangelist. The evangelist, named before the pastor, has a more important role in carrying out the Great Commission. It is rebellion against the New Testament plan, it is substituting human wisdom for the divine order when we try to get along without full-time, anointed, dedicated, Spirit-filled evangelists.

If we want revivals, we must pray for God to send the laborers and particularly that He will fit each one for the task God has for him to do. If we want to have a great time of revival so that every principal city and town in America will be shaken, then we must pray that God will raise up evangelists with the holy oil of God upon them, the breath of Heaven, the fullness of the Spirit.

3. For the Greatest Revivals, God's People Must Unite on Soul Winning

In the Bible account of the great revival at Pentecost, and

before and after it, one simple phrase is repeated again and again—"with one accord."

As they waited in the ten-day prayer meeting, "these all continued *with one accord* in prayer and supplication, with the women, and Mary the mother of Jesus, and with his brethren" (Acts 1:14).

Jesus had previously taught these disciples, "If two of you shall agree on earth as touching any thing that they shall ask, it shall be done for them of my Father which is in heaven" (Matt. 18:19). He said, "Where two or three are gathered together in my name, there am I in the midst of them" (Matt. 18:20).

Evidently the power in believing prayer increases in geometric ratio with the number of those really united in prayer. Two can agree and get anything. And it becomes clear that the more Christians we get to unite, really be of one accord in prayer, the more certain will be the great revival and the more fruitful its results.

Only one hundred and twenty of the disciples were united in heart at the end of the ten days' prayer meeting, when the day of Pentecost was fully come. They had started out with much less than that—just the disciples and the half brothers of Jesus and His mother and a few other women (Acts 1:14). But that handful of Christians, united in heart, could really ask "with one accord" for the pouring out of God's power.

Again we see the same beautiful phrase used in Acts 2:1, "And when the day of Pentecost was fully come, they were all *with one accord* in one place" as they prayed through the ten days and when the power of God came. Unity of heart, even the gathering in one place, were important for the great revival.

Of course all of us are glad for single churches to win souls in their regular services and to have special revival services whenever God leads. The local congregation is a divinely instituted unit. Yet oftentimes there is great lack of blessing because people are more absorbed in their own local church plans than in the much larger and more important issue of great revivals and in seeing multitudes saved.

It is well, then, for God's people, those who believe the same Book, who are saved by the same blood, who have been given the same Great Commission and are of like precious faith in these essentials, to unite in saving souls.

I do not ask that people throw away their convictions. But people can honestly differ on the matter of baptism and be sincerely united in pleading before God for a great revival. People may honestly differ as to whether a church government should be local and democratic congregational form or the rule by an episcopacy, yet unite if they love the Lord and believe the Bible and accept responsibility for the Great Commission, in great citywide revivals. On the day of Pentecost "they were all with one accord in one place."

May God bring the same blessed state to pass in cities and towns all over America! A certain unity of heart on the main thing—soul winning—is essential if we are to have the greatest revivals.

Even the great rejoicing and blessing of the continuing revival were enjoyed with the same unity of heart after Pentecost, for Acts 2:46 says, "And they, continuing daily *with one accord* in the temple, and breaking bread from house to house, did eat their meat with gladness and singleness of heart." Thank God for the unity of heart among God's people!

We can have denominations without having a sectarian spirit and isolation among believers. Christians can work together to get people saved and can rejoice together when sinners are saved. God had in mind great citywide movements; and when groups can be gathered and centered on this blessed end and purpose, then God can give the revivals.

Let me say here that this is one reason why I feel a cooperative or union campaign, when fundamental churches and pastors officially set out to work together in soul-winning effort, is better than an independent revival campaign where an evangelist makes independent plans and preaches the Gospel. Better independent campaigns than none at all, and better a few saved than none; but the greatest revival results have always depended somewhat on how many born-again Bible believers one could enlist in the same prayer and effort.

In Acts 4:24, again the people of God were "with one accord." That verse says, "And when they heard that, they lifted up their voice to God *with one accord,* and said, Lord, thou art God, which hast made heaven, and earth, and the sea, and all that in them is." When persecution and trouble came, the people of God were still with one accord and they prayed with one voice and heart! How could such a revival close! How could God quit giving His blessing! The revival continued, and multitudes of people were saved, including chief priests and thousands of others.

Soul winning is the main thing for any Bible-believing Christian who is really surrendered to the will of God. The foolish talk of infidels that there are some three hundred denominations and that every one of them understands the Bible differently is not really true. There are minor matters in which there is very great variety of opinion, in Christian doctrine and in Bible interpretation. But there is no room for much difference among sincere Bible believers on the great principal doctrines: that all men are sinners, that Christ died to save sinners, that the blood of Christ atones for sin, that men need to be born again, that there is a Heaven for those who, trusting in Christ, are born again, and a Hell for those who will not repent and trust Christ. There is no room for difference of opinion about the fact that God has given to His people the Great Commission and that we are to get the Gospel to every creature.

I have been for many years working with Bible-believing

Christians of many denominations. I have found that Baptists, Presbyterians, Methodists, Mennonites, Christian and Missionary Alliance, Assemblies of God, Salvation Army, Nazarenes, the Reformed Church, the Christian Church, Lutherans, Evangelicals, Congregationalists and many others, when they truly believe the Bible and have been born again, can happily unite in soul saving. **(EDITOR'S NOTE: Things have changed since Dr. Rice made this statement. Some of these groups are now members of the National Council and World Council of Churches.)**

And the isolation of sectarian pride and denominational prejudice, often promoted by self-seeking denominational leaders so that people are discouraged from uniting in soul-winning work, greatly hinders revival. Let every local church and every denomination do all it can to win souls. But God still wants His born-again, Bible-believing people to work together wherever possible to the saving of multitudes of sinners. That was His plan at Pentecost; it is His plan now.

I do not say that Christians should yoke up with modern infidels who deny the Bible and the deity of Christ, who themselves are not converted and do not seek to convert others. To yoke up with unbelievers is a sin. I do not ask that Christians anywhere compromise on essential doctrines and convictions. I simply ask what God asks—that Christians put soul winning first and do everything possible to reach the unsaved. That involves being "with one accord" with other Christians who have the same motives and purposes. And it will often involve uniting with other such Christians in great citywide or areawide campaigns.

It is well to remember that down through the centuries the the great revivals were never confined to one denomination and, in given cities, were not confined to any particular local church.

The Wesleyan revivals permeated England. Wesley, whenever possible, preached in the Church of England church houses, while he fellowshiped also with independent groups like the Moravians. Only near his death did Wesley consent to the organization of a denomination as such, separate from the Anglican Church.

Although Spurgeon was a Baptist and pastor of a Baptist church, his work was largely interdenominational, citywide, nationwide, worldwide.

In Marion, Ohio, an old saintly pastor heard me preach who had been converted under Spurgeon's ministry and trained in Spurgeon's Pastors' College. After saying some things which burn in my heart today but which I shall not repeat here, this Rev. Robert Hughes told me that the union campaign we were then in reminded him of the time when Spurgeon, an Anglican bishop or two, and others, were on the same platform in a united, soul-winning campaign in England.

Everybody knows that the work of Moody, Torrey, Charles G. Finney and Billy Sunday cut across all sectarian lines. They called for the people who believed the Bible, people who were born again, those who wanted to obey Christ in soul winning, to get together for revival. Moody and Sunday alike insisted that, when they were called to a city for a revival campaign, the pastors should unite in the invitation, and they generally did.

Great revivals have everywhere brought together mighty crowds. That means then that the best revivals will be held in large neutral auditoriums, not in a local church. No synagogues could hold the crowds that attended the ministry of Jesus. The crowds that heard John the Baptist by the Jordan River could not have collected in any porch of the Temple. The revivals under the leadership of Moody, Torrey, J. Wilbur Chapman and Billy Sunday would have been impossible had men insisted that the services be conducted in their own church. The enormous crowds that gathered in the fields to hear Whitefield and Wesley could not have been accommodated in any cathedral of England.

Let us learn God's lesson—that His people ought to get together and make large plans to reach every creature with the Gospel. That means mass evangelism, with anointed and specially called and experienced evangelists. It means that Christians who hold to the simple fundamentals will cooperate. It means that countless multitudes can be gathered to hear the Gospel in city auditoriums, under great tents, and in other large public places, when such people would never attend a church and would go to Hell if their only chance to be saved were in local church services.

In my union revival campaign held in Kleinhan's Music Hall, Buffalo, seating 2,800, there were 997 public professions of faith. What a blessed time we had! The converts were dealt with very carefully in an inquiry room, and it was discovered that over three hundred of the converts had no church preference whatever! That meant that more than one-third of these converts would never have attended a revival in a local church. Neither they nor their parents nor anybody near and dear to them attended a church so that they could have a preference.

If we expect to reach the drunkards, the harlots, the atheists, the Jews, the Catholics, we must make provision in great central and neutral places where God's Bible-believing Christians will unite in getting the Gospel to sinners, to whole cities full of sinners, and so winning thousands who would otherwise never be won.

Oh, for a oneness of heart among the people of God on the main business of soul winning!

4. For Great Revivals We Must Have Evangelistic Preaching of a Special Flavor and Power Suited to the Crowds and the Occasion

A certain kind of preaching marks God's anointed evangelist.

It is a mistake to think that simply preaching on the plan of salvation will bring a revival. Such preaching alone will neither revive the people of God to get them on praying ground and endued with soul-winning power, nor will it convict and convert hardened sinners.

Elijah could have a mighty revival at Mount Carmel, but it would be shortsighted to ignore the kind of preaching and warning Elijah had done which preceded the falling of the fire. The boldness of Elijah in condemning sin was so proverbial that, when the widow's son died in whose house Elijah lived, she said unto Elijah, "What have I to do with thee, O thou man of God? art thou come unto me to call my sin to remembrance, and to slay my son?" (I Kings 17:18). And just before the marvelous demonstration of God's power on Mount Carmel, Elijah said to wicked King Ahab, "I have not troubled Israel; but thou, and thy father's house, in that ye have forsaken the commandments of the Lord, and thou hast followed Baalim" (I Kings 18:18).

It is astonishing to see the man of God whom Ahab has sought three years to slay, now giving the orders and Ahab running quickly to call the 450 prophets of Baal, 400 prophets of the groves which ate at Jezebel's table, and all the people of Israel to Mount Carmel at Elijah's word!

Elijah could pray down the fire of God from Heaven, for God knew that immediately Elijah would command the people, "Take the prophets of Baal; let not one of them escape," and would bring these prophets of Baal and kill them at the brook Kishon (I Kings 18:40).

There is a distinctive character to the evangelist's message, and it involves particularly a boldness in condemning sin and calling men to repentance.

Obadiah was a good man, a believer in Elijah's time, the governor of the palace. He hid out one hundred prophets of God by fifty in a cave, and fed them on bread and water to deliver them from wicked Jezebel. But since he did not have the heart to condemn sin, he could not bring a revival.

Jonah preached to Nineveh; and his message from God was, "Forty days, and Nineveh shall be overthrown" (3:4).

All the foolish talk that preachers should give "a positive message," by which modernists and pussyfooters mean a soft message that pats sin on the back and doesn't hurt anybody's feelings, never names a sin nor calls a sinner to repentance—that kind of talk ignores the clear teaching of the Word of God. And this so-called "positive preaching," which never names a sin nor condemns it nor calls Christians to forsake their backsliding nor sinners to repent, never did bring a revival and never will.

Jesus won the woman at the well of Sychar in Samaria, but the sword point that reached the woman's heart was Christ's plain revelation that He knew she was living in adultery with another man to whom she was not married, though she had been married five times! And the evidence that the woman gave to the men of Sychar was, "He told me all that ever I did."

There was iron in the preaching of John the Baptist. To men who were outwardly the best churchmen of his day, John the Baptist said,

"O generation of vipers, who hath warned you to flee from the wrath to come? Bring forth therefore fruits meet for repentance. . . . And now also the axe is laid unto the root of the trees: therefore every tree which bringeth not forth good fruit is hewn down, and cast into the fire."

He preached that God's fan is in His hand,

"And he will throughly purge his floor, and gather his wheat into the garner; but he will burn up the chaff with unquenchable fire."—Matt. 3:7-12.

That is evangelistic preaching by a Spirit-filled preacher, a typical evangelist.

John the Baptist faced Herod and said pointedly that he sinned in taking his brother's wife.

What kind of preaching was that which Peter did at Pentecost? Bible preaching, of course, preaching that told how to be saved, but it had the sharpness of the Roman short sword and the crushing power of a battle-ax! "Him...ye have taken, and by wicked hands have crucified and slain." Again he said, "Therefore let all the house of Israel know assuredly, that God hath made that same Jesus, whom ye have crucified, both Lord and Christ" (Acts. 2:23, 36).

In the next sermon Peter accused the people as follows: "But ye denied the Holy One and the Just, and desired a murderer to be granted unto you; And killed the Prince of life, whom God hath raised from the dead; whereof we are witnesses" (Acts 3:14, 15).

And in the first sermon at Pentecost, the application was, "Repent" (Acts 2:38). In the second sermon it was likewise, "Repent ye therefore" (Acts 3:19). They were to repent in order that their sins might be blotted out.

Spirit-filled Stephen preached like an evangelist:

"Ye stiffnecked and uncircumcised in heart and ears, ye do always resist the Holy Ghost: as your fathers did, so do ye. Which of the prophets have not your fathers persecuted? and they have slain them which shewed before of the coming of the Just One; of whom ye have been now the betrayers and murderers: Who have received the law by the disposition of angels, and have not kept it."—Acts 7:51-53.

I do not wonder that they were cut to the heart, that they hated Stephen and killed him; but that Gospel cut Saul of Tarsus to the heart too deep for him to ever be cured, and he turned to God.

Every evangelist who has been mightily used of God in soul winning has been sharp in his denunciation of sin and explicit and plain in naming it.

Gamaliel Bradford, biographer of D. L. Moody, acknowledges that Moody preached much on the love of God, but he reminds us also that D. L. Moody was sharp and powerful in his preaching against sin and says that Hell was always in the background of Moody's preaching. All the biographers of Moody agree that he was unrelenting in his demand that people make restitution for wrongs, that he condemned the theater roundly, that he preached on drunkenness many times, and that his sermons on sowing and reaping were convicting and almost terrifying. Moody clearly condemned even Sunday newspapers, condemned membership in secret orders.

Charles G. Finney was relentless in preaching against sin, and his preaching was often terrifying so that people fell from the pews to their knees and cried out to God for mercy.

Most people remember the sharp preaching of Billy Sunday against sin.

Those who heard Gipsy Smith after he was eighty may have forgotten that, when he was in his prime and had great revivals, his preaching on repentance and on restitution was bold, specific and powerful in condemning sin. One of the most moving messages I ever read was a sermon preached by Gipsy Smith in a citywide campaign in Kansas City, Missouri, on "Washing Stripes" or "Making Wrongs Right."

Dr. R. A. Torrey was so specific and bold in his preaching against the dance that society people in an Australian city took it up, and for a joke invited Torrey to visit one of their dances. He went and prayed in public, then preached powerfully. Torrey was equally plain in preaching against the theater, against the lodges and other sins and hindrances.

Evangelistic preaching must be the kind that gets Christians to turn from their worldliness and waywardness so they will have power with God and influence with men, and it must be the kind that will cause sinners to repent.

I have just read again one of the biographies of D. L. Moody, *The Wonderful Career of Moody and Sankey in Great Britain and America.* The author is rather amazed that for the first eight or nine days of the revival, Moody preached to Christians, showing them their sins, laying on their hearts a burden for soul winning and teaching them how to pray. No one can be much of an evangelist who does not learn to prepare Christians for revival.

An evangelist in the nature of the case must learn certain methods which go with a revival.

We well understand that God could have saved men without using human instruments, if He had chosen to do so. He could have had the angel show Cornelius and his household how to be saved without sending all the way to Joppa for Simon Peter, who was temporarily at the house of Simon a tanner. But God chose to use human beings as instruments and human methods. God could have saved sinners without the instrumentality of preaching, yet "it pleased God by the foolishness of preaching to save them that believe" (I Cor. 1:21).

God has ordained that people should be gathered in crowds to hear the Gospel, that some man of God should preach to them with boldness and power. It is the plan of God that lost people should be urged to trust Christ, then to make an open confession of Christ before men (Matt. 10:32; Rom. 10:9, 10). It is God's plan that Christians should do personal work. Nothing can be clearer than that one who hears the Gospel is to tell it to others. Every Christian is to take part in the carrying out of the Great Commission. That means that the man who does not try to run sinners down and get the Gospel to sinners could not be much of an evangelist.

An evangelist must seek to get the Christian people together to pray and prepare for revival. He must seek to teach Christians to go out and compel sinners to come in to hear the Gospel. He must, one way or another, try to get the Gospel to everyone in a community. That involves promotion, enlistment, propaganda or advertising. No good evangelist is content to preach to small crowds or content to preach to Christians only when there are sinners to be reached.

Ultradispensational friends scorn the public invitation to accept Christ and confess Him openly before men. But this method of D. L. Moody, R. A. Torrey, J. Wilbur Chapman and all the great evangelists is ordained of God. A great deal of leeway is allowed, so each one may follow the leading of the Spirit, but no one could do the work of an evangelist to advantage who does not someway get sinners to decide in their hearts and to claim Christ openly before men. That was done at Pentecost and has been done everywhere else in great revivals—in Bible times and in modern times.

One, to be an evangelist, must learn the methods of evangelism, methods which God has blessed and which inherently go with the evangelistic message and urgency and boldness.

In the nature of the case, evangelistic preaching is not formal preaching. There should be a brightness, a sincerity, a forthrightness, an urgency about the preaching of a man who has set out to keep people out of Hell and bring them to trust Christ and claim Him openly as Saviour. There should be a holy boldness. There should be tears and compassion. As a result, the preaching will be all the more personal, direct and powerful.

O God, raise up evangelists, and teach all preachers to "do the work of an evangelist," as Timothy was commanded to do (II Tim. 4:5).

5. Revivals Wait for People to Have the Mighty Power of the Holy Spirit for Soul Winning

R. A. Torrey's favorite theme was "The Baptism of the Holy

Ghost," the mighty power of the Holy Spirit to come upon a Christian as a special enduement, subsequent to conversion, to enable him to win souls! Were that the favorite topic of preachers today, we would have more revivals.

"The Baptism of the Holy Ghost" was also the favorite theme of D. L. Moody. He himself definitely knew that he had been endued with power from on high. He could name the day when, long after his conversion and after two years of waiting and pleading with God, he received such overwhelming visitation of the power of God that he was compelled to say, "Lord, that is enough! If I have any more, it will kill me!" Moody knew that his power was a special miraculous enduement of the Holy Spirit.

Charles G. Finney uses similar terminology about the baptism of the Holy Spirit and tells us that again and again he would set apart a day for fasting and prayer, "for a new baptism of the Holy Ghost."

I have deliberately used the term, "the baptism of the Holy Ghost," which is offensive to many. I personally prefer the term more often used in the Bible, "filled with the Spirit" or "filled with the Holy Ghost"; but we had as well face the plain fact that the people to whom the term, "the baptism of the Holy Ghost," is offensive as a name for a special enduement of power from on high, find the blessing as offensive as the name.

I am not speaking about talking in tongues. I am not speaking of any so-called eradication of the carnal nature. I am speaking about an enduement of power which can be had by Christians as a special blessing to be sought and had after conversion, or perhaps occasionally at conversion, but certainly separate from it.

What happened to the disciples at Pentecost was what Jesus had promised, "Ye shall be baptized with the Holy Ghost not many days hence." The Scriptures seem to teach that the baptism of the Holy Ghost, the fullness of the Spirit, the pouring out of the Holy Ghost, the gift of the Spirit, the enduement of power from on high are all one and the same thing. (For fuller discussion see my large book, *The Power of Pentecost.)*

But I am not here arguing for terminology. I do not care whether you say you are baptized with the Holy Spirit or full of the Spirit or that you are endued with power from on high. But I am desperately anxious that those who set out to win souls have a supernatural enabling, an empowering from Heaven for the task.

The promise of Jesus in Acts 1:8 comes as powerfully to us as to the disciples to whom He first addressed it: "But ye shall receive power, after that the Holy Ghost is come upon you: and ye shall be witnesses unto me both in Jerusalem, and in all Judaea, and in Samaria, and unto the uttermost part of the earth."

How presumptuous we are to suppose that New Testament Christians needed a special enduement of power, but that for us, college degrees and seminary training are sufficient! How foolish to suppose that the Galilean fishermen needed the power of the Holy Ghost, but we need only personal magnetism, culture and personality! When for these preachers the Word of God was not enough unless it was preached in the power of God, who can honestly believe that orthodoxy is all that God requires of us?

No Christian can be a personal soul winner unless he has power from God. And no evangelist can lead in blessed revivals with power except he be endued with power from on high.

6. Great Revivals Wait on People Who Are Willing to Prevail in Prayer

The classic revival text, II Chronicles 7:14, says, "If my people, which are called by my name, shall humble themselves, and pray, and seek my face, and turn from their wicked ways; then will I hear from heaven, and will forgive their sin, and will heal their land." Actually that whole verse speaks of prayer. If God's people shall first "humble themselves," they get on praying ground. Then when they pray, they ask for specific things. Then when they "seek God's face," they keep on pleading with God, begging God, waiting on God in prayer. And when they "turn from their wicked ways," they are removing the hindrances to prayer. Prevailing prayer is the secret of revival.

Necessarily I put this to follow the need for the power of the Holy Spirit, because after one knows that he needs the mighty power of God from on high to make him a soul winner, he must be willing to wait on God for that power.

I have no sympathy with those who say that at Pentecost the disciples needed to wait ten days in fasting, prayer and pleading, but that now we can have the same kind of power without any heart-searching, any penitence, any self-denial, without any long period of heartbroken prayer. I do not believe it! It does not seem sensible, and certainly historically that theory has been proven incorrect.

I have never known of any great revival in which there was not mighty, prevailing prayer. God does not give the mighty power of the Holy Spirit except to such people as have hungered and thirsted for God's power and waited patiently before Him until in His mercy He made them fit to be filled with power.

Recently I had occasion to recommend a young preacher to hold a revival campaign. I had confidence in him because, in a conference on evangelism when all of us were on our faces in prayer, I happened to be near this young preacher. I heard him begging God for forgiveness for his coldness, his powerlessness. I heard him promise God that he would never give up without having the power of God upon his ministry.

When he went to the revival effort to which I had recommended him, he found most discouraging circumstances. He called the people to prayer, and hours were spent in waiting on God. With plain preaching and with day and night praying, the opposition melted away, and God's blessings came mightily upon the people. Souls were won, and a church saved from division and strife.

I recommended this same young man for another revival effort, and the pastor wrote to tell how, in the midst of most difficult circumstances, he had called the people to prayer and had waited on God until power and unity came. Souls were saved and the work built up.

Too long we have been afraid of fanaticism. God give us some fanatics! Too long we have been afraid of wildfire when in truth we had no fire. Too long we have been on the defensive.

Many of us have been so afraid that someone would think we talked in tongues that we did not fret because all around us people were going to Hell. Some of us were so anxious that no one would think we claimed sinless perfection, that we ignored the power of the Holy Spirit. We did not seek His power and did not have it. Many of us would rather be respectable than powerful. Many of us would rather please men than please God and win souls. I say, we have been on the defensive too long.

I know some have misused this doctrine of the fullness of the Spirit. But that only illustrates how vital the doctrine is. Men cannot win souls without the power of God. Men cannot have revival without an enduement of power from on high. And this power comes in answer to prevailing prayer.

R. A. Torrey tells how a few young men met night after night and prayed until the revival of 1905 came in Wales, with Dr. Torrey leading. In that revival about one hundred thousand souls were won to Christ. Others will remember the haystack prayer meeting where some college students prayed in the lee of a haystack in the rain and started much of the missionary movement.

In England a bedridden saint of God prayed until God brought Moody from America to England, then prayed until hundreds of souls were saved in her church.

Charles G. Finney tells how Abel Clary followed him in revival meetings and prayed, often not attending the services but waiting and weeping before God for His power. Father Nash also was moved to pray mightily for the Finney revivals, and Finney himself ascribed the power of God which came upon him largely to the prayers of men such as these, as well as his own prayers.

If we are to have revivals, we must prevail with God in prayer.

Let us sum up the truth of this chapter. God waits on men for revivals. God is ready to do His part. The harvest is white, but the laborers are few. We should continually pray that God will send laborers into His harvest.

And we might sum up very simply His requirements. In Jeremiah 29:12, 13 we are told: "Then shall ye call upon me, and ye shall go and pray unto me, and I will hearken unto you. And ye shall seek me, and find me, when ye shall search for me with all your heart." We can find God's power, His might, His miraculous manifestation in revival if we simply seek Him with all our hearts.

God wants His people to seek revival with a holy abandon. Paul suffered the loss of all things and counted them but dung. No wonder God could use him to save souls! Paul went "night and day with tears," both "publickly, and from house to house" in his preaching at Ephesus (Acts 20:20, 31). Paul could wish himself accursed from Christ to win the Jews (Rom. 9:3)!

The disciples in Bible times set out facing martyrdom with holy joy. What did it matter to them that their goods were destroyed? What did it matter to them that they were hounded and persecuted, were thrown into dungeons, that they could have none of the comforts of home and family which other men have?

They went as gladly to the soul-winning task as a bride to the wedding altar or as a soldier returning home!

This holy abandon which God requires of those who would be His laborers would make it so that human love would seem incidental. A man for love of Christ would appear to hate father, mother, wife, children, brothers, sisters, houses, lands, yea, and his own life also (Luke 14:26)! Oh, this holy business of winning souls ought to get such a hold on a Christian's heart that nothing else in this world could much matter! This is the one business that makes Heaven rejoice, that adds stars to the crown of the Lord Jesus, that brings eternal glory to the soul winner.

So in Christ's dear name, let us offer ourselves living sacrifices to be the laborers God can use to win souls and bring about revival in America.

Soul Winner's Fire

Soul Winner's Fire

John R. Rice

SWORD of the LORD
PUBLISHERS

P.O. BOX 1099, MURFREESBORO, TN 37133

Printed in the United States of America

Table of Contents

Preface 7

1. "He That Winneth Souls Is Wise" 9

2. God's Way in Soul Winning 21

3. The Compassionate Heart 41

4. The Soul-Winner's Fire 45

5. Praying for Revival 59

6. Evangelistic Preaching 75

7. The Soul-Winner's Feet 91

8. Unsaved Brothers! 103

Preface

As a fifteen-year-old boy, I had my first taste of the joy of soul winning. I persuaded a friend to confess himself a sinner and look to Christ for salvation. Since that day it has been the longing of my soul to bring people to trust in Christ as their personal Saviour.

These chapters appeared at various times in THE SWORD OF THE LORD. Each one was planned for a particular time and occasion; now they have been selected for this book as centering around soul winning and revival. I trust the dear Lord will use them to warm and make tender the hearts of God's people in a deep concern for a lost world.

Three principal thoughts seem especially urgent to me: first, that every Christian ought to win souls; second, that we ought to have a holy passion, a tearful and compelling earnestness, an apostolic fervor of soul; and third, that we must have a divine enablement of the Holy Spirit.

By saving souls we do not mean getting people to join the church, or to be merely reformed, or to go through certain religious rites. We believe that the whole world lies in sin. People are all undone, lost, ruined sinners who cannot save themselves. Not an outward change in the life, but an inward change in the heart, a new birth by which one becomes a born-again child of God, with all sins forgiven—that is what every man

and woman, and every child who has reached the age of account-ability needs. Christ died on the cross to put away the sin of the whole world. Those who trust in Him, in penitent faith accepting Him as their Saviour, depending on Him for forgiveness of their sins and everlasting life and a home in Heaven, are saved and become the children of God.

So to be a soul winner means to cause people to realize their need of Christ as personal Saviour and to lead them to commit themselves wholly to Him, with heart faith. A sinner who does so trust Christ is a forgiven child of God, and one who leads the sinner to make this heart decision is a soul winner.

Oh, the blessed rewards God has for the soul winner!

Nothing is clearer in the Bible than this: every Christian can and ought to win souls. Andrew won Peter. Philip won Nathanael. Jesus won the woman at the well of Sychar in Samaria, and she in turn won so many of her townspeople. Every Christian may have the marvelous privilege of winning souls.

Dear reader, if God stirs your heart, will you not start out at once to win souls to Christ?

It is the humble prayer of the author that God may use these simple messages to start soul-winning fires and to cause many Christians to introduce lost sinners to the Saviour. Grant it, O God!

JOHN R. RICE

"The fruit of the righteous is a tree of life; and he that winneth souls is wise."—Prov. 11:30.

It is the wise person who takes the long look. How foolish to think only of today with its passing pleasure or profit! Esau is a classic example of the man who thought only of the pleasures of today. He sold his birthright for a mess of pottage. Afterwards he found no place of repentance, though he sought it carefully with tears. He threw away his opportunity to be the head of a great race, the ancestor of Jesus Christ, for a bowl of chili. On that account, the Bible calls Esau that "profane person." Whatever faults Jacob had, he did take the long look.

Jacob was given spiritual wisdom, and sacrificed, suffered and sweated to receive the promised blessing in the uncounted years ahead. The best estimate of these two—the folly of Esau and the wisdom of Jacob—is expressed in the words of the Lord: "Jacob have I loved, but Esau have I hated."

Abraham was wise; Lot was foolish. Abraham counted himself a sojourner and lived in tents all his days, as did Isaac and Jacob, heirs with him of the same promise. Hebrews 11:13-16 tells us:

"These all died in faith, not having received the promises, but having seen them afar off, and were persuaded of them, and embraced them, and confessed that they were strangers and pilgrims on the earth. For they that say such things declare plainly that

they seek a country. And truly, if they had been mindful of that country from whence they came out, they might have had opportunity to have returned. But now they desire a better country, that is, an heavenly: wherefore God is not ashamed to be called their God: for he hath prepared for them a city."

That heavenly wisdom of Abraham, who by faith took the long look, will never be fully justified until the New Jerusalem comes down from God out of Heaven, and Abraham dwells in eternal happiness in the land of Palestine, made new like the Garden of Eden, in the presence of Christ and the Father with all the redeemed. On the other hand, Lot, who was enamored by the riches of this world, moved into Sodom and there saw the ruin of his home, the death of his wife, and later was guilty of drunken shame with his own daughters. Lot sought the things of today, but Abraham looked to the morrow. Lot chose the things that are seen, which are temporal, while Abraham chose the things that are unseen, which are eternal (II Cor. 4:18).

Every day I see those who take the short look and live only for today. Their thoughts and efforts are centered on food, clothing, jobs, business, pleasure, which are enjoyed for a moment or a day or a year, and then vanish away.

The Wisdom of the Soul Winner in the Light of the Worth of a Soul

"He that winneth souls is wise." We may put it down, on the authority of Holy Writ, that the best wisdom of this world is not shown by the banker nor by the statesman nor by the educator nor by the millionaire businessman, but by the humble soul winner. All other labor is insignificant beside the supreme labor of winning souls. All other efforts are as good as wasted when the results they bring are considered beside the eternal and glorious results of soul winning.

The Saviour Himself indicated that one soul is worth more

than all the world: "For what shall it profit a man, if he shall gain the whole world, and lose his own soul? Or what shall a man give in exchange for his soul?" (Mark 8:36, 37).

Certain considerations help us to see the value of a soul, and I want to suggest them for your prayerful meditation. Our fathers were accustomed to pray, "Lord, roll on us the weight of immortal souls." Again and again I have heard that heartfelt petition as men besought God to give them a Heaven-born concern for the salvation of sinners. That prayer I heard often in my childhood, and I make it my own again today.

Soul winning is such a delicate art, it requires such a heavenly wisdom, it weighs so little in the minds of worldly men, that we are not likely to win souls unless we consider some appalling and glorious facts that bear on the subject. Suppose we think about the fact of Hell, the ruin and misery of this world, the death of Christ, and the glories of Heaven, as they bear on soul winning.

The Fact of Hell

I suppose the most horrible, concrete fact in all the world is that of Hell. The doctrine of Hell has a most prominent place in the Bible. Even Jesus Himself, who spake as never man spake, the tender and lowly One, the forgiving, the healing, the comforting Jesus, referred again and again to the place called Hell. The most startling things ever said in the Bible about it came from His lips.

It was Jesus who said that the worm does not die and the fire is not quenched in Hell.

It was Jesus who said that men should be cast both soul and body into Hell.

It was Jesus who opened for us the lid of Hell and let us hear the cries of the doomed rich man who lifted up his eyes in torment and begged for one drop of water to cool his tongue,

as he was tormented in flames!

If any man has a heart, a soul, he ought to be profoundly moved at the thought of one human being going to that place!

Let us be honest about it; the Bible does teach that Hell is a place. It teaches that men are conscious there, that men remember there, that they cry out, beg for water, long to warn their loved ones, "lest they also come into this place of torment." The Bible does teach that the smoke of their torment in Hell ascends up forever and ever, and that they have no rest day or night. It does teach that all the impenitent who die without Christ wake up in the terrible world of eternal punishment. The Scripture makes clear that at the resurrection of the unjust, the unsaved dead will come out of Hell only long enough to get physical bodies and then be sentenced forever to the unending doom of the lake of fire (Rev. 20)!

If they believe the Bible, honest people will not quibble about a literal Hell. If Hell is not a fact, then the inspiration of the Bible is not a fact. If Hell is not a fact, then the deity of Christ is not a fact, for He believed in and preached about Hell.

The Red Cross takes up collections for storm sufferers and victims of floods and drought. Congress passes laws and appropriates money for the relief of the distressed. A recent report of some government officials indicated a good deal of anxiety because some families were so poor that they could only attend the movies once a week and other nights must remain at home! Other social activities appeal to the tenderhearted on the basis that some children do not have as much milk to drink as others, and some do not have lunch money, and some boys do not have clubs, "older brothers" and outings as do the children of the better privileged. In fact, the term "underprivileged" is used again and again these days, as if to be "underprivileged" was the greatest of disasters.

We may well help the poor, but no want or poverty, no distress

of mind or body is to be compared for a moment with the torture of the damned who go to Hell. The most awful fact is the fact of Hell and that some whom we know, who live in the same houses or go to the same schools or work in the same business or are our daily companions, will die and spend an eternity away from God, eternally unforgiven, eternally sinning, and eternally doomed. That one fact will enable you to see what God meant when He said, "He that winneth souls is wise."

If one who reads this has yet any tenderness of heart, any love for his neighbor, any of the milk of human kindness, then he will see some of the spiritual wisdom in winning souls.

I do not wonder that modernists who deny the fact of Hell, or who scoff at the idea of literal fire, do not win souls. Not believing the Bible, which is the wisdom of God, it is not strange that they miss the wisdom of soul winning. Let him who would be wise consider the eternal doom of the lost.

Disappointments and Unhappiness of This World

This present world is a failure, which fact is not hard to prove. That homes have failed is evidenced by the ever-mounting divorce rate. About one in every two and a half marriages ends in divorce, and many other couples live in stark tragedy and bitterness of soul.

Our jails are full of boys and girls. Suicides are high among high school teenagers, proving that both home and school have failed.

Governments have failed. They cannot put down crime. They cannot control graft. More than three-quarters of the population of the globe have been killing and being killed. Unbalanced budgets, mounting taxes, show the failure of the governments of the world. And disease, suicide, crime; heartless, conscienceless wickedness everywhere prove the failure of this present civilization. It is a sad, bitter, wicked world, and it offers no peace to the human heart.

I am impressed more and more with the sad, stark tragedy that stares out of the faces of people. As I preach, and the faces of people relax into the grim, sad, lonely lines of despair, I realize that this world has wrought tragedy in the heart of every person who ever put his hope in it.

Youth starts out so gay, so optimistic, with so many delightful prospects, with visions, dreams, air castles, laughter and high ambitions; but before youth merges into mature manhood or womanhood, life has become a grim business of making ends meet, or wringing some drops of joy out of the fleeting pleasures of a day. And old age comes on to bring, in most cases, a sadder disillusionment, which results either in the bitter, querulous resentment of the aged or the calmer resignation of defeat.

This is a sad, bitter, wicked, disappointing world. It does not give men and women, boys and girls what they cry out for, what they hunger for, what they need!

Here, then, is a weighty argument for winning souls. The Gospel of Jesus Christ is the only sure road to peace!

One Sunday night a young man stood in my service during the invitation time and said to a friend, "I have given up hope of ever being happy." This friend said to him, "There is no real happiness except in Jesus Christ!" Peace, soul peace, real rest for the weary and heavy laden, can be found only in Jesus Christ! You may give your wealth to the poor, you may die a martyr in a good cause, you may relieve human distress and earn the gratitude of millions; but no philanthropist ever did so much for any man as he who told him the Gospel and taught him to trust in Jesus and obtain peace of heart and forgiveness of sins!

The pleasure, the wealth and all the good things that this world can give, fail men. How important, then, to offer troubled, sinning people the soul peace that comes with salvation! If you will be wise, remind people of the words of Jesus:

"Come unto me, all ye that labour and are heavy laden, and

I will give you rest. Take my yoke upon you, and learn of me; for I am meek and lowly in heart: and ye shall find rest unto your souls. For my yoke is easy, and my burden is light."—Matt. 11:28-30.

Here is reason enough for winning souls and proof that he that winneth souls is wise.

Sufferings of Christ

What weighty reasons there are for winning souls! What crushing arguments prove the wisdom of the soul-winner's course! I press on your mind another and perhaps the most compelling of all reasons for winning souls! The sufferings of Christ prove the eternal worth of a soul.

The modernist doubts a literal Hell and the eternal torment of the unsaved. Very naturally so, for the modernist doubts that the blood of Jesus Christ was shed as the only possible atonement for man's sin. But he who believes the Bible must see in the sufferings of Christ how greatly He valued a soul and how wise with the wisdom of God is the winner of souls.

The torture of Jesus by the Roman soldiers, by the mob and by wicked Jewish leaders preceding and during the crucifixion was hellish with all the venom of Satan. Unless there were some immeasurable profit to be gained, some infinite good to be bought by the sufferings of Christ, then His life and death were the folly of Jesus and the wickedness of God! If Christ does not keep souls out of torment and purchase for them eternal happiness, then He died *like* a fool. If by the offering of His Son, God the Father did not redeem men from the torments of Hell to everlasting life, then to put the lovely and innocent Jesus on the cross was the most awful wickedness! Oh, the death of Christ proves the worth of a soul!

Christian, if you can go through the Garden of Gethsemane with Jesus to win a soul, then you are learning a little of the

wisdom of God. If, like Paul, you can bear in your body the marks of the Lord Jesus to win a soul, then you are learning the lesson of eternal wisdom which will bring the eternal fruit of joy.

John 3:16 proves the worth of a soul. Jesus' thirty-odd years away from the angels, homesick for Heaven, the poorest of the poor, 'despised and rejected,' 'a man of sorrows and acquainted with grief,' setting His face like a flint toward the cross—that is concrete evidence of how important saving a soul is and how wise is the soul winner. The sufferings of Christ for sinners form one of the best arguments for soul winning. If you would be wise like Jesus, then win souls, for that was the supreme passion of His heart.

This is what He meant when He said, "For the Son of man is come to seek and to save that which was lost" (Luke 19:10).

Glories of Heaven

At the beginning of this chapter, I indicated that true wisdom takes the long look. Proverbs commands the improvident, "Go to the ant, thou sluggard; consider her ways, and be wise," because the ant provides for tomorrow. So with the soul winner. He must somehow forget today in order to provide joy for many a tomorrow. Soul winning does not pay much in United States dollars.

The soul winner has many blessed rewards in this world. He has the great joy of the Holy Spirit's conscious presence, for no one ever won souls without an enduement from Heaven. He has the joy of answered prayer, for who ever won souls without beseeching God for wisdom and power? It is sweet to know that God has heard, and to have the burden lifted after long pleading. The soul winner enjoys the gratitude of those he wins. I remember with glad heart the affectionate thanks I have received from many I have won to Christ. I treasure a great number of letters written out of a heart full of gratitude and

love by those I was privileged to snatch as brands from the burning with the Gospel of Christ.

The soul winner has much joy in this world, I say, and "he that winneth souls is wise," very largely because he believes the Word of God and knows that there will be rewards commensurate with the importance of the task—rewards in the world to come.

This is the meaning of Daniel 12:3, "And they that be wise shall shine as the brightness of the firmament; and they that turn many to righteousness as the stars for ever and ever." The rewards of the soul winner are eternal.

The man who works day and night in acquiring a fortune may wake up someday to find the fortune gone overnight. Even if he can hold it in the clutch of his withered hand, finally the monster Death will drag him away unwillingly, and his riches will slip between his palsied fingers. Men do not carry their wealth into the grave.

The fame of this world is hard won, and a man may lose in a week or a year what he has toiled for during a lifetime.

President Wilson earned the plaudits and praise of the civilized world, and sat on the highest pinnacle of fame when he went to Paris to dictate the terms of worldwide peace. Christian gentleman, idealist, statesman and orator, he held for a moment the limelight of the world. But a few months later he died a brokenhearted, disillusioned man, defeated by his opponents, forsaken by former friends, broken in health and neglected. It is well that he could say, "I am willing to wait for the verdict of mankind," for certainly the sweetness of fame had turned to wormwood and gall.

Fame of Earth

How easy it is to illustrate the vanity of fame! President Hoover was swept into office by the most overwhelming vote this

nation had ever seen. But after only four years in office, he was denied a second term and was crowded out by the even more crushing victory of Franklin D. Roosevelt. The rewards that men slave for, scheme for, yea, even sometimes sell their souls for, are rewards that flee away and are found no more, like the dew that melts in the heat of the rising sun.

But not so the eternal rewards of a soul winner. He shall shine "as the brightness of the firmament," and "as the stars for ever and ever," says the Word of God.

Jesus Himself took the long look. Nothing could possibly have happened in the years of Christ's ministry that could pay Him for the loss of coming to earth and the torture of the cross. But in Isaiah 53:11 we are told that "he shall see of the travail of his soul, and shall be satisfied." Well did Jesus with heavenly wisdom know that all the travail of His soul, the pouring out of His soul unto death, would be paid for later, "when the saints go marching in." Jesus knew that, though He had made Himself poor for our sakes, one day the riches of the universe would be His to enjoy again as the Creator of them all. He was despised and rejected, but well He knew that one day He would be crowned King of kings and Lord of lords, and rule the nations with a rod of iron. He knew that all the Father gave Him would one day be His, so He was content.

Jesus, then, is the great pattern for soul winners. Concerning this, Hebrews 12:1, 2 tells us:

"Wherefore seeing we also are compassed about with so great a cloud of witnesses, let us lay aside every weight, and the sin which doth so easily beset us, and let us run with patience the race that is set before us, Looking unto Jesus the author and finisher of our faith; who for the joy that was set before him endured the cross, despising the shame, and is set down at the right hand of the throne of God."

The inspired writer of Hebrews tells us that, for the joy that

was set before Him, Jesus endured the cross and despised the shame. He looked forward to the joy in Heaven, so He despised the shame of the cross and endured it gladly. The soul winner must have the same wisdom.

I well know that the course of a soul winner will not bring me the wealth of this world. I once thought that if I won many souls I would gain the fame and honor of Christian people everywhere. Alas, I find that is not true. The churches honor the scholar more than the soul winner. In denominational councils the man who can raise money for schools and hospitals is more valued than he who can keep the drunkard and the harlot out of Hell. The pay of the world for soul winning is not large. But, thank God, I can take the "long look," as Moses did when he led the children of Israel out of Egypt and was content not to be called Pharaoh's daughter's son, or be like Paul who gave up his place as a blameless Pharisee, a leader of the Sanhedrin at Jerusalem, and became the despised but soul-winning apostle to the Gentiles. Moses had insupportable burdens. Paul so suffered that he said, "If in this life only we have hope in Christ, we are of all men most miserable." Both endured as seeing Him who is invisible. They knew there is a life beyond the grave, when the soul winner will have his payday. "He that winneth souls is wise," and there will be eternal glories and rewards for the one who has the wisdom to turn many to righteousness.

My Christian friends, if the cost of soul winning seems too great, then I urge you to take private lessons from the Holy Spirit, for I Corinthians 2:14 tells us, "But the natural man receiveth not the things of the Spirit of God: for they are foolishness unto him: neither can he know them, because they are spiritually discerned." The Holy Spirit can show you the things of God, the worth of a soul, and help you to be a soul winner. No one ever wins souls except by the power of the Holy Spirit. Do not be deceived by the foolish wisdom of this world.

"For the preaching of the cross is to them that perish foolishness; but unto us which are saved it is the power of God. It pleased God by the foolishness of preaching to save them that believe." —I Cor. 1:18, 21.

Let those who would be wise win souls; and when the soul winner hears the word of the Saviour, "Well done, thou good and faithful servant: thou hast been faithful over a few things, I will make thee ruler over many things: enter thou into the joy of thy lord," then he will have just begun to enjoy the eternal rewards and the glorious returns of his investments.

"He that winneth souls is wise"!

"He that goeth forth and weepeth, bearing precious seed, shall doubtless come again with rejoicing, bringing his sheaves with him."—Ps. 126:6.

Soul winning is the main job of a Christian. The saving of sinners is the thing nearest to the heart of God. For that purpose Christ came to earth, lived, died and rose again. Even now the angels in Heaven rejoice more over one sinner that repents than over ninety-nine just persons who need no repentance. Soul winning is the eternal business. One sows now, then reaps throughout the endless ages of glory.

How may I win souls? should be the chief concern of every child of God. The Scripture says, "Let him that heareth say, Come." And the Great Commission is given to every Christian. He is to go into all the world and make disciples.

The Bible has much to say about how to win souls. Here in Psalm 126:6, God's way of winning souls is clearly laid out. A meditation on this passage, directed by the Holy Spirit, should certainly make clear God's infallible method in the winning of souls.

This is a psalm of revival:

"When the Lord turned again the captivity of Zion, we were like them that dream. Then was our mouth filled with laughter, and our tongue with singing: then said they among the heathen,

The Lord hath done great things for them. The Lord hath done great things for us; whereof we are glad. Turn again our captivity, O Lord, as the streams in the south. They that sow in tears shall reap in joy. He that goeth forth and weepeth, bearing precious seed, shall doubtless come again with rejoicing, bringing his sheaves with him."

"When the Lord turned again the captivity of Zion, we were like them that dream." The captivity referred to must be the Babylonian captivity. We do not know the author of this psalm, but we know it is inspired by God. David wrote many psalms. Solomon, Moses, Asaph and others wrote some. The inspired writer here recalls the happy revival when the remnant under Nehemiah and Ezra returned from Babylon to build again the walls of Jerusalem and the Temple. It seemed too good to be true—it was almost like a happy dream when God turned the captivity of Zion.

Then their mouths were filled with happy laughter. It was not frivolous laughter, but the deep, joyous laughter so close to tears, so close to the shouting of praise. I have never yet broken out into uncontrollable shouting of praise, but sometimes I have been so happy that I could not refrain from laughter. Sarah must have felt so when God gave her the promised boy in her old age and she called him Isaac, "Laughter!" Many of us look back with mingled joy and longing to the times of great revival and blessing, when our mouths were filled with laughter and our tongues with singing.

"Then said they among the heathen, The Lord hath done great things for them. The Lord *hath* done great things for us; whereof we are glad." The heathen were impressed with the marvelous deliverance which God gave His people. Real, Heaven-sent revivals are like that. Outsiders know when God has visited His people. A great moving of repentance among the people of God, of tears, of restitution and reformation, times of joy and bless-

ing and reconciliation, make a profound impression upon a community. Such had been the revival to which the psalmist here refers, and then his heart cries out to God for a return of revival. "Turn again our captivity, O Lord, as the streams in the south."

Beware of Spiritual Bondage

There are other captivities worse than being carried into Babylon. Our churches, our hearts, our prayers are cold. The Bible becomes a dull Book. The ministry becomes a thankless task— a burden to be borne. Our services become mere form, our songs, meaningless. We feel the parching drought of worldliness. Our souls long for a breath from Heaven. We need a rain of the Holy Spirit upon God's people. We are carried captive by our sins and are crushed by the world about us. O God, turn our captivity again!

The psalmist prays a big prayer and asks for a great revival. "Turn again our captivity, O Lord, as the streams in the south." Possibly he has in mind the Nile River, rising in Lake Tana in Ethiopia, then flowing down through the hills to the broad plains of Egypt, where every year, until conquered by the British dam, it overflowed all the banks and watered the lowland. It irrigated the valleys and enriched the soil with overwhelming flood tides of resistless water! May God send that kind of revival! As the song says,

> **Mercy drops round us are falling,**
> **But for the showers we plead.**

Or the psalmist may have had in mind the Euphrates and Tigris Rivers, great broad streams that flow together and then sweep majestically on southeastward to empty their mighty burden into the Persian Gulf. We need to pray, expect and try to have revivals that are as mighty as "the streams in the south."

"They that sow in tears shall reap in joy," the Scripture says.

Revivals and soul winning are always matters of sowing and reaping. It costs to be a soul winner. Soul winning should be a matter of the deepest concern. If a soul winner is willing to sow in tears, he will certainly be able to reap in joy.

In verse 6, we have a clear outline of God's way to win souls and the certainty of results: "He that goeth forth and weepeth, bearing precious seed, shall doubtless come again with rejoicing, bringing his sheaves with him."

Analyze that verse and you will find these five parts in God's plan of soul winning:

1. "He that goeth forth"—the GO in soul winning.

2. "And weepeth"—the BROKEN HEART in soul winning.

3. "Bearing precious seed"—the WORD OF GOD in soul winning.

4. "Shall doubtless come again . . . bringing his sheaves with him"—the CERTAINTY OF RESULTS with God's method.

5. "Rejoicing . . . bringing his sheaves with him"—the JOY OF THE REAPERS, or a soul-winner's reward.

The "Go" in Soul Winning

God's Word puts going as the first requirement in soul winning. How like the Great Commission, when Jesus said, "Go ye into all the world" (Mark 16:15), and again, "Go ye therefore" (Matt. 28:19). The main reason Christians do not win souls is that they simply do not get at it. The one who wins souls is the one who tries to win souls, the one who talks to sinners, the one who makes it his business.

Many have the impression that the best man or woman is the best soul winner—that the Christian who has the highest moral standards, pays his debts, avoids worldliness, attends church, tithes, etc., will automatically be the best soul winner. If it were true, then every Pharisee would have been a wonderful soul winner, but they were not. And many a Christian today prays, reads

his Bible, attends church and carefully watches his daily life, yet never wins a soul. That is tragic but true.

How often in revivals a good sister or brother rises to testify and says, "I want to live such a godly life that sinners will see my daily walk and be saved!" The fact is, living a godly life is not the way God has appointed to get sinners saved. Living a good life is vitally important for the one who would be a soul winner, but the first condition of soul winning, divinely appointed, is this—get up and go after sinners!

Soul winners ought to know the Bible, but the best Bible students are often not the best soul winners. Many, many times in revivals I have noticed that preachers would sit in the services, enjoy the sermons, pray in public and show an active interest, but would win very few sinners to Christ. But in the same revival I have seen a young person who had not been long converted, who knew little about the Bible and had little time to grow in Christian grace, yet who persistently and earnestly went after his friends until he won far more souls than the preachers. I have known a fifteen-year-old girl to win more souls in a revival than a half-dozen sincere preachers, and the reason was that she obeyed the command of the Scriptures to go after that which was lost.

If you want to be a soul winner, the first thing to do is to "go!"

I have known mothers and fathers to see their unsaved children grow up in the midst of prayers, Bible reading and moral teaching, yet never once earnestly, lovingly and persistently press an immediate decision for Christ. Among the hundreds of sinners I have dealt with, no cases are sadder than the unsaved sons and daughters of ministers. Young people tell me how they were accustomed to family prayer in the home, how they believed with all their heart in the sincerity of mother's and father's faith; yet it would seem that neither ever went after his or her children for definite and immediate decision. There

is no possible substitute for the "go" in soul winning. Doubtless Paul was the greatest of all the apostles, and his greatness lay most of all in that he was "in labours more abundant."

Soul winning is not a matter of talent. People do not win souls because they are educated or are peculiarly fitted for it by nature or have magnetic personalities. Those who win the most souls are those who most persistently and with the greatest abandon go after sinners.

We must realize that soul winning is not done in human power and wisdom but the power of the Holy Spirit convicts and converts a sinner. But remember that Jesus said, "Go. . .and, lo, I am with you alway, even unto the end of the world" (Matt. 28:19, 20). The obedient heart who sets about the Master's business, obeying His plain command to win souls, is far more likely to have the power of the Holy Spirit upon him. Going is God's first requirement for soul winning.

One who would win souls must "be instant in season, out of season" (II Tim. 4:2). The best soul winners are those who go when it is and when it is not convenient. "Blessed are ye that sow beside all waters" (Isa. 32:20) is just another way of saying, "Blessed is the soul winner who tries to reach every sinner possible." Again, "He that observeth the wind shall not sow; and he that regardeth the clouds shall not reap" (Eccles. 11:4).

You may think you do not know enough Scripture, but in a few minutes you can learn John 3:16, and that has led to thousands of conversions. Learn it and go. You may feel you do not know what to say. Ask God to give you the message and go! You may not know to whom you should speak, but if in loving obedience you go, the Holy Spirit will direct your steps and your words. "He that goeth forth" is the one who will win souls.

It is said that in the last years of the war between the states, a farmer was drafted into the Confederate army. He did not know the drill manual, did not know how to keep step on the

march, nor how to salute. Nor did he know any of the bugle calls. But he brought his squirrel rifle, and when the command was given to attack, he charged the Yankee lines, joining in the rebel yell. However, the gray-coated Confederates were outnumbered and were soon driven back. The bugle blew "retreat," and the thin gray line withdrew to safer ground.

As the battered soldiers treated their wounded, prepared their camp and threw up breastworks in the late afternoon, someone said, "Poor old Jim! He was either killed or taken prisoner in the first battle he was ever in! Too bad he didn't know the bugle call to retreat and ran right into that nest of Yankees."

But about sundown they saw two tired fellows coming over the hill. The one in front had on a blue uniform and the man behind wore a gray. Somebody had taken a prisoner! As he saw the camp, he prodded his prisoner with a bayonet and somebody shouted, "It is Jim! Jim's got a prisoner! Where did you get him, Jim?" The farmer recruit drew up angrily. He felt they had all deserted him in the first battle! "Where did I get him?" he said. "Why, the woods are full of them! Why don't you get one yourself?"

The world is full of sinners, and you can take them alive for Christ, if only you will go after them.

Somewhere near you is a poor, lost soul, someone who would listen to you, someone who is burdened, someone who realizes he needs Christ. That soul is not saved because nobody has gone to tell him the message of salvation.

"Go" is the first command of God to the soul winner. "He that goeth forth" is the man who returns with sheaves. If you want to be a soul winner, then commit yourself to this holy business and go after sinners. Other things are necessary, but this is most necessary. If you would be a winner of souls, then you must go forth.

The Broken Heart in Soul Winning

"He that goeth forth and weepeth," the psalmist says, will

come back with sheaves, rejoicing. Beyond all doubt, this is another essential for the soul winner. If going forth is the first requirement of a soul winner, perhaps even the going involves a broken heart. If we care as we ought, we will go. A broken heart will send us forth.

It is amazing that we have few tears when there is so much to weep about. Have you ever felt the compassion that Jesus had as He looked on the multitude? Have you ever experienced what was in His heart as He wept over Jerusalem, and said, "O Jerusalem, Jerusalem, thou that killest the prophets, and stonest them which are sent unto thee, how often would I have gathered thy children together, even as a hen gathereth her chickens under her wings, and ye would not!"? The love of the shepherd for the lost sheep, the tender compassion of the father for his prodigal son, exemplify the broken heart of God and of Christ over sinners. To win souls, we must go, weeping.

Sometimes preachers are ashamed to weep; more often our hearts are too cold to weep over sinners. It was not so with Paul. To the assembled elders of Ephesus, he urgently said, "Therefore watch, and remember, that by the space of three years I ceased not to warn every one night and day with tears" (Acts 20:31). Paul warned people night and day. In verse 20 of the same chapter, he declares that he taught "publickly, and from house to house." He put the "go" in soul winning. But best of all, he went with tears! The one who will come back rejoicing with sheaves is he who sows in tears.

Often I am amazed at the callousness of my own heart. How strangely absorbed we become in the things about us until we have little concern about souls—to be eternally blessed or to be eternally tormented!

> Would you care if some friend
>   You had met day by day
> Should never be told about Jesus?
>   Are you willing that he

**In the judgment should say,
"No one ever told me of Jesus"?**

When I first began preaching, I remember how I wept. I was embarrassed about it. This was wholly unlike the college debating, the commencement addresses and other public speaking to which I had been accustomed. The tears flowed down my cheeks almost continually, and I was so broken up that sometimes I could scarcely talk.

Then I grew ashamed of my tears and longed to speak more logically. As I recall, I asked the Lord to give me better control of myself as I preached. My tears soon vanished, and I found I had only the dry husk of preaching left. Then I begged God to give me again the broken heart, the concern, even if it meant tears in public, and a trembling voice.

I feel the same need today. We preachers ought to cry out like Jeremiah, "Oh that my head were waters, and mine eyes a fountain of tears, that I might weep day and night for the slain of the daughter of my people!" (Jer. 9:1).

The personal soul winner needs a broken heart. The cold and callous sinner can, it may be, answer all your arguments and withstand all your pleas, but he has no argument against tears. If you have a holy compassion given of God and wrought by the Holy Spirit in your heart, until tears flow down your face as you talk to sinners, then you have a magnet that must tug at the heart of the coldest and hardest of unbelievers. After all, nothing can prove you and your message better than a love like Christ had for sinners. It is not hard to believe that God so loved the world, that He gave His Son, if those of us who tell about it have some of the same love to transform our appeal and give urgency to our message. May God give us tears!

Do You Care for the Dying?

Humanly speaking, there must be a multitude who are un-

saved because no one especially cares. Many a man has felt in his heart the cry of the psalmist, "No man cared for my soul!"

A college senior told me, weeping, after I had just won him to Christ, "Nobody seemed to care whether I was saved or not!" One of the standing complaints that the sinner and the backslider have against our modern churches is that, when they go to church, no one seems to care. No one shakes hands with them, no one seems glad to see them.

A seventeen-year-old boy in Waxahachie, Texas, told Mrs. Rice that no one had ever in his life talked to him about being a Christian. His mother and father were church members, he had often attended Sunday school and church and revivals, yet no one had ever urged him to trust Christ and be saved. Surely it must have been that no one cared very much.

Several years ago I lived in Ft. Worth on Seminary Hill, and made that my headquarters as an evangelist. In the Southwestern Baptist Theological Seminary located there, I had taken my training. Mrs. Rice and I often attended the Seminary Hill Baptist Church (now the Gambrell Street Baptist Church). She attended a class for women taught by Mrs. Scarborough, a fine teacher, whose illustrious husband had been president of the seminary for many years. He was a great soul winner, an earnest man of God, and his wife a blessed, good Christian.

In the class was an unsaved woman. My wife became concerned about her and said to me one day, "Will you go with me to see this lost woman and try to win her?" I agreed to go, but with a great deal of anxiety. She lived among preachers. Her next-door neighbor on one side was a preacher, I think; on the other side lived a Christian educational worker. Three or four doors away lived the president of the seminary. I lived not far away, and so did many other preachers. This unsaved woman had been attending the services. I felt that surely she must be gospel-hardened. It seemed to me likely that she had been ap-

proached many, many times about her soul in that warm evangelistic atmosphere.

With some dread we prepared to go visit her and try to win her to Christ. My wife engaged a woman to stay with the children a whole afternoon, and after prayer we went to call on the unsaved woman, prepared for a long and hard battle to win her to Christ.

She met us at the door with a friendly smile. She seemed pleased that we had come to see her. We are so often cowards when we come to speak about Christ, and that afternoon I looked about me to find some point of contact that I might come gradually to the question of salvation. On the table I saw a nice new Bible, and I commented upon it.

She said, "Yes, my mother gave me that last Christmas."

Then I said, "I understand you are not a Christian. Wouldn't it be wonderful if you were a Christian, so that you and your husband could read the Word of God together every night?"

Her face was very grave as she answered, "We are not Christians, but we do read the Bible every night. Every night since last Christmas we have read a chapter in this new Bible."

Somewhat taken back and nonplused, I started over again. "But if you were a Christian, you and your husband could get down together and ask God to bless you and lead you right and keep you safe through the night. Wouldn't it be fine to be a Christian and have family prayer?"

Tears came into her eyes as she said, "I'm not a Christian, but we do pray. Every night my husband and I read a chapter in this Bible, then get down on our knees and pray."

I hardly knew what to say. Here was a woman whom I had supposed was gospel-hardened. I supposed that many, many times she had turned down the Saviour. Living in the midst of Christians and special workers, I thought that surely she must have been urged many times to trust in Christ. But instead of

being hardened, she and her husband were daily reading the
Bible and praying. And even then she was in tears!

So I left off all devices and plainly asked the question, "Then
why is it that you have turned down Jesus? Why is it you are
not a Christian?"

Breaking out into sobbing she said, "I *want* to be a Christian,
but I don't know how!"

My heart was stirred. To my shame I found that right here,
a few blocks away from me, was a woman who daily read the
Bible and prayed and tried to find God. Around her were preachers and their wives and others dedicated to lifetime Christian
work as gospel singers, Christian education workers and missionaries. All of us were occupied with our own affairs and never
took time to tell this lost woman how to be saved.

I took up the new Bible and said, "Well, God bless you; you
are going to find out how to be saved." I turned to the third
chapter of John and read the wonderful story about how one
must be born again, how God loves sinners, and how those who
believe in Christ have everlasting life and shall never perish.
In five minutes she was a happy, rejoicing Christian.

This incident has come back to my mind many times to remind me of this question, "Do you really care about sinners?"
We are so professional, so formal, that we let people all around
us go to Hell. If we had a broken heart over sinners, if we went
forth weeping to find those who need the Saviour, we would
feel responsible to find out who was lost.

Many are hardhearted and indifferent. Many do not want to
discuss their sad, lost condition. But if we go with tears and
hearts full of tender love for sinners for whom Jesus died, we
will find those who can be won.

How shameful it will be for many Christians when they hear
the plaintive cry of lost sinners at the judgment of God, "No man
cared for my soul"! (Ps. 142:4). I know that all who reject Christ

are without excuse. Men ought to seek the Saviour and find Him, for He is not far from every penitent heart. But I know also that any Christian who does not love and seek sinners is also without excuse. He is untrue to His Saviour, ungrateful for his own salvation, and disobedient to the Great Commission that God has given him.

May God give us tender, broken hearts and weeping eyes as we go out to win souls.

Tears touch the heart of God. He said to Hezekiah, "I have heard thy prayer, I have seen thy tears: behold, I will add unto thy days fifteen years" (Isa. 38:5). If tears touch the heart of God, we may be sure they make a way into the hardest hearts. Nothing proves a soul-winner's sincerity like his broken heart, his tearful concern. I know that there is a difference in my preaching when God gives me a heavenly compassion for sinners, until I yearn over them in the tenderest, brokenhearted anxiety.

"He that goeth forth and weepeth" is the man who will come back rejoicing with his sheaves. The broken heart is indispensable for the soul winner. And if you do not have a broken heart, a concern for sinners, and tears over their lost condition, then I suggest that you wait before God until the Holy Spirit gives you this Christlike concern, this shepherd heart to seek the lost ones. Wait before the Lord until He gives you tears out of His boundless, world-embracing, brokenhearted love for sinners; then go forth.

The Word of God in Soul Winning

The soul winner must go forth not only weeping, but "bearing precious seed." In the parable of the sower, the Saviour tells us, "The seed is the word of God" (Luke 8:11). This is the precious seed that the soul winner must carry if he is to come back with sheaves.

How important it is that we take the good seed, the only seed

that has the divine power to spring up in the human heart with the fruit of salvation! The would-be soul winner must know ahead of time that he cannot win souls by human wisdom, human influence, personal magnetism or tact. He goes not to reform men, but to save them. A reformation might take place without a supernatural, divine act in the heart. Men have been known to leave off drinking, cursing, or even a career of crime, under the moral influence of some strong character or some great life. But that is not salvation. Unless there is a supernatural change of heart, a regeneration, a new birth, the sinner is still a lost sinner, a rejecter of Christ, a rebel against God, justly condemned and Hell-bound.

Dear soul winner, you must have heavenly help in this business of saving sinners. "For the weapons of our warfare are not carnal, but mighty through God to the pulling down of strong holds" (II Cor. 10:4). You must take supernatural weapons for this warfare, supernatural seed for this sowing. You must take the living, supernatural Word of God. "For the word of God is quick, and powerful, and sharper than any twoedged sword, piercing even to the dividing asunder of soul and spirit, and of the joints and marrow, and is a discerner of the thoughts and intents of the heart" (Heb. 4:12). Remember the word of God to Jeremiah: "Is not my word like as a fire? saith the Lord; and like a hammer that breaketh the rock in pieces?" (Jer. 23:29).

Depend upon the Word of God to bring conviction. You cannot outtalk a sinner. Do not depend upon long, drawn-out arguments. Place your dependence upon the sharp Word of God. This is holy seed and within every verse there is the germ of eternal life. The soul winner must have confidence in the living Word of God. It is inspired of God. The Word of God reveals every sinner's condition. It shows the love of God. Its promises are so faithful that faith comes by hearing the Word of God. If you go forth weeping, sowing this seed, you may expect a blessed harvest.

The soul winner ought to learn by memory many Scriptures. He should saturate himself in the message of the Word of God. He should speak in terms of the Word. He should surrender himself to the Holy Spirit who is the Author of the Word. When the Spirit wields the Sword of the Spirit, then a mighty work is done.

Often, some wife has said, "O Brother Rice, I hope you can say something that will touch my husband's heart." Let us not think that illustrations, logic, songs or poems will win souls. These are useful and blessed of God only as they carry the *Word*, and as they shed light and understanding upon the Word of God. Blessed is the soul winner who quotes a Scripture, or better yet, who points out a suitable verse to a sinner and has him read it. There are Scriptures to fit every case, and the well-prepared, Spirit-led soul winner will use the Word of God with mighty effect.

Once in our home a group agreed to pray while a young woman went to see a lost girl friend. We prayed until we were assured that God had heard; then I went to find the young woman. I found the lost girl standing in a kitchen door looking at John 5:24 in a Testament held open before her face by the Christian young woman.

As it dawned upon her that by simply receiving Christ she could have everlasting life and never lose it, the dear girl said, "Oh, I never knew that was in the Bible; I did not know it was as easy as that!" Tearfully, she trusted the Saviour, and all of us rejoiced together. The Word of God did the work.

Dear soul winner, as you go and weep over sinners, take with you the precious Word of God, the seed, the power of God unto salvation to everyone who believes.

The Certainty of Results

The Scripture says, "He that goeth forth and weepeth, bear-

ing precious seed, shall *doubtless* come again with rejoicing, bringing his sheaves with him." There is a certainty about results when we go in God's way. God's plans are infallible. Anybody can be a soul winner, if he is willing to go in the way God has laid out here in His Word. The word *"doubtless"* here means without any doubt.

You may have to plead with ten sinners to win one, or with a hundred to win ten, or with a thousand to win a hundred. When the sower of whom Jesus spoke went forth to sow, some seed fell by the wayside and was carried away by the birds, without sprouting. I know that many sinners will never listen seriously to the Gospel. Satan takes the seed out of the heart before it has time to take root. Other seed fell among stones. Some hearts are too hard, it seems, for the Word of God to take any permanent root. In other sad cases where people receive the Word it is so choked by the cares of this world and the deceitfulness of riches that it brings no fruit to perfection. We need not expect every sinner we talk to will be saved. But, thank God, some seed will fall in good soil and bring forth fruit, some thirty, some sixty and some an hundredfold.

Did you ever "drop corn" on the farm? If so, you planted two, three, or four grains in each hill. Only one good stalk of corn is desired in a hill, but a crow may get one seed and a cutworm another, and some seed will not sprout. So to insure a good stand, one must use more seed than he expects to come to full fruitage.

The cotton planter plants cotton seed thickly in a row, and when it comes up it is thinned out to a proper stand. Not every seed comes to mature fruitage, but the one who uses plenty of good seed makes a crop.

The soul winner will have disappointments. We will never win all the lost. "Wide is the gate, and broad is the way, that leadeth to destruction, and many there be which go in thereat" (Matt. 7:13). More people will be lost than will be saved. We will never

get the world converted. But the soul winner who goes forth weeping, bearing precious seed, will snatch some brands from the burning. He will come back with his sheaves.

If you go out to seek lost people, you will find some are not at home, and others will not listen. A thousand hindrances will prevent the consummation of your purpose. But where one family has moved, you will find another with lost members. Where one will not hear, you will find somebody else eager for the message. You may have to turn from the rich to the poor, from the merry to the sad, before you find a willing audience for your message. You may have to turn from your own loved ones to find a stranger. If those about you will not hear, you may have to go to those in the hospitals and jails. But you may be sure that "he that goeth forth and weepeth, bearing precious seed," shall certainly come back with souls. It will take going, it will take a broken heart, and it will take the life-giving Word of God; but this combination never fails.

> Going forth with weeping, sowing for the Master,
>   Though the loss sustained our spirit often grieves;
> When our weeping's over, He will bid us welcome,
>   We shall come rejoicing, bringing in the sheaves.

The Soul-Winner's Joy

When one goes forth and weeps, and bears precious seed and comes back with sheaves, then how fitting that divine inspiration should say he shall "doubtless come again with *rejoicing*, bringing his sheaves with him"!

There is no joy like the soul-winner's joy. The shepherd who comes home with the one lost sheep "calleth together his friends and neighbours, saying unto them, Rejoice with me; for I have found my sheep which was lost." The woman who loses a piece of silver and finds it "calleth her friends and her neighbours together, saying, Rejoice with me; for I have found the piece which I had lost." And when the prodigal son comes back to the

father, they kill the fatted calf and the home is marked by a feasting and rejoicing over the boy which "was dead, and is alive again...lost, and is found."

So we are told that "likewise joy shall be in heaven over one sinner that repenteth, more than over ninety and nine just persons, which need no repentance"; and again, "Likewise, I say unto you, there is joy in the presence of the angels of God over one sinner that repenteth." It is only fitting that they that sow in tears should reap in joy. So when we share the compassionate heart of the Saviour, God allows us to share the joy which is in the presence of the angels. It was the soul-winner's joy that Jesus had in mind when He was willing to die for sinners. He "for the joy that was set before Him endured the cross, despising the shame" (Heb. 12:2). He had in mind the joy of reaping.

In the marvelous fifty-third chapter of Isaiah, where we are told that Jesus would bear our iniquities and that with His stripes we should be healed, because He would pour out His soul unto death, we are also told that "He shall see of the travail of his soul, and shall be satisfied." Therefore, the Lord Jesus will come rejoicing, bringing in the sheaves, and all that have had a part in the sowing and a share in His weeping will rejoice with Him "when the saints go marching in." When 'many shall come from the east and west, and shall sit down with Abraham, and Isaac, and Jacob in the kingdom of heaven,' what a time of rejoicing that will be for all who sowed the precious seed and watered it with tears!

Others have the fame and plaudits of this world. Let Congress make the laws; let vulgar and immoral movie stars have the limelight on TV and in the nation's press; but when the soul winner comes back with the drunkard, saved and made sober, or with the harlot made pure or even with a little child transformed by being born again, the soul winner has the best of the bargain. And if we catch some gleams of joy here in the

midst of our weeping, what a joyful reaping when the Saviour comes and gathers up His jewels and we see for the first time the fullness of our reaping!

The soul winner must take the long look, and by faith look forward to the time when he will be paid a hundredfold for all his tears, all his sorrows, all his self-denials.

If you are defeated, discontented, unhappy; if you have lost the joy of the Lord and you do not enjoy prayer and the Bible and Christian service as you once did, then you need to give yourself with a holy abandon to going after sinners, weeping, bearing precious seed. When you come back, as you doubtless will, with sheaves, then you will come with rejoicing. Lost joy will be restored to the Christian who wins souls.

Just now the morning mail comes and with it a letter, enclosing a copy of my booklet, *What Must I Do to Be Saved?* with a decision slip signed. The man who signs his name as taking Christ as his personal Saviour says in the letter, "This pamphlet was handed to me by Mr. F. W. W____; he insisted that I read every word, which I did." Just now I feel part of the joy I have been talking about over a sinner's getting saved. There is no joy like coming back with sheaves.

Here is God's way of winning souls, and here are the divinely appointed results, so let us put in practice this precious verse: "He that goeth forth and weepeth, bearing precious seed, shall doubtless come again with rejoicing, bringing his sheaves with him."

The Compassionate Heart   **3**

"They that sow in tears shall reap in joy."—Ps. 126:5.

Hear these remarkable words, "In tears!" The tears of a broken heart are necessary equipment of the soul winner. The certainty of returning with joy depends, says Holy Writ, on going with tears. There are other requirements for the one who would be a fisher of men. He must go, he must bear precious seed, but the thing so often lacking is the broken heart. Indeed, I make bold to say that it is the broken heart that drives one out, that makes him go. The broken heart will sow the seed that will bring forth fruit. Yea, even the same broken heart will make the homecoming joyful.

There is joy in the surcease of a broken heart. The broken and compassionate heart, the humble and contrite spirit please God, attract the sinner; and the contact between these two results in the changed heart and saved soul of a sinner and brings honor to the Saviour.

See the example of Jesus. Never was there such a compassionate winner of men! He saw the people as sheep having no shepherd and "had compassion on them." He wept over Jerusalem. He sought the fallen woman to forgive her and the publican to make him a preacher. His compassion would not let Him eat. He found "meat that ye know not of" in the winning of souls. His compassionate heart would not let Him sleep, for

He must needs go into a mountain and pray all night or rise
a great while before day to pray for the lost. His compassionate
heart would not let Him die, even, till the repenting thief on
the neighboring cross was forgiven and won to Himself and
Heaven. The prodigal son was a sinner, and the forgiving, griev-
ing father was like Jesus. Christ was the Shepherd, and the sinner was the poor lost lamb, at the mercy of the cold and the
beasts. As the shepherd seeks the sheep until he finds it, rescues
it, and rejoices over it, so Jesus with the sinner.

> **They crowned Him with thorns,**
> **He was beaten with stripes;**
> **He was smitten and nailed to the tree.**
> **But the pain in His heart was the hardest to bear,**
> **The heart that was broken for me.**

No marvel, then, that when He died on the cross for sinners
and the soldiers opened His side with a spear, they found a heart
literally broken. O Saviour, teach us to love sinners, to weep
over them, to find pillows hard and food tasteless and life not
worth living, if they be not saved! Send us out with compassion
and tears to win the lost!

How Paul wept over sinners! Hear him say, "Remember, that
by the space of three years I ceased not to warn every one night
and day with tears." Night and day! Night and day with tears!
Hear him say, "Brethren, my heart's desire and prayer to God
for Israel is that they might be saved." And again he said: "For
I could wish that myself were accursed from Christ for my
brethren, my kinsmen according to the flesh." A stoning, a ship-
wreck, a life-and-death fight with lions in the coliseum, a Philip-
pian jail at midnight, with his bleeding back and shackled feet,
could not quench Paul's tears for lost men nor distract his compassionate heart till they were saved.

All the great winners of men have had compassion. Moody,
Spurgeon, Torrey and Finney succeeded beyond other preachers
in winning souls mainly, if not solely, because of this compas-

sion. Charles Alexander showed it in his singing. John Vassar, Bible agent, tract distributor and soul winner rare, oh, so rare, had this compassion and yet almost no equipment by nature in his personal work. No one will win souls without it. The preacher, the teacher, the everyday Christian will do well to cultivate this compassionate heart. He may have all else without the broken heart, but will not, cannot, win the lost to a Saviour who died for them.

Once there was a preacher on the streets of a Texas town who strangely stirred and melted the hearts of men in his unlettered street preaching. The people heard him gladly, and you will not marvel when you know that they called him "Weeping Joe." I do not know, nor want to know, his other name, for no other name can so well recall the tears and prayers and the heart-broken, compassionate love of Jesus which he had for a lost world.

O Saviour, give us the broken heart, that going forth, weeping, we may come again with rejoicing, bringing precious sheaves!

"For since I spake, I cried out, I cried violence and spoil; because the word of the Lord was made a reproach unto me, and a derision, daily. Then I said, I will not make mention of him, nor speak any more in his name. But his word was in mine heart as a burning fire shut up in my bones, and I was weary with forbearing, and I could not stay."—Jer. 20:8, 9.

The soul-winning testimony of a child of God depends upon fire from Heaven. Isaiah found himself totally unprepared and unable to speak for God. "I am undone," said he, "I am a man of unclean lips, and I dwell in the midst of a people of unclean lips" (Isa. 6:5). But a seraph took a coal of heavenly fire from off the altar in the Temple, touched his lips and said, "Lo, this hath touched thy lips; and thine iniquity is taken away, and thy sin purged." Then Isaiah heard the call of God and said, "Here am I; send me." No man is fit to preach nor to witness for Christ until he be touched with fire from Heaven.

Of John the Baptist, Jesus said, "He was a burning and a shining light" (John 5:35). Moses was called to his work by the God who spoke to him out of a burning bush; and that burning bush, flaming but never consumed, is a type of every prophet of God touched by a supernatural fire from God.

The fire of God fell on Mount Carmel in answer to the prayer of Elijah, and this heavenly fire was a sign to the people that

Elijah was God's prophet and that his message was true. The people fell on their faces and said, "The Lord, he is the God" (I Kings 18:39).

The one hundred and twenty disciples who were filled with the Holy Ghost at Pentecost had outward, visible tongues of fire sitting upon them, symbols of the Holy Spirit as the Enduer and Anointer of His people for service.

One who would speak for Jesus needs fire from Heaven! The call, the preparation, the passion, the power of a soul winner depend upon the fire of the Holy Spirit!

How many preachers have had the experience of Jeremiah? He cried out against the wickedness of his day and warned of the judgment of God that was certain to come to Israel. But for such preaching Jeremiah was derided and reproached. In Jeremiah 20:8, he says, "For since I spake, I cried out, I cried violence and spoil; because the word of the Lord was made a reproach unto me, and a derision, daily." He was not a popular preacher— no preacher is popular if he preaches all the counsel of God. Jesus said, "Woe unto you when all men shall speak well of you." When Jesus was despised and ready to be crucified, He said to His disciples, "The servant is not greater than his lord."

Sometimes the burden of the ministry is almost insupportable. Under the fires of criticism that every true preacher faces, he must choose one of three courses. He can compromise, soft-pedal, use smoother words; say not so much about sin and repentance and judgment, and thus continue in the ministry without the continual harassment that was the lot of such prophets of God as Jeremiah, Elijah and Paul. Or a preacher may resign himself, as the best Bible preachers did, to suffer malice, reproach and ridicule of wicked sinners and worldly church men, and continue faithfully to preach. The third course open is to leave the ministry, which hundreds of preachers have done, not having the fortitude to face continual opposition, yet with too much

conscience and honesty to compromise Christ and dilute His message.

Jeremiah Quits the Ministry

This was the case with Jeremiah. He decided to quit the ministry. In Jeremiah 20:9, we are told, "Then I said, I will not make mention of him, nor speak any more in his name."

Jeremiah had prophesied that Judah should be carried away captive for their sins (Jer. 18:15-17; 19:8, 9; 20:4-6). Besides, Jeremiah had been a "blue-law" preacher, insisting on strict observance of the Sabbath (Jer. 17:19-27). The people had agreed among themselves, "Let us not give heed to any of his words" (Jer. 18:18).

Jeremiah's prophecies about the destruction and desolation of Jerusalem aroused Pashur, a priest, chief governor of the house of the Lord. "Then Pashur smote Jeremiah the prophet, and put him in the stocks that were in the high gate of Benjamin, which was by the house of the Lord" (Jer. 20:2). Brave man of God that he was, when Jeremiah was released from the stocks, he continued to preach. But the public whipping and exposure in the stocks was followed by such derision on the part of the people that finally Jeremiah's heart was broken and he said, "I will not make mention of him, nor speak any more in his name." Jeremiah decided to leave the ministry!

Do not blame him too quickly. He was a well-born man, a priest, intelligent and cultured. This was his first great persecution. Small wonder that he decided to speak no more in the name of the Lord, but to let people go their way to destruction, with no further admonition, since they would not heed his warning.

The Fire in Jeremiah's Bones

But when Jeremiah decided not to make mention any more of the Lord, nor to speak in His name, he found a seething

volcano within him, a fire shut up in his bones! He said, "I will not make mention of him, nor speak any more in his name. But his word was in mine heart as a burning fire shut up in my bones, and I was weary with forbearing, and I could not stay." Outward circumstances and his relation to the people tempted him to quit the ministry; but inward circumstances, the fire of God upon him, would not let him stop speaking in the name of the Lord. Jeremiah was not only in the ministry; the ministry was in him! He was like the black man who had the billy goat by the horns and cried, "Somebody come and help me turn this animal aloose!"

There are just too many preachers who can preach or not preach, just as is convenient. They are like the "moderate drinker" who boasts of his liquor that he "can take it or leave it alone." There are too many preachers who will preach if they are well paid but will not preach without a job.

When I was a boy I was amazed that country preachers, pastors of half- and fourth-time country churches, rarely went to their own churches to preach on the fifth Sunday of the month. They were not "employed" for that week!

And all over America are scores of men not preaching. They say they are called of God to preach and would gladly accept a paying position in the ministry, but they never preach on the street nor in the jails nor in shops or factories; never do house-to-house soul winning!

It may be there are not enough well-paying jobs for all the preachers. It may be that all who are called to preach cannot preach to large and enthusiastic audiences with the acclaim of men. But there are enough dying men to hear the message of every preacher who will tell the story of Christ and redemption. It is as true today as in the time of Jesus, that "the harvest truly is plenteous, but the labourers are few." It is still true that we should "pray ye therefore the Lord of the harvest, that

he will send forth labourers into his harvest."

I have a special burden for ministers of the Gospel. The greatest problem of the churches is the preacher problem. "Like priest, like people." Our preachers are usually good men, often learned men, unselfish, self-sacrificing, sincere men; but that is not enough. Preachers lack the divine fire, the Christlike passion, the John the Baptist boldness, the Pauline urgency, the Holy Spirit enduement of power that will fire the churches of God. They lack the supernatural evidences that accompanied New Testament preachers.

The miraculous, the supernatural is missing in the average preacher's life and message and results. God have pity on us! What all of us need and must have to please God and do His work effectively is the fire in our bones that Jeremiah had.

We have depended on culture and learning, but schools and literature do not make prophets like Jeremiah! We have depended on organizations and institutions, but they do not bring the power that came at Pentecost and converted 3,000 souls in a day. Our colleges and seminaries send out preachers; but do the same signs and wonders attend them as were shown in the ministry of Barnabas and Saul, who went out, "being sent forth by the Holy Ghost" (Acts 13:4), with a miraculous, supernatural commission, with explicit instructions that came during fasting and prayer, with the miracle-working power that proved they were from the Lord?

My Christian friend, do you see any difference in the results of your testimony and that of New Testament saints with the fire from Heaven burning in their bones? You deacons who read this, or other officers of the churches, how does your life and soul-winning witness compare with that of Stephen the martyr, and Philip who evangelized Samaria? There is a holy something, a divine ingredient, a resistless, supernatural Energy—which usually we do not have—that called and led, impassioned and

empowered the saints of Bible times! Oh, may He send it upon us! We need the Word of God to burn within our hearts like a fire in our bones, so that we cannot stay.

Most so-called Christian work these days is done in the power of the flesh, not in the power of God. God struck dead Aaron's sons, Nadab and Abihu, because they took strange fire, that is, common fire, not divinely kindled, into the Tabernacle (Lev. 10:1, 2). God struck down Uzzah because he put forth his unanointed hand to steady the ark of God (II Sam. 6:6, 7). King Uzziah, not called of God to be a priest, intruded into that holy work and burned incense in the Temple, and for that he was smitten with leprosy (II Chron. 26:16-21). And the ministry of many a man today is lifeless and dead. The Lord has departed from him, though he, like Samson, may not know it. Too often the Gospel we preach has a barren womb and dry breasts; sons and daughters are not brought forth into the kingdom of God, and the starving saints are not fed! Oh, for fire from Heaven!

The Divine Call

There are not too many preachers; nay, I do not believe there are enough. The Scripture commands, "Let him that heareth say, Come" (Rev. 22:17). And every born-again child of God should, like the converted maniac of Gadara, go home to his friends and his father's house and tell what great things God has done for him. We need, not fewer preachers, for the world is dying and the white harvest is wasting. We should pray the Lord of the harvest to send forth laborers into His harvest. Mothers should give their newborn sons to the ministry, and fathers should bring up their children in the nurture and admonition of the Lord, longing and pleading that God will use them in His own service. There are not too many preachers.

But there *are* too many preachers preaching without a divine call, a supernatural commission from Heaven. It ought to be said of every preacher, every Sunday school teacher, every soul

winner, as it was of John the Baptist, "There was a man sent
from God, whose name was _____."

Do you know why the Word of God was in the heart of
Jeremiah as a burning in his bones? Read Jeremiah 1:4-9:

*"Then the word of the Lord came unto me, saying, Before I
formed thee in the belly I knew thee; and before thou camest forth
out of the womb I sanctified thee, and I ordained thee a prophet
unto the nations. Then said I, Ah, Lord God! behold, I cannot
speak: for I am a child. But the Lord said unto me, Say not, I
am a child: for thou shalt go to all that I shall send thee, and
whatsoever I command thee thou shalt speak. Be not afraid of
their faces: for I am with thee to deliver thee, saith the Lord. Then
the Lord put forth his hand, and touched my mouth. And the
Lord said unto me, Behold, I have put my words in thy mouth."*

Jeremiah was called to preach before he was born! God "sanctified" him, "ordained" him to be a prophet unto the nations.
Then in due time the word of the Lord came to him saying he
must preach, and God Himself reached down and touched
Jeremiah's mouth saying, "I have put my words in thy mouth."
God promised detailed instructions, definite leadership, daily
preparation. Jeremiah was to go where he was sent, and to speak
what was told him, and God promised to deliver His prophet.

If anyone who reads this expects to work for God with blessing, get your Bible down and read again how God called Moses,
Isaiah, Elisha and Saul of Tarsus. Read how Jesus called the
fishermen to leave their nets, and said, "Follow me, and I will
make you fishers of men." Some of you have had this call of God.
Some of you *know* that your ministry was never a matter of
human preference. We need to go back again to the starting
point and let God put His words in our mouths and hearts and
fire in our bones.

Do you remember one spot of holy ground where you needed
to take the shoes off your feet, because God spoke to you from

a burning bush? Do you remember the time, like Gideon, when the angel of God spoke to you, and the fleece was first wet, then dry, to prove the call of God? Did you, like Gideon, ask for the "miracles which our fathers told us of" again? and did you receive assurance that the power of God, which was on the prophets of old, would be on you?

Do you remember the time when God lifted you out of sin, put a burning coal to your lips and said, "Lo, this hath touched thy lips; and thine iniquity is taken away, and thy sin purged," as He did to Isaiah when God called him? Did God somewhere strike you down and say to you, as he did to Saul, "I will send thee far hence unto the Gentiles"? Did Jesus ever say to you, as He said to the eleven disciples the day of His resurrection, "As my Father hath sent me, even so send I you"; and did His holy breath blow upon you as He said, "Receive ye the Holy Ghost"? The one hundred and twenty tarried ten days in the upper room, until the day of Pentecost was fully come. Have you waited upon God until you received power to be His witness?

O preachers, officers of the churches, Sunday school teachers, soul winners, Christians, we are not fit to serve God until we receive a divine commission, a breath of Heaven, a holy flame! I thank God I know, as definitely as I know I am writing this chapter, that God called me to preach, that He anointed me from my mother's womb to be a soul winner. "To this end was I born." Oh, may I never forget it. I need again that call burned into my soul.

The Soul-Winning Passion

One who would work for Christ must have not only a divine call but a passion that will not let him quit. The fire you once had will not do for today. One who speaks for Christ must speak as one having authority. He must know that his message is of God. Too many of our sermons are like a supper of leftovers—

too long away from the fire! A newsboy cannot sell a paper one day old. God forgive the preacher who expects results from a ministry that has not been touched by the fire of God for weeks or even years!

If a man preaches because he chooses to, he may preach pleasant and lukewarm platitudes to those who come to hear him in a comfortable building and pay him for his trouble; but only the man who preaches because he must, the one with fire in his bones, will preach to men who hate him or deride him or ignore him on the streets, in their homes, in the parks, jails and shops—everywhere.

Paul commanded Timothy, "Preach the word; be instant in season, out of season." For a long time I really wondered at that strange command. Timothy was to preach the Gospel when it was convenient and also when it was not convenient. He was to preach the Gospel when men heard and preach it the same when they would not hear. He was to preach when men supported him and also preach with the same burning passion when he must make tents for bread! The preacher with fire in his bones not only awaits an opportunity; he makes one. *He must preach!*

This was what Paul meant when he said:

"For though I preach the gospel, I have nothing to glory of: for necessity is laid upon me; yea, woe is unto me, if I preach not the gospel! For if I do this willingly, I have a reward: but if against my will, a dispensation of the gospel is committed unto me."—I Cor. 9:16, 17.

Paul was a bondslave to Jesus Christ, enslaved by the Gospel! He was a debtor both to the Greeks and to the barbarians, both to the wise and to the unwise; for he said, "A dispensation of the gospel is committed unto me." God had placed a holy deposit in Paul's heart that blazed until his dying day, so that he could say, "Woe is unto me, if I preach not the gospel!"

Paul did not mean that God would punish him if he did not

preach. I do not think he feared, as some preachers do, that ill
health and financial distress would come upon him if he did not
preach. Instead, Paul meant, "I am miserable when I can't
preach. Life is not worth living if I cannot win souls! I would
willingly die to see my brethren, the Jews, saved. I have unceasing sorrow in my heart. I could wish myself accursed from Christ
for the sake of lost sinners."

That passion, that compassion was wrought in the heart of
Paul by the Holy Spirit, as it was in the heart of Jeremiah.
Without some of that no man or woman is fit to win souls nor
able to do much of that holy work.

My beloved readers, this is a divine matter about which I write.
We did not save ourselves, call ourselves nor equip ourselves.
We need to wait before God until the dross is burned out of our
lives, until self-will is dead and the self-life is conformed to the
death of Christ, before we can wholly follow the Lord Jesus.

I say frankly that the passion for soul winning, that holy, loving, tearful "MUST" that has burned with consuming flame in
the heart of some soul winners, is a supernatural enduement
from God. Schools do not give this. Organizations cannot build
it. It is supernatural, not natural; divine, not human.

What we need is to tarry before God and so confess and forsake our sins until we are anointed from Heaven. Then the Word
of God will be in our hearts like a fire in our bones, as it was
with Jeremiah.

O Thou holy God, Thou dying, risen, living Saviour, Thou seeking Spirit, give us this holy passion for sinners, this compelling
Gospel, this fire from Heaven!

God's Word in the Preacher's Heart—
the Supernatural Message

Jeremiah said, "But his word was in mine heart as a burning
fire shut up in my bones." The term, *"his word,"* was supplied

by the translators, but that is actually the sense of the Scripture. God had said to Jeremiah, "Behold, I have put my words in thy mouth"; and again and again, many, many times in the book of Jeremiah we are told, "Then the word of the Lord came unto me, saying . . ." (1:4); or, "Moreover the word of the Lord came unto me, saying . . ." (1:11). See also Jeremiah 2:1; 3:6, etc. The words of Jeremiah were literally the words of the Lord.

In Jeremiah 30:2, the Lord commanded Jeremiah, "Write thee all the words that I have spoken unto thee in a book." Jeremiah did, and this proves the verbal inspiration of the Bible. Word-for-word inspiration is God's way of revelation. But it teaches far more than that. When Jeremiah spoke, he spoke the words of the Lord. The message is God's message.

I have heard preachers quote, "My word . . . shall not return unto me void" (Isa. 55:11), and say that, if a man simply preaches the truth of the Bible, God is certain to bless it. But that is a false interpretation of that Scripture. That verse really means that what God has promised He will bring to pass. It is utterly false to suppose that the Word of the Lord, preached by a cold-hearted, unanointed preacher who preaches in human wisdom and for selfish purposes, will bring its proper fruit, the same as if preached by a man whose heart is set aflame by the Holy Spirit. It takes the power of God to preach the Word of God. The Word of God is not a sword of man but the sword of the Spirit.

All the Bible is God's Word, but it must burn in the preacher's heart. Many coldhearted Pharisees spent a lifetime studying the Bible, teaching the Bible and trying to follow the Bible; but they were blind leaders of the blind, Jesus said. They compassed land and sea to make a proselyte, then made him twofold more the child of Hell than themselves! The lawyers, Jesus said, experts in the law of Moses, would not enter into the kingdom and yet would not permit others to enter. They had the Word of God, yes, but only the letter of it, not the Spirit. The letter of the law

killeth, but the Spirit makes alive. The bare, cold outlines of scriptural facts, as preached by many a preacher, deaden, kill and damn. The Word of God, which comes only through the brain and mouth of a preacher or personal worker, is blighting, fruitless, powerless. In order to be blessed to the hearer, the word of God must be preached from *the heart*! Jeremiah said, "His word was *in mine heart* as a burning fire shut up in my bones." A preacher's heart is far more important than his head. It is heart preaching that has power, not head preaching.

In Kansas City during the great Gipsy Smith revival years ago after the service an old preacher came into the room where the Gipsy was sitting. Thousands were being blessed and hundreds saved. The older minister placed his hands upon the evangelist's head and felt about it. "I am trying to find the secret of your success," he said.

"Too high! too high! My friend, you are too high," Gipsy said. "The secret of whatever success God has given me is not up there but down here," and he placed his hand upon his heart!

I heard this man preach, this gypsy, born in a tent, won by his gypsy father. Gipsy Smith never had a day's schooling from men, yet he preached to the multitudes for sixty years. As he preached, I saw tears course down his cheeks, and my own heart was stirred, warmed and blessed. The Word of God must be in the heart.

Soon after I entered the ministry, I was asked to preach. Somewhat distressed about facing a great Sunday night crowd, I said to a great old minister, Brother G. I. Brittain, "I don't know what to preach tonight." He replied, "And don't you know where to go to find out?" I saw the point, and instead of racking my brain to make a sermon, I went to God in earnest prayer, seeking and begging for a message from Heaven.

This does not belittle the Bible—it adds emphasis to the Bible. Study the Bible? Yes, with all your heart. Preach the Bible? Yes,

preach it, all of it; it is God's Word, the infallible, verbally-inspired revelation of God Himself. But preach it with tears, with passion, with fire—preach it from a burning heart set on fire from Heaven!

The apostles were strictly Bible preachers. It is amazing how much Scripture that fisherman Peter used in his sermons recorded in the book of Acts. But mark you; these great preachers, these flaming preachers, these incessant, daily preachers, placed more importance on prayer than on preaching. They asked the multitude to select seven men whom they might appoint over the business of caring for the widows, and "we will give ourselves continually to prayer, and to the ministry of the word" (Acts 6:4).

The Word of God in the brain may lie dormant and unfruitful, but the Word of God in the heart burns like fire in the bones, until one is weary with forbearing and cannot stay! It is the Word of God in the heart, so living, so burning, that one must say, "Woe is unto me, if I preach not the gospel!" Christians need to spend enough time with God that the message of God may really take possession of the heart.

Natural preaching of a supernatural Word will not do. We need a supernatural element in our testimony, a miraculous fire in our ministry. In other words, we need to be filled and transformed by the power of the Holy Spirit so that the message, the power and the fruit are God's.

May God kindle a fire in our bones so that we cannot stay but *must* tell out God's message!

"A prayer of Habakkuk the prophet upon Shigionoth. O Lord, I have heard thy speech, and was afraid: O Lord, revive thy work in the midst of the years, in the midst of the years make known; in wrath remember mercy."—Hab. 3:1, 2.

A revival of Bible religion—how precious and glorious it is! The greatest event that can ever happen on this earth, aside from the return of Christ Himself, is an old-fashioned, Heaven-sent, Holy Spirit revival, when God comes near to the hearts of many men, saving sinners and renewing and rejoicing the hearts of His own people. Revivals are necessary. They are part of God's plan in dealing with His people and with all mankind. Revivals ought to be the chief concern of pastor and people in every church. God calls and prepares evangelists, revivalists. Ephesians 4:11, 12 says:

"And he gave some, apostles; and some, prophets; and some, evangelists; and some, pastors and teachers; For the perfecting of the saints, for the work of the ministry, for the edifying of the body of Christ."

God gives evangelists for the work of edifying the saints, as well as for winning sinners. That proves that God is in favor of revivals.

All of us wish we could stay on the mountaintop. Surely Chris-

tians may have blessings day by day. God has provided victory for a Christian all the time. There need be no relapses, no periods of defeat, no fruitlessness. There is abundant power for every Christian. Yet the plain, simple fact is that all God's people need reviving frequently. People do not stay on the mountain of transfiguration, but must return to the valley of suffering.

Revival is a law of nature. Just now

> **The melancholy days have come,**
> **The saddest of the year,**

as the poet says. Green leaves have turned yellow and buff and red and brown. Soon they will all be drab and sear. The sap is gone from the trees. The crops are harvested in the fields. But next spring we will have a revival of leaf and bud and flower and fruit. Seedtime and harvest, sowing and reaping, summer and winter, is the unfailing law of nature. In the millennial reign of Christ we may have eternal summer—the tree of life will bring forth her fruit every month, and the leaves are for the healing of the nations. But as long as Christians have two natures; as long as we live surrounded by manifold temptations; as long as our adversary Satan goes around like a roaring lion seeking whom he may devour (for "we wrestle not against flesh and blood")—that long the saints of God will need periods of refreshing, of revival.

Those who despise revivals ignore the way in which God has dealt with His people. Again and again throughout the Bible we find accounts of how God sent mighty revivals upon His people—Elijah at Mount Carmel, Daniel in Babylon, Nehemiah in Jerusalem after the captivity, kings Hezekiah and Josiah in Judaea before the captivity; John the Baptist by the river Jordan, Peter and others at Pentecost, Philip in Samaria—all experienced mighty revivals. Bless God for the revivals recorded in the Bible! In fact, the history of God's dealings with the race shows that, when God sent His prophets to warn the people, the

inevitable result was either revival or judgment. Today, sure-ly, the only thing that can prevent the terrible wrath of God upon America is a Heaven-sent revival of His blessing and power, a mighty turning to God.

Let no one condemn revivals. You say they do not last? That is not altogether true. Every soul saved in a Heaven-sent revival will shine throughout eternity with a marvelous luster, and all the toil of revivals will be paid for in the coinage of another world. But let us admit that the warmth and the fervor, the new dedication and consecration which we experience in revivals need to be sought again and again. That part of a revival waxes, then wanes, and another revival is needed soon, we frankly admit.

But this does not prove that revivals are a failure; it is simply an argument for the need of *another* revival, when the first one has waned.

Every traffic *"Safety First"* campaign is temporary. For a time motorists drive more carefully, but soon the inspiration and warning wear off. Has the campaign failed? No, it has saved many lives. The temporariness of the campaign only proves there must be other campaigns.

Plowing is a temporary business. The farmer turns over the soil that in the loosened seedbed seeds may sprout and plants take root. Weeds are turned under. Soon, to be sure, weeds will grow again, and the ground will become packed and hard and will need another plowing. But, meantime, the crop has grown. Food and clothes are made possible by the farmer's plow, even though the work is only temporary. Because the plowing is only temporary is another reason for plowing again.

Revivals, periods of more earnest seeking after God, more fre-quent and fervent praying, examining our hearts, mortifying the deeds of the flesh, judging our sins—such revivals are in the plan of God for all of us.

Let no church or pastor be satisfied without seeking to have special times of revival. Revivals are not usual, but unusual; not ordinary, but extraordinary. The bane of Christian living and work—the sin which is most certain to befall us—is that our service for Christ may become just a form without the substance—professional, habitual, commonplace and ordinary. The same prayers that once came from the heart now come only from the lips. The Bible reading that was once the fervent seeking after God's truth becomes merely a dutiful habit. Then there is need for a revival.

"O Lord, I Have Heard Thy Speech, and Was Afraid"

Habakkuk lived in a time of terrible declension and worldliness. It was just before the captivity of Judah. The prophecy begins with this title, "The burden which Habakkuk the prophet did see." "Burden" means a message of weight and sorrow, a promised punishment. The second to fourth verses of the first chapter of the prophecy say,

"O Lord, how long shall I cry, and thou wilt not hear! even cry out unto thee of violence, and thou wilt not save! Why dost thou shew me iniquity, and cause me to behold grievance? for spoiling and violence are before me: and there are that raise up strife and contention. Therefore the law is slacked, and judgment doth never go forth: for the wicked doth compass about the righteous; therefore wrong judgment proceedeth."

Habakkuk, amazed and grieved at the sin, violence and idolatry about him, cries out to God for judgment and punishment on the people. Then in chapter 2, the answer of God is given. Verses 6, 9, 12, 15 and 19 promise separate and terrible woes upon Israel. Then in our text in chapter 3, Habakkuk cries out, "O Lord, I have heard thy speech, and was afraid: O Lord, revive thy work in the midst of the years, in the midst

of the years make known; in wrath remember mercy."

A TIME OF WICKEDNESS, WORLDLINESS, BLOODSHED AND THE WRATH OF GOD IS A GOOD TIME FOR REVIVAL! In fact, such times cry out for revival. The more a revival is needed, the more willing God is to give it. The more a revival is needed, the more will some people realize the need. Christians will be led more earnestly to pray. Some sinners will be more willing to listen. The preacher's sharp message against sin will be more emphatic, more startling, yet more quickly believed by some who have found that the way of the transgressor is hard and have seen the fruits of sin.

When Habakkuk heard the woes which God pronounced upon His people, the warning of God frightened him and led to earnest prayer for revival.

Let preachers consider and take notice! Revivals, old-fashioned, Heaven-sent revivals, are ordinarily preceded by plain, sharp, dogmatic, positive preaching. The preacher who faithfully, fearlessly and with a holy abandon condemns sin in high places and in low, among the saints of God and in the wicked world about him, will cause conviction on the part of sinners, and a keen hunger and thirst for revival on the part of God's people. Penitent seeking after God follows faithful proclamation of the divine warning. Nineveh repented only after Jonah preached, "Yet forty days, and Nineveh shall be overthrown." The marvelous revival under John the Baptist came from such preaching as this:

"And now also the axe is laid unto the root of the trees: therefore every tree which bringeth not forth good fruit is hewn down, and cast into the fire. I indeed baptize you with water unto repentance: but he that cometh after me is mightier than I, whose shoes I am not worthy to bear: he shall baptize you with the Holy Ghost, and with fire: Whose fan is in his hand, and he will throughly purge his floor, and gather his wheat into the garner; but he will burn

up the chaff with unquenchable fire."—Matt. 3:10-12.

That was a plain warning of the wrath of God against sin, that the Jewish religious leaders, yea, even the nation itself would be cut down like a fruitless tree if it did not repent and get right with God. More than that, there was a plain warning of the fires of Hell—that Jesus will "burn up the chaff with unquenchable fire."

The great revival under Hezekiah was preceded by such plain preaching as this in II Chronicles 29:6-9:

"For our fathers have trespassed, and done that which was evil in the eyes of the Lord our God, and have forsaken him, and have turned away their faces from the habitation of the Lord, and turned their backs. Also they have shut up the doors of the porch, and put out the lamps, and have not burned incense nor offered burnt-offerings in the holy place unto the God of Israel.

"Wherefore the wrath of the Lord was upon Judah and Jerusalem, and he hath delivered them to trouble, to astonishment, and to hissing, as ye see with your eyes. For, lo, our fathers have fallen by the sword, and our sons and our daughters and our wives are in captivity for this."

Other Old Testament revivals were preceded by the reading of the law, with solemn judgments promised upon those who should depart from God.

Let preachers then take heart. In the time of war, the time of sin and worldliness, of unbelief and modernism, of gambling and drunkenness and adultery—that is the time for revivals, provided the prophets of God will be true in declaring God's wrath on sin. If preachers will be true to God, then people will cry out, "O Lord, I have heard thy speech, and was afraid," and will beg God for a revival.

"O Lord, Revive Thy Work"

My brother, the work is the Lord's. We have a right to expect

Him to repair it, to renew it, to bless it.

First of all, what happened to me was of God. When I was an undone sinner, it was God who loved me and prepared salvation for me at the fearful price of the death of Jesus on the cross. It was the Holy Spirit who sought me, who ran me down, who knocked so insistently and pleaded so tenderly that I surrendered and was saved. It was the blood of Christ that paid my debt and cleansed me from all sin. My salvation is all of grace. "Not by works of righteousness which we have done, but according to his mercy he saved us." If my heart is not as warm as it ought to be, if my service is not pleasing and acceptable to God, then nothing is more reasonable than that I should come to God for His remedy.

I do not blame God for my faults. He is not responsible for my sins. My failures are not His failures. Yet, in some sense, I am not my own. The problems of my Christian life are not my problems after all, but His. I am bought with the blood of Christ. The work is Christ's. I am "his workmanship."

When buying a new car, you receive a warranty for ninety days. During that time any defective part must be replaced free of charge. If some adjustment was not properly made or if there was some fault in the manufacture of the automobile, you may drive back to the dealer and have the matter attended to at his charge.

But how much better is the guarantee that God gives a sinner when He saves him! The Lord not only took care of the first cost, but all the upkeep on your salvation! It is everlasting life that He promised, and even the more abundant life! Troubled, backslidden reader, the work you need done is God's work. You have a perfect right to lift up your poor, feeble hands to Him and cry out, "O Lord, revive *Thy* work. I am Yours. I need a blessing. I need spiritual food and drink. I need new cleansing, new love, new joy, new power! Father, I am Your child. I have

nowhere else to go. *Lord, revive Thy work.*"

As conversion is a divine business, so is the call to preach. There is a romance about preaching the Gospel. There is a heavenly fragrance about telling sinners that the risen, glorified Christ died for them, and teaching the people of God what their calling and inheritance are.

But preachers do not stay on fire for God. We sometimes find that the Gospel is not as sweet to our own ears as it once was. We may serve others at God's table yet ourselves go hungry. Preachers need revivals. But we have a right to go to the Lord and say, "O Lord, revive thy work in the midst of the years." We who have been called to preach have a right to a fresh vision, a fresh anointing, a fresh commission.

Many great business firms feel personally responsible for their salesmen. And every so often a salesman is taken to "the home office" or to "the factory" for fresh inspiration and reward.

When an automobile manufacturer puts out a new model, special sessions are held for automobile dealers and salesmen. They are given the facts about the new model. They are given the best sales talk. They see with their own eyes the beauties of the lovely machine. They test for themselves its wonderful performance. They return to sell it with enthusiasm and inspiration. The automobile manufacturer knows that he is responsible for his dealers.

So, my brother preacher, we have a right to go to God and ask Him for new help, just like Elijah fleeing from Jezebel, or like John the Baptist languishing in prison. We are His workmanship. May God revive His own work in the hearts of His preachers!

"...In the Midst of the Years, in the Midst of the Years Make Known"

Years ago at many a baptizing by a riverbank they sang the old song:

> Oh, how happy are they
> Who the Saviour obey,
>   And whose treasures are laid up above;
> Tongue can never express
> The sweet peace, joy and rest
>   Of a soul in its earliest love.

Even the Scripture speaks of the first love. The church at Ephesus is warned of God, "I have somewhat against thee, because thou hast left thy first love" (Rev. 2:4).

Do you remember the sweetness, the fresh ecstasy when you first trusted Christ? Do you remember how you loved Christians, how you longed to see sinners saved? Do you remember with what fervor you prayed, and how rich were those passages in the Bible with which you first became familiar after you were saved?

Oh, that God would give us again the freshness of our beginnings! Preacher, do you remember your first sermons, your first revivals? How sweet is the first love!

It is "in the midst of the years" that we need revivals. A watch, when first wound, may keep accurate time; but if it goes too long without winding, it begins slowly to lose time. A preacher who goes too long without winding does not have the power he once had! Christians need rewinding, i.e., reviving "in the midst of the years."

Tendency to Backslide

It is a strange thing, this tendency to backslide after one has long been settled in the Christian life. I have seen many a young Christian give up cigarettes or picture shows or gambling, and do it gladly, do it easily, to begin the soul-winning life. But little by little, later on, the older habits laid aside have a tendency to reappear "in the midst of the years." I have found that the drunkard, wonderfully saved, often leaves his old companions, gives a fervent testimony wherever he goes, and

experiences all the power and victory of a Christian life for weeks or months or sometimes years; and then, when he ceases to be afraid of the old habit, when he is off his guard, when he has settled down into a more or less routine service, he may slip into the old sins again.

Christian, look out for the settled period "in the midst of the years." Then is when we should pray earnestly for a revival. Then is our time of danger.

Many a man marries a lovely girl and lives with her happily through the strenuous early years of married life. He must work hard in business. He loves his wife. There is the holy thrill of new babies and the responsibilities of fatherhood.

But after awhile, "in the midst of the years," when a man is well established in business, when his home seems safe and his children are maturing satisfactorily, many a man falls prey to the siren voice of an evil woman.

How many homes are broken after the children are grown! How many a man takes up gambling or crooked business after he has made a success in life! Those middle years, those settled years, are times of great need for revival.

I believe that a nation is in great danger after it has passed the first stages, when the government is settled, when its frontiers are developed, when prosperity and independence are safely assured, when danger seems a thing of the past. Then there comes the slow decay of manhood, corruption in politics, worldliness in the church, atheism in the school and license in the home. When America was young, we believed in God. Our greatest danger has come "in the midst of the years." Oh, the need for revival in the midst of the years!

"In Wrath Remember Mercy"

God had expressed His wrath on the sins of Judah. Captivity and woe were promised. There is every evidence that the wrath of God is on the world today.

A view of the world shows a dark picture. Murderous communism has overrun much of Europe. The nuclear bomb and other war techniques threaten to destroy the entire civilization. We are in days of wrath!

Government of the people, by the people and for the people is disappearing from the earth. Drugs and drunkenness are increasing as are crimes of every kind, and accidents. Even nature shows the wrath of God upon His wicked creatures; drought, flood and pestilence add to the terrors of unemployment. We are in days of wrath! Preachers ought to preach this fearlessly.

I expect judgment to fall upon America. Communism rears its defiant head, seeking to bring anarchy and atheism to our land, to overthrow our government and close our churches. I say, these are days of wrath, and every preacher should be a warning prophet.

But, thank God, days of wrath can be days of mercy, too! Let every Christian pray, "O Lord, revive thy work in the midst of the years, in the midst of the years make known; in wrath remember mercy." Troublous, sinful days are just the days to pray for revival.

I have found that people's hearts are terribly hard in these wicked days. Many men will not hear the Gospel. Many women will laugh in a preacher's face. Many youths scoff at religion and Heaven and God. But I find that, where the chastening hand of God has fallen, there oftentimes men listen to the Gospel! When I preach a funeral sermon, I preach revival, and you may be sure that there are broken hearts who will hear it. Days of wrath and judgment are also days of mercy. When God stretches out His hand, He does it in mercy as well as in wrath. We should expect sinners to turn to God as a result of every great calamity.

In Wichita Falls, Texas, some years ago, I came upon an awful scene one night, just after a car had turned over with four young people. The car was ruined. One young woman was so badly

injured that she spent months in the hospital, though that night we did not know how seriously she was hurt. I took them in my car to their homes at midnight. When I suggested that we have a time of prayer and thank God that I was not bringing home to the mother a dead girl, they were eager to pray. They knew it was a warning from God. Two of that number were happily converted, and the other two—backslidden Christians—made confession of their waywardness and promised to attend services the following Sunday, to line up with God's people and serve Him. They knew that it was a time of wrath, and they sought mercy.

My dear reader, the time of judgment is a time to call on God for a revival.

In the jails, I have seen hundreds claim Christ as their Saviour. There are several reasons why I liked to preach to people in jail. One reason is, they needed it. Another reason is that they couldn't get away. But the best reason is that they wanted the Gospel. A man who is sentenced to several years in the penitentiary listens very respectfully when you preach that the way of the transgressor is hard; and in many, many cases he rejoices to know that his sins, though scarlet, can be made as white as snow.

Take heart, my friends. I believe that we are in days of wrath, but I know that we have a right to pray that God will send a mighty revival in such a day as this.

The great Dwight L. Moody never tired of telling how God blessed and saved souls as he went among the wounded soldiers of the Union Army, following the great battles of the Civil War. They were ripe for the Gospel.

The clouds are heavy on every side. Christians must be grieved and heavyhearted, if they feel that they are their brothers' keepers, and if they have loved ones unsaved. Then let us pray, like Habakkuk, that God will revive His work in the midst of

these evil years, and that in these days of wrath He will remember mercy.

"A Prayer of Habakkuk"

How shall we have a revival? Dear reader, let us pray! Habakkuk prayed for a revival. At Pentecost, the apostles and others waited and prayed for a revival. In Nineveh, they fasted and prayed day and night, so that neither man nor beast ate nor drank. They put on sackcloth and ashes and ceased every man from his violence. And God heard from Heaven and repented of that which He had planned to do and did it not.

Let it be settled once for all that revivals are divine manifestations. A revival is a miracle of God, not natural, but supernatural; not ordinary, but extraordinary; not human, but divine. Only God can give a revival.

Elijah well said to the men on Mount Carmel about the sacrifice, "Put no fire under." God must put the fire on the altar if we are really to have a revival. Elijah could repair the altar that was torn down; he could lay the wood in order; he could slay the bullock and dress it, but only God could give the revival fire!

Before Pentecost the apostles had been breathed upon; and when Christ was glorified, according to promise, they received the Holy Ghost to live in their bodies (John 7:37-39; 20:22). Jesus had opened their understanding that they might understand the Scriptures and had taught them in all the Scriptures the things concerning Himself (Luke 24:27, 44, 45). They had received their Great Commission, but even then the revival did not come until with all their hearts and with one accord they continued in prayer and supplication (Acts 1:14).

An old, old song that I used to hear when a boy in country churches impressed me greatly:

Brethren, we have met to worship,
  And adore the Lord our God;
Will you pray with all your power,
  While we try to preach the Word?

All is vain unless the Spirit
  Of the Holy One come down;
Brethren, pray, and holy manna
  Will be showered all around.

Brethren, see poor sinners round you,
  Trembling on the brink of woe;
Death is coming, Hell is moving—
  Can you bear to see them go?

See our fathers and our mothers
  And our children sinking down;
Brethren, pray, and holy manna
  Will be showered all around!

That may be old-fashioned, but according to the Word of God, it is true. Habakkuk prayed! It is PRAYER to Almighty God that brings revivals!

In these modern days, people think much of a trained ministry. We are strong on organization and on equipment. There is a subtle change going on in our thinking, and we begin to persuade ourselves that mass revivals are over, that God does not work miracles any longer, that what preachers need is more culture, not more Christ. Psychology seems more important than power, and organizing is a good deal easier than agonizing! "The supper room" is more popular than "the upper room" in the modern church. But after all, there is only One who can bring us out of our difficulties in our nation, in our homes, and in our churches, yea, in the depths of our own hearts. We need a revival! Only God can give it. Then I beg you who read this, let us pray!

If a lost sinner is reading this who is undone, away from God, and has never found peace, then I remind you that you have a right to pray for salvation. Romans 10:13 says, "For whosoever shall call upon the name of the Lord shall be saved." If you want

forgiveness, salvation and peace, you can have it today wherever you are, if you will ask God for it. The publican in the Temple prayed, "God be merciful to me a sinner," and went down to his house justified (Luke 18:13, 14). The thief on the cross cried out to Jesus, "Lord, remember me when thou comest into thy kingdom," and Jesus forgave him and said, "To day shalt thou be with me in paradise" (Luke 23:42, 43).

It is God who forgives sinners. It is God who changes the heart. God will save you today, right now, if you will trust Him. Jesus said, "Him that cometh to me I will in no wise cast out" (John 6:37).

You can have a revival of your own just now as you sit in your chair, if you will call on the God of revivals. Christians everywhere can have revivals, if earnestly, persistently, with holy abandon, with heart-searching confession and humility and surrender, they pray, as did Habakkuk:

"O Lord, I have heard thy speech, and was afraid: O Lord, revive thy work in the midst of the years, in the midst of the years make known; in wrath remember mercy." — Hab. 3:2.

Evangelistic Preaching

"I charge thee therefore before God, and the Lord Jesus Christ, who shall judge the quick and the dead at his appearing and his kingdom; Preach the word; be instant in season, out of season; reprove, rebuke, exhort with all longsuffering and doctrine. For the time will come when they will not endure sound doctrine; but after their own lusts shall they heap to themselves teachers, having itching ears; And they shall turn away their ears from the truth, and shall be turned unto fables. But watch thou in all things, endure afflictions, do the work of an evangelist, make full proof of thy ministry."—II Tim. 4:1-5.

"Do the work of an evangelist." This message is given to a pastor. Paul said, "I besought thee to abide still at Ephesus, when I went into Macedonia, that thou mightest charge some that they teach no other doctrine" (I Tim. 1:3). Timothy was evidently a pastor, still Paul says to him, "Do the work of an evangelist." "Preach the word; be instant in season, out of season; reprove, rebuke, exhort with all longsuffering and doctrine."

Most of our finest soul winners have been pastors. We think sometimes that the evangelist is the man to win souls, and the pastor is merely to feed the sheep; but there is nothing like that in God's program and plan. When God sets men on fire to win souls, they often, yea, generally, have been pastors. For instance, Charles Spurgeon was never known as an evangelist, yet the

tens of thousand he won to Christ prove that he did the work of an evangelist, though his entire ministry was given as a pastor.

Many people think of R. A. Torrey as an evangelist, but for years he was pastor of the Chicago Avenue Church, which eventually became the great Moody Memorial Church. His was pastoral preaching.

Charles G. Finney was a pastor for several years in New York City and elsewhere. The great soul winners have been pastors—Talmage and Len Broughton and George W. Truett and H. A. Ironside, and many others whose names I could mention.

To please God, a pastor must do evangelistic preaching. And I make bold to say that any man whom God calls, whatever gifts God may have given him should be used for winning souls. The Saviour said, "Follow me, and I will make you fishers of men." Whenever God calls a man to follow Him, He means to make him a soul winner.

I know preachers who have said, "Well, I am going to settle down and become a teaching pastor." Such a pastor is a backslider, "at ease in Zion," lukewarm, not willing to pay the sacrificial price to be a real soul winner—blood, sweat, tears, separation, consecration, purging, and day by day denying self (Luke 9:23), going "outside the gate," bearing the reproach of Christ.

Though now in full-time evangelistic work, it was only in 1940 that I closed a pastorate of nearly eight years. In those years, some 7,000 or 8,000 people made professions of faith under the ministry of that church and pastor. Now I say, not to take any credit, that God intends the head of a local congregation, an overseer and pastor and bishop, to be a soul winner, and to train and send out soul winners.

Evangelistic Preaching Must Boldly Attack Sin

Now what kind of preaching is evangelistic? I suggest, first,

that pastors must preach against sin if they are to have many saved.

The other day in a service my dear wife talked to a woman about her soul who had no conception about the plan of salvation. My wife said later, "I didn't know where to begin with her." I said, "You must remember, when dealing with a sinner, you begin with the fact of sin."

A man may say, "I don't believe as you do. I am not a member of your church." Never mind; the one common ground on which to approach every sinner is the fact of sin. That is where God begins, and that is where God wants preachers to begin. Preachers ought to condemn sin.

A certain preacher said about my preaching, "That man knows nothing about grace." I know about grace, but one way I know about grace is that I know what an awful, Hell-bound, *Hell-deserving* sinner I was and am. I know how God saved me from the torments of the damned. There is no grace unless there is first sin. No use preaching grace unless first men know they are wicked, Hell-bound sinners. Only the grace of God can save, but grace saves only convicted, confessed sinners.

We need to preach against sin; Bible preachers did. Elijah hated sin. When he prayed down fire from Heaven, he took the prophets of Baal down to the brook and slew them himself. Elijah was known everywhere as a hard preacher. He told Ahab that God would destroy every man of his whole family, and the kingdom would be changed. Elijah was known as God's man, preaching against sin.

There is Jeremiah. We learn in the book of Jeremiah that he said, "I cannot speak: for I am a child." But God told him He would give him a face of brass against the people. "Do not fear their faces nor their words; but preach. Whether they hear or whether they forbear, preach what I give you. I will put My words in your mouth, and they will know a prophet of God has

been among them." Oh, may God give us men like Jeremiah, who was called to preach plainly against sin!

New Testament preachers preached the same way. By the river of Jordan John the Baptist preached, "Repent." Some people think that is out of date. They talk very wisely about the "baptism of John," as if that were Old Testament, as if that were law. Don't you believe it! That was the only baptism Jesus had. That was the only baptism that Peter had, and James and John and the rest of the apostles, and all the New Testament Christians of that day.

John the Baptist preached New Testament sermons. He preached grace, he preached the Gospel, but he preached first that men are awful sinners and must repent! He preached, "The axe is laid unto the root of the trees." And when some came to be baptized who didn't show any evidence of a changed heart toward sin and toward God, John the Baptist rebuked them, saying, "O generation of vipers, who hath warned you to flee from the wrath to come? Bring forth therefore fruits meet for repentance" (Matt. 3:7, 8).

Preachers today don't like to look into the faces of the people in the pews and declare, "You bunch of snakes, you generation of vipers, who has warned you to flee from the wrath to come?" But John the Baptist did. He was sometimes personal in it. He came face to face with King Herod and said, 'It isn't right for you to have your brother's wife. It is shameful, adulterous.' It cost him his freedom, and he was put in prison, and eventually it cost him his head; but he was a preacher without fear or favor, and he was honored of God. Jesus said that never was one born of woman who was greater than John the Baptist.

Now to be evangelistic in our preaching, we must first preach against sin. Bible preachers won souls because they preached against sin.

Jesus also denounced sin. If you want to know how Jesus

preached, read Matthew 23. Seven times He calls the scribes and Pharisees hypocrites. "Woe unto you, scribes and Pharisees, hypocrites." He calls them "whited sepulchres." He calls them "blind leaders of the blind." He says they are "wolves in sheep's clothing." He says, "Fill ye up then the measure of your fathers. Ye serpents, ye generation of vipers, how can ye escape the damnation of hell?"

That is how Jesus preached. He took a rope, tied knots in it, made a good whip, then drove out of the Temple the worldly and covetous moneychangers. He called it a "den of thieves"! He not only scattered the beasts of burden, the doves and the sheep that people sold, but He turned over their tables! He didn't say politely, "Will you please take the tables and step outside?"

Can't you see those covetous old Pharisees chasing the coins that rolled over the marble floor, when Jesus kicked the tables over and cracked that whip and drove the people out? I say, Jesus preached plainly against sin. You can't have people saved unless first you bring a consciousness of sin and preach the wrath of God on sin and call for repentance from sin.

That dear woman at the well of Sychar in Samaria was won because Jesus showed her she was a sinner. Jesus was ever so tender, ever so kind, but when she found the Saviour and went to tell the people about it, the thing that stuck in her mind, the thing that broke her heart and transformed her life was that Jesus knew all about her sin! She went back and told the men, "Come, see a man, which told me all things that ever I did" (John 4:29). Jesus didn't really say to her, "You are an adulterous harlot; you have already lived with five different men, and are living with one now who is not your husband," but He made her say it. He put His finger on the hellish sin in her life.

Nobody is going to have conviction settle on congregations where he preaches and have hardened sinners, bootleggers, fallen women, convicts and dope fiends saved, without preaching

on sin. No preacher will reach these proud and haughty evolutionists and atheists unless he preaches against sin.

Sin is the point of contact between the preacher and the sinner. It is God's point of contact, too. You must do something about sin. You must repent, turn away from sin. That is how Jesus preached.

Peter stood and preached at Pentecost to the crowd that crucified the Saviour, perhaps looking straight into the eyes of the soldier who put the spear in His side. He was certainly looking into the eyes of the priests, Pharisees and leaders of the synagogue who had mocked Him while He died. He afterwards said to them, "You killed the Prince of life and desired a murderer to be granted unto you. You have crucified and slain the Lord of glory, but God has raised Him up, whereof we are witnesses." When later they called Peter and John to account, saying, "Ye have filled Jerusalem with your doctrine," they said, "We ought to obey God rather than men." God give us more Peters and Johns who will preach boldly to the Pharisees of this day! We need preaching against sin.

Stephen stood and preached, "Ye stiffnecked and uncircumcised in heart and ears, ye do always resist the Holy Ghost: as your fathers did, so do ye." It cost Stephen his life; but He was filled with the Spirit of God, and he preached against sin. Such preaching by Stephen, I have no doubt, convicted the young man Saul so that he never got away from Stephen's dying testimony and his piercing words, until he met Jesus on the road to Damascus and became Paul the apostle! What if Stephen had failed that day! He preached sharp against sin. His hearers became so angry that they literally "gnashed on him with their teeth" (Acts 7:54).

How boldly Paul preached against sin! Paul stood before Felix; "and as he reasoned of righteousness, temperance, and judgment to come, Felix trembled" (Acts 24:25). If we preached more on

judgment, temperance and righteousness these days, we, too, could cause sinners to tremble as Paul did!

Paul, you say, was a preacher of grace? He was also a preacher of "righteousness, temperance, and judgment." The people trembled, even the rulers. Though Paul had chains dangling from his handcuffs and anklets, yet they trembled when he preached against sin in the power of the Holy Spirit.

How flaming, how personal, how insulting was Paul's preaching sometimes! Standing in the court of Sergius Paulus, Paul faced Elymas the sorcerer and announced, "O full of all subtilty and all mischief, thou child of the devil, thou enemy of all righteousness, wilt thou not cease to pervert the right ways of the Lord?" (Acts 13:10). And in answer to such boldness and faith, God struck the vile sinner blind, and the deputy was wonderfully saved.

If you do not go for that type preaching, then remember that it followed days of fasting and prayer, when Paul and Barnabas, "being sent forth by the Holy Ghost, departed" on this missionary journey. Spirit-filled preachers must hate sin and say so. God will back up such men with wonders and signs and with great conversions, as He did then.

What kind of subjects shall a man preach on in evangelistic preaching? Preach on booze! Paul preached on "temperance" (Acts 24:25). There is plenty in the Bible like, "Wine is a mocker, strong drink is raging: and whosoever is deceived thereby is not wise" (Prov. 20:1). Some people say, "I don't believe in a preacher's getting into politics." Politics or no politics, an honest pastor must denounce the horrible sin of the liquor traffic, if he is to see God move wonderfully in saving drunkards.

One dear woman said, "O Brother Rice, we have the dearest preacher. He doesn't meddle in either politics or religion!" What she meant was that he never expressed himself on any civic question where there was a difference of opinion and never got on

any question of doctrine where there was a difference of opinion.

No preacher can please God who stays out of controversy. God has a controversy with sin. It is sin that nailed Jesus to the cross. It is sin that is populating Hell. It is sin that fills every graveyard, every hospital, every jail. It is sin that blights every home that is broken by divorce. *It is sin* that a preacher must hate, denounce, expose! God hates sin; and if a preacher doesn't hate it, people will not repent of sin. Preach on booze! Preach on the scarlet sin, adultery. Some cheeks will turn red with shame, and some won't like it; but it will bring repentance.

Preach on the dance. Tell people that it is rotten with sin. Tell them they dance because they enjoy the lust, the deliberate inflaming of passion! Yes, preach on the dance.

Preach on the movies. Tell people what they are and what they will do; that they are made by vile, lewd people, holding up rotten moral standards, breaking down respect for marriage, pure love, hard work, God and the Bible. Denounce the lust, the crime, the bawdy vulgarity of the movies.

Preach against the lodges. Tell people that God commands Christians: "Come out from among them, and be ye separate."

Preach against evolution and false cults. Preach on death, sin, Hell, judgment! Such preaching with boldness, with love, with tears, with Scripture, and with faith will bring great revivals and will save hardened sinners.

Some preacher says, "I like to preach on John 3:16—'God so loved the world.'" That is fine. But here is another verse from the Bible: "For our God is a consuming fire." Why not preach that, too? Or, "It is a fearful thing to fall into the hands of the living God" is also in the Bible. So is, "For the wages of sin is death." Here is another one in the Bible: "Be sure your sin will find you out." Here is another one in the Bible: "Be not deceived; God is not mocked: for whatsoever a man soweth, that shall he also reap."

May God give us grace to preach against sin!

Somebody says, "An evangelist can do that, but a pastor cannot." But I would remind you again that for these years as a pastor, I have preached the same, using the same texts and the same kind of language—plain, sharp and clear. Others say, "You will make somebody mad." Of course you will. "They will quit giving money." Of course they will. But is that your goal in preaching? "Somebody will leave the church." Certainly they will; maybe even you will have to leave. Sure! John the Baptist lost his head. Stephen was stoned to death. Paul was put in prison. Jesus Christ was crucified.

God have pity on a preacher who is not willing to suffer for real convictions. May God put *men* in the pulpit these days, not sissies!

The pulpit has lost the confidence and respect of the world these days. We have soft-spoken preachers who never hurt anybody's feelings, never offend anybody, never cross anybody, never awaken anybody, never arouse anybody, *and rarely save anybody!*

Allow me to give you a personal reference. Last fall a wicked woman came to hear me preach. She had cursed God and said she would never serve Him because her mother had died. As she talked about it later, she said, "Oh, that preacher!"—with hate in her voice as she said it—"I have lost nine pounds going to hear him preach! I don't know why I come back."

Our preaching should make people sleepless at night, cause them to lie awake, stare into the dark, afraid to go to sleep. It should be preaching that makes people go to their closets in prayer. We need to break up the ground before we sow the seed. God give us preachers like that. These "panty-waist," sissy-britches, peace-at-any price preachers; these "good-Lord and good-Devil," milk-and-cider preachers will never bring a revival. All the world is under judgment and the wrath of God.

My dear preacher-brethren—God bless you! My preacher-brethren, reprove and rebuke, as well as exhort. Preach Bible doctrine!

Evangelistic Preaching Must Be of Red-Hot Earnestness

What else about this preaching? If you want the Lord's power and blessing on you in saving souls, you must mean business. Evangelistic preaching must have a certain fervor of heart that involves tears in preparation and perhaps in delivery; that involves a straightforwardness, a zeal which makes it so that when he preaches an evangelistic message he may speak so fast that he will mispronounce the words and sometimes lose the trend of his well-prepared discourse. He may not say what he had planned, but he is led by the Holy Ghost. He may appear awkward and what he says may be more or less abrupt and uncouth.

God give us back the fervor, the tears, the boldness of men of God of other days! We must have a mean-business attitude about our preaching that will make it colorful, informal and unorthodox as to the method, though orthodox always as to God's message.

Why shouldn't a preacher stand or sit, cry or laugh or sing while he preaches? People on the stage do it. Why can't a man laugh and weep for joy over Heaven? Why can't he blaze against sin? Why not an informal sincerity to get results? Why must a preacher have a sonorous voice, a stilted attitude, a pious smirk and platitudinous commonplaceness in the pulpit?

God give us men who mean business in the pulpit! I did when I played college football. I did when I was out in business. Then why shouldn't I mean business as a preacher of the Gospel?

That means that our preaching will sometimes have to be sensational. If we preach as we ought about sin, death, judgment, the second coming, and the wrath of God, we will sometimes be

called sensational. The people said about Paul and Barnabas, "These that have turned the world upside down are come hither also." Remember, Peter and John were dragged before the Sanhedrin, and the priests said, "Ye have filled Jerusalem with your doctrine." When there is a riot and a preacher now and then gets put in jail and someone spits in his face or throws rotten eggs and tomatoes; when drunkards, harlots, convicts and dopeheads are saved, then you are going to have a sensation. Don't avoid it, but pray God to arouse and alarm people.

I don't mean trick and fake sensational stunts. I mean the boldness of God, the fire of the Spirit, the kind of preaching that brings men to their knees, with tears of repentance, trusting in Jesus Christ, or which sends them out in hate, gnashing their teeth, as they did with Christ and Stephen.

Depend on the Miracle-Working Word of God

O my fellow preachers, believe the Word and press it hot on people's hearts. "He that goeth forth and weepeth, bearing precious seed, shall doubtless come again with rejoicing, bringing his sheaves with him" (Ps. 126:6). Take the Word of God. Plant it, believe it, expect God to bless it. Depend on the Word of God. Memorize a lot of it. When you come to preach, claim the promises. Then when you give an invitation, give the actual words of the Scripture to cling to, and get men to meet God on His promises. It isn't hard to be saved. The reason people are not saved is that in their wicked hearts they are not willing to turn from sin and take God at His Word. Use the Word. It is "quick, and powerful, and sharper than any two edged sword" (Heb. 4:12). "Is not my word like as a fire saith the Lord; and like a hammer that breaketh the rock in pieces?" (Jer. 23:29).

Pull for Results Always

We must mean business, and that means we will pull for

results. O my brothers, let us so preach so that if an unsaved person is present we will seek to win him while we can. And if you preach to a crowd and there are no unconverted present, then urge the Christians to do all they can in winning souls. You can't preach to the sinners if they are not there, but you can preach to the people who will reach sinners and bring them in. Let's set people on fire for winning souls. Let's pull for results.

I preached many funerals, especially when I was pastor and had a daily radio service. I made God a promise: I would never preach a funeral service without making plain the plan of salvation and urging men to repent. I have given an invitation at many, many funerals and had people saved.

As a young woman came down the stairs from a dance hall on the second floor at Magnolia and Hemphill Streets in Fort Worth, Texas, her husband met her and jealously stabbed her to death. I was called to preach the funeral. That nightclub crowd, that underworld crowd, that wild and profligate crowd, that wayward-daughter and prodigal-son crowd, packed the funeral parlor. I preached the plan of salvation. As I called for sinners, eight came down to claim Christ as Saviour.

"But people will be offended," a preacher says. Then announce ahead of time that that is the only kind of sermon you will preach. I promised God I wouldn't preach one kind of Gospel in a revival meeting and another kind at a funeral. I will never preach into Heaven some old profligate, ungodly wretch who would not repent while he had an opportunity.

Get people saved when you marry a couple. Get people saved at funerals. Get people saved in Sunday school classes. Get people saved in the morning as well as in the evening service. Get people saved at Rotary clubs, at Kiwanis luncheons. Anyplace a preacher has a right to speak, he has a right to talk about salvation.

Dr. L. R. Scarborough had a way of saying, "Any end of the

Gospel is good, just so it is the hot end." Deliver the Gospel hot and win souls!

A Definite Enduement of Holy Spirit Power Essential to Soul-Winning Preaching

Another word about evangelistic preaching is this: It must be preaching with a definite enduement of Holy Spirit power. Magnetism won't do it; personality never saved a soul; psychology never won a sinner.

I read an article the other day by a man who was lamenting that in these days we can't have revivals, that there is a great falling away. He said: "We had so many preachers; we had chalk talks, motion pictures, special music—all those—yet we didn't get but about fifty people saved."

They didn't have a musical saw at Pentecost, but three thousand people were saved. John the Baptist didn't win them by wearing a cowboy suit and bringing a long lariat into the pulpit. Elijah didn't set out to Mount Carmel with a boy prodigy who could play an accordion. It takes more than these incidentals, more than cowbells and tricks and solos. *It takes the fire of Almighty God!* Nobody is going to win souls and have a revival, unless he has an anointing from God.

When Jesus came to be baptized and waited and prayed, the Holy Ghost came on Him like a dove, and Jesus was anointed. Then He went back to the synagogue in Nazareth and read Isaiah 61:1:

"The Spirit of the Lord God is upon me; because the Lord hath anointed me to preach good tidings unto the meek; he hath sent me to bind up the brokenhearted, to proclaim liberty to the captives, and the opening of the prison to them that are bound."

Jesus never worked a miracle nor preached a sermon nor won a soul *until He was anointed!* Perfect and sinless and holy He

was, but He began His ministry after He was anointed to preach.

Sometimes preachers preach so dully and lifelessly that people say, "I am afraid he has not been called to preach." That isn't the answer. He has been *called* but not *anointed*. He has been called, but he hasn't answered, hasn't been fitted.

Let us learn a lesson from Peter, James, John and the other apostles. Before Pentecost they were saved and had been given the Great Commission. Christ had opened their hearts to understand the Scriptures. They were filled with joy at the appearance of the resurrected Saviour. "Then were the disciples glad, when they saw the Lord" (John 20:20). Jesus had breathed on them and said, "Receive ye the Holy Ghost," and He had come in to dwell in their bodies (John 20:22). The indwelling of the Spirit began when Christ was exalted in a resurrection body, as He promised in John 7:37-39. Yes, the apostles had everything— salvation, a call, training, instructions, the indwelling Spirit and joy—*everything but soul-winning power!* So Jesus commanded them, "Behold, I send the promise of my Father upon you: but tarry ye in the city of Jerusalem, until ye be endued with power from on high" (Luke 24:49).

What they needed was *power from on high!* Beloved brethren, we too need the supernatural, miracle-working power of God upon our ministry.

I am not talking here of a jabber in tongues nor of an ecstasy of feeling nor of sinless perfection. I do not mean that we are to seek a self-centered "experience" so that we may go about boasting that we are holier than others; and I do not care whether you call it *a baptism, a filling, an anointing, a pouring out of the Spirit,* or *a gift.* But God help us to see that we need the power of God, power to witness, so that souls will be saved, churches revived, and God become real and His presence blessed to thousands. "Ye shall receive power, after that the Holy Ghost is come upon you: and ye shall be witnesses unto me both in

Jerusalem, and in all Judaea, and in Samaria, and unto the uttermost part of the earth" is what Jesus promised in Acts 1:8.

O preacher-brethren, we need power, power with God and power with men! Any theology, however orthodox, that leaves out the need for a holy enduement of the Spirit's power as manifested in the soul winning of the New Testament, is a barren desert with rainless clouds, a dry waterhole and a broken cistern! It is wicked presumption, modernism of the heart, infidelity in practice!

Whatever of self-judgment, of confession, of restitution, and self-crucifixion; whatever waiting on God, whatever surrender, whatever faith it takes, the one essential that the soul-winning man or woman must have is the power of the Spirit of God to attract, convict, enlighten and save sinners!

If it is to be greatly blessed of God and work soul-saving miracles, evangelistic preaching must boldly attack sin, must have holy earnestness and fervor, must depend upon the Word of God, must aim for definite results, and must have a definite enduement of the Holy Spirit.

Brethren, let us do God's kind of preaching and win souls. *"Do the work of an evangelist"!*

"And your feet shod with the preparation of the gospel of peace." —Eph. 6:15.

Soul winning begins with the feet! To our proud, haughty, human minds it would seem proper that soul winning would demand the most brilliant minds, the greatest education, the strongest possible backing of wealth and influence. But not so! Instead, soul winning is made a prosaic matter of the feet! That is the way of God. He has chosen by the foolishness of preaching to save men, instead of by the wisdom of angels or even the wisdom of this world. He has chosen the weak to confound the mighty. So soul winning is very largely a matter of consecrated feet.

A little reflection will show that the same principle is taught many times throughout the Bible. In the Great Commission the first two words are, "Go ye." Going is before teaching, preaching or baptizing! In Psalm 126:6, where God gives a wonderful outline of soul winning, we are told, "He that goeth forth and weepeth, bearing precious seed, shall doubtless come again with rejoicing, bringing his sheaves with him." Again, going is before sowing or reaping, or weeping or rejoicing.

God certainly demands that we put feet in soul winning. And when He wanted to make soul winners out of some fishermen, He said, "Follow me, and I will make you fishers of men."

Following comes before fishing, just as going comes before sowing. Walking comes before talking in God's plan.

In Luke 14 the work of a soul winner is clearly pictured. A man made a great supper and bade many. Now notice the activities of the servant (the model soul winner), and his lord's commands to him. "And he sent his servant at suppertime to say. . . ." You see, "going" comes before "saying." Again, "So that servant came, and showed his lord these things." Soul winning is not all glory. A lot of it is coming back for further orders, when our message does not bring results.

Notice again: "Then the master of the house being angry said to his servant, Go out quickly into the streets and lanes of the city, and bring in hither the poor, and the maimed, and the halt, and the blind." "Go out" must be before "bring in." The feet have much to do with soul winning.

Then we find that the servant, after going out into the streets and lanes of the city, came back and reported that there was yet room. Notice the command, "And the lord said unto the servant, *GO* out into the highways and hedges, and compel them to come in, that my house may be filled." The same servant who had gone from house to house for the guests first invited and who then searched all the streets and lanes of the city for the poor, the maimed, the halt, and the blind, at last set out for the highways in the country and up and down the hedges to compel the people to come in! And between times he returned again and again to report to his boss.

That servant's main business was not inviting but going. Going took more time than anything else. Getting out the Gospel is largely a matter of footwork. And remember that one command was "go out quickly." I am sure that that servant was valued by his master, not for his eloquent speech nor for his tender pleading, but for faithful going!

And so all Christians are commanded to have "your feet

shod with the preparation of the gospel of peace"!

Beautiful Feet

The feet of a soul winner are beautiful in God's sight. The Spirit of God tells us in Isaiah 52:7:

"How beautiful upon the mountains are the feet of him that bringeth good tidings, that publisheth peace; that bringeth good tidings of good, that publisheth salvation; that saith unto Zion, Thy God reigneth!"

Again, Nahum 1:15 is a similar passage, praising the feet of those who carry the gospel message.

"Behold upon the mountains the feet of him that bringeth good tidings, that publisheth peace!"

In Romans 10:15 we have the same message:

"And how shall they preach, except they be sent? as it is written, How beautiful are the feet of them that preach the gospel of peace, and bring glad tidings of good things!"

How can one preach except he first goes? Of what use is a mouth with a sweet message, unless the feet carry it? How beautiful are the feet of the soul winner!

I can well understand how the dear Saviour Himself washed the feet of the disciples. He meant it as a lesson in humility, yet someway He made the feet of a preacher grand and beautiful. The feet of the apostles trudged over the then-known world, carrying the Gospel.

Every preacher, every missionary, every soul winner ought to read carefully the story of Paul's missionary journeys with this in mind, that Paul spent more time walking than he did preaching, and his feet got more exercise than his mouth! Paul not only preached publicly but also "from house to house" (Acts 20:20).

I was profoundly impressed one day in reading Acts 20:13, 14:

"And we went before to ship, and sailed unto Assos, there intending to take in Paul: for so had he appointed, minding himself to go afoot. And when he met with us at Assos, we took him in, and came to Mitylene."

Paul was minded to go "afoot" from Troas to Assos, a distance, I suppose, of eighteen or twenty miles. I think it likely that on the crowded ship he would have no quiet place in which to meditate and pray, no time to seek the will and power of God. So he provided that his lesser companions should have the comfort of the ship while he walked.

And to make it more interesting yet, remember that in the same chapter the preceding verses tell how the night before he had preached until midnight, then brought back to life the young man who fell out of the third-story window, ate a midnight lunch and talked on till daylight! Following that, then, Paul felt the need to walk a day-long journey to the next preaching place!

Beautiful feet of Paul! They were soul-winner's feet. No wonder Paul could say of himself, "In labours more abundant." We often miss the point, so clearly taught in the Bible, that there is a severe price in toil to be a soul winner.

I can easily get a preacher willing to fill a pulpit and preach a sermon, but it is a difficult thing to get somebody to do house-to-house visitation—harder still to get Christians to take tracts and walk block after block giving out the message of life or spreading revival circulars and handbills. Christians do not realize that walking is the first part of soul winning.

Pearls are found in oysters in the bottom of the sea; diamonds are found in the dirt far below the surface of the ground in Africa; and the soul-winner's joy is found in the midst of drudgery and toil. Precious souls are not won without going after them. It takes consecrated feet to be a soul winner!

Oh, may you who read this develop feet that are beautiful in the sight of God, feet over which new converts in Glory will rejoice and say, "How beautiful are the feet of them that preach the gospel of peace, and bring glad tidings of good things!"

Have your feet been shod with the preparation of the Gospel of peace?

May I urge everyone who longs to win souls to set yourself to pay a price. You envy the soul-winner's joy and well you may, but it costs far more than you know! Do not think lightly of his work. Perhaps you see only the platform work, the public speech, not the enormous amount of drudgery and going, the footwork that is necessary for anybody to be a soul winner for Christ.

"Shod With the Preparation—"

There are too many barefooted Christians. There are too many would-be soul winners who are not shod with the preparation of the Gospel of peace. Once "Uncle William" Mullins said about a certain problem that he faced, "Now this is going to be a battle of wits!" His wife, Mamie, replied, "That is just like you, William, entering into a battle half-armed." There are too many half-armed Christians entering into the battle with the Devil. The lesson here is that, if you want to win souls, then get ready.

I well remember that the first garments my dear father put on each morning were his socks. He didn't want his feet to get cold. And so a Christian every day is to prepare his mind and heart for soul winning. Put the shoes of the Gospel on your feet before you start out for the day!

First, I think this means that you need a new dedication to soul winning every day. The little song we sang in Sunday school a long time ago is good for every Christian:

> **I washed my hands this morning**
> **So very clean and white,**
> **And held them up to Jesus,**
> **To work for Him till night.**

> **Little feet be careful**
> **Where you take me to;**
> **Anything for Jesus,**
> **Only let me do.**

Your body is the temple of the Holy Spirit, which you have of God, and you are commanded to glorify God in your body. Then let God have your feet! Dedicate them to Him each day to carry the Gospel. A fire hose with a high pressure nozzle may shoot a stream of water hundreds of feet high, and that may do for putting out fires; but it will not do for carrying water to the sick and dying. That you must carry by hand, and perhaps hold the cup while they sip. My dear friend, you cannot shoot the Gospel to China from the home base; somebody must carry it there.

It is well enough to enclose tracts in letters. Every way to get out the Gospel is good, but some people will never be reached without the clasp of a warm hand or the earnest, searching gaze and the quiet word or sometimes the tear of one whose trudging feet have carried the Gospel in person.

Strangely enough, the Gospel goes better by retail than by wholesale. I believe in mass evangelism, but do not misunderstand mass evangelism. The great revivals are made up principally on the human side of thousands of details, steps taken, planning, inviting, advertising, sweating, crying and praying; and then the public preaching and singing often get all the credit!

So if you want to win souls, put your shoes on your feet every day. That means to store your mind and heart with Bible verses that you can take to those whom you seek to win. That means to plan your work. Depend upon the Holy Spirit to direct where you should go, whom you should see, and what you should say. Watch for the "breaks" in the game. Many a football game has been decided because an alert player blocked a punt or fell on the ball or snatched a pass not intended for him.

I have known some preachers who were unprepared when called upon to preach. I have always thought it shocking that any preacher should not have bait on his hook and his gun loaded all the time. The Christian's mind should be so set on soul winning, and his heart so prepared for soul winning, and his will so surrendered to the Spirit's leadership, that he can win souls at every opportunity.

Will you permit a bit of personal testimony? Some time ago I was called to a funeral of an old man whom I did not know, yet one who had plainly told his loved ones he was ready to meet Christ, his Saviour. I had never seen the man who died; I did not know a one of his relatives or friends at the funeral. I did not know a single pallbearer, except one that I took with me; yet my heart was greatly moved, and I felt led to preach on John 3:16. I thought that surely these dear troubled souls, most of whom were unsaved, would be comforted by the thought that God so loved them as to give His Son.

At that funeral I preached a gospel sermon, almost as I would preach it in a revival campaign. I asked those who needed Christ to hold up their hands for prayer. Most of those present did. I asked those who would take Christ as Saviour to claim Him openly. A number did. When I returned from the cemetery (where I had the joy of winning two others), I thought back to the early morning when in my private devotions I had asked the Lord to help me win somebody that day. I tried to set my heart on soul winning. Through His mercy and help, I had in a small measure shod my feet with the preparation of the Gospel of peace.

Again, very humbly, permit me to give another illustration. One Saturday night I was called out of bed at 11:30 to marry a couple. I had risen at 5:30 in the morning; and at 6:00 I had gone to work on the open-air lot, preparing for the revival, digging holes for the light poles, cutting weeds, moving benches,

setting light poles, and helping to build the giant screen for gospel pictures. It had been a busy, heavy day, and yet somehow my heart was moved to hunger over sinners and to pray for them. I had retired rather sadly because I had not won a soul that day.

When I went to the door and found that a dear friend had brought his sister and her sweetheart so I could perform the ceremony, I prayed while I dressed that God would give me wisdom. The young couple loved each other very dearly. It showed in their faces and in every act.

After the marriage ceremony, during which both were awed and moved by the Scriptures read and the sanctity of the step they were taking, I urged upon them the need to take Christ as Saviour both into their home and into their hearts. The young man first and then the girl claimed to trust in Christ.

After a time of counsel and as they were about to leave me at the door, the young man said, "Brother Rice, I am sorry to keep you up so late, but you have made me so very happy, and I believe that you are happy in our happiness!"

I do not win as many as I should, and I do not know how many opportunities I missed on that Saturday; but I do know that God helped me in the eleventh hour, at the time when these young hearts were tender, because early in the day I had committed myself to winning of souls and had shod my feet with the preparation of the Gospel of peace!

How many we could win if we were ready! Jesus won the woman at the well of Samaria because "he must needs go through Samaria." He had prepared and planned ahead of time to win that dear soul and others. He won her because His mind was not on food, as were the minds of His disciples, but on needy souls. He could say, "I have meat to eat that ye know not of" because He had shod His feet with the preparation of the Gospel of peace.

O my dear Christian, take time to get ready every day for soul winning! Study your Bible, ask God to cleanse your heart, seek divine wisdom in your plans. Secure the right tracts to give out, ask the Holy Spirit to give you the right words to say.

Philip the evangelist walked all the way from Samaria down to the road that leads from Jerusalem to Gaza which is desert (Acts 8). It must have been a long, tiresome journey, particularly for a great evangelist who was called away from the thrill of a marvelous revival. But Philip went. He had beautiful feet in God's sight! I am sure they seemed so to the eunuch, also. And the compassionate heart of God was so moved in love toward Philip that on the return journey He caught him away, and he was carried back by the Spirit to Azotus. He had been faithful in walking, so he got a ride, carried by the Holy Spirit! But the long walk of Philip would have been wasted if he could not have begun at Isaiah 53, the same Scripture that the eunuch was reading, and preached unto him Jesus!

Philip walked, but before he went walking that day he put on his shoes. He had his feet shod with the preparation of the Gospel of peace. He knew his Bible, he was led by the Spirit, and he had his heart prepared in sincere love for sinners.

A preacher can well afford to read his Bible. Elisha could well afford for a time to be simply the servant "which poured water on the hands of Elijah" (II Kings 3:11). Timothy could well afford to wash Paul's feet and write his letters, before he got to be the bishop of the great church at Ephesus. Any would-be soul winner can well afford to study his Bible, wait before God in prayer, and be filled with the Holy Spirit. Put on your shoes, brother, put on your shoes!

"The Gospel of Peace"

The soul-winner's feet are to be shod with the preparation of the Gospel of peace. The good news is so sweet that the soul win-

ner must enjoy it himself. The messenger of a king may carry a package or a letter whose seal he dare not break, but it is not so with God's messengers. The soul winner must know the Gospel that he is to take to the sinner. He must be able to say, "I have tried it myself." If you seek sinners, you must be saved yourself, and the sweet Gospel that won you must be fresh in your heart.

When Samson found the honey in the carcass of the lion he very properly carried some to his mother and father. But he carried it in his own hands, eating as he went! My dear brother, there is honey enough for all. Eat it and be filled with the Gospel of peace as you carry it to others.

Here is a strange thing, my brother! No verse of Scripture will ever be so sweet to you as that one which you have used in pointing some other soul to Christ. A preacher never understands other parts of the Bible as well as that portion of the bread of life which God has led him to break for others. The sweetest verses in my Bible are those used when I have preached with tears and power, and when others have been blessed.

It is a Gospel of peace that you carry, and part of the soul-winner's preparation is the sweet enjoyment of the assurance of his own salvation. One who rejoices that his name is written in Heaven may get other names written there, too.

This Is Part of the Christian's Armor

And now comes a surprising lesson. The soul-winner's shoes are part of his armor, part of his defense against Satan. In this same passage, Ephesians 6, we read in verses 10-15:

"Finally, my brethren, be strong in the Lord, and in the power of his might. Put on the whole armour of God, that ye may be able to stand against the wiles of the devil. For we wrestle not against flesh and blood, but against principalities, against powers, against the rulers of the darkness of this world, against

spiritual wickedness in high places. Wherefore take unto you the whole armour of God, that ye may be able to withstand in the evil day, and having done all, to stand. Stand therefore, having your loins girt about with truth, and having on the breastplate of righteousness; And your feet shod with the preparation of the gospel of peace."

Verse 15 tells how to be strong in the Lord and in the power of His might, as commanded in verse 10. It is part of the whole armor of God mentioned in verse 11, and these shoes are to be put on "that ye may be able to stand against the wiles of the devil." Verse 12 tells us that we have a terrific battle on, not against flesh and blood, but against principalities, against powers, against the rulers of darkness, etc. Satan and all his evil spirits are around about the Christian. Therefore for his own safety, verse 15 tells us, the Christian must *have his "feet shod with the preparation of the gospel of peace"!*

In war and in football we are told that the "best defense is a good offense." The Christian who retires from the field of battle and lets souls go unhindered to Hell, is not safe from temptation; rather he is in greater danger. The Christian who really puts up a fight against Satan and snatches men as brands from the burning, will find that all about him God has put a wall of protection.

How many times I have been almost defeated, discouraged, downhearted, without a message to preach; but when I gave myself to personal soul winning and had the joy of seeing some saved, what joy, what close touch with God! How much easier it is to pray when you win souls! How much easier it is to resist temptation when your feet are shod with the preparation of the Gospel of peace!

The only safe place for a Christian is in the line of duty, and that is always in a path of soul winning. A young man called to preach said to me one day, "Brother Rice, if I do not preach

I can't even live like a Christian." No doubt he was telling me the truth. One who follows the Spirit in soul winning can have the help of God in time of need. But if with a willful heart you pick your own path outside the will of God, you throw yourself open to a thousand evils and make yourself a prey to Satan and his evil spirits.

So, my brother, put the shoes of the Gospel on your feet and set out to win souls. Dedicate your feet to the blessed business of carrying Christ to sinners, and see that they are "shod with the preparation of the gospel of peace."

8

Unsaved Brothers!

"Then he said, I pray thee therefore, father, that thou wouldest send him to my father's house: for I have five brethren; that he may testify unto them, lest they also come into this place of torment."—Luke 16:27, 28.

One of the most moving passages in the Bible is Luke 16:19-31, where Jesus tells us of the rich man who died and was buried, "and in hell he lift up his eyes, being in torments." If we believe the Bible, we must take this account at face value. Jesus did not call it a parable. He gives the name of Lazarus, who lay at the rich man's gate full of sores. Lazarus was a real person, and the story is not fiction. The rich man was a real person. Doubtless, Jesus would have given his name, too, but for the loved ones or friends of the rich man who would be grieved or embarrassed. This account is a true story of what happened to two men, one who went to Heaven and the other who went to Hell.

Many say they do not like deathbed stories, but such men will have one of their own one of these days. It is foolish not to face the fact of death and the eternal certainties that are beyond death for the saved and the lost. Preachers should preach, as Jesus did, about a Paradise where the saved are comforted and consciously happy, and about a Hell where the unrepentant are "tormented in this flame," as the rich man said that he was.

Those who would be Christians must believe in a literal Hell

of eternal, conscious torment for those who do not repent of their sins and seek salvation. No argument against a literal and eternal Hell of torment can weigh against the plain statement of the Lord Jesus Christ. Those who do not believe what Christ said should certainly not call themselves Christians nor pretend to believe the Bible. And those who would win souls must carry in the background of their minds this fundamental fact: men without Christ are lost, Hell-deserving and Hell-bound, and will lift up their eyes in Hell, tormented in flame, if they are not led to repent, to turn and trust Christ before they die unsaved.

What Do People Think About in Heaven?

We are all mightily interested in the unseen world. Our interest in those we love does not cease when they die. We know from the Bible that the soul does not cease to exist at death. There is life beyond death. Even savages instinctively know that this is true; and only the hardened, perverted, embittered and wicked cynic denies the eternal existence of the soul. The most natural thing in the world is to wonder what they are doing, these ones we have loved and lost awhile. Scores of times bereaved souls have come to me asking for light from the Word of God on what their loved ones are doing, whether they are happy, what they think, whether they know what is going on here on earth.

The saved in Heaven are deeply concerned about the race we run here on earth. The millions of angels who are our guardians and ministering spirits come and go constantly between earth and Heaven, as Jacob saw them in his dream. The rejoicing in the presence of the angels of God over one sinner that repents (Luke 15:7, 10) is shared by the saints of Glory. Heaven is concerned about soul winning. The love with which "God so loved the world" is shared by every redeemed soul in Heaven. The

concern of Christ, the tender compassion of Him who poured out His soul unto death, the great love of the Saviour who is the Advocate and High Priest of every believer, are shared by the saved who are spiritually in the likeness of Christ. We know, then, that soul winning must be the chief concern of people in Heaven.

What People Think About in Hell

In Hell, too, people see things as they are; they face eternal verities. And that being true, people in Hell are concerned about soul winning.

The rich man in Hell died as he had lived, an unrepentant sinner. He did not love God when he lived, and he did not love God after he died. People do not repent in Hell. People are not good in Hell. As the tree when cut falls in the direction it leans, so men in Hell are still the same kind of men that they were when they lived. God's mercy is withdrawn, and good influences are absent; but the wicked, rebellious, sin-loving, Christ-rejecting soul of the sinner is still the same.

When he lived the rich man loved his five brothers. When he died he still loved his five brothers. He evidently led them in sin while he lived. Now that he is in Hell, he does not want them to "come into this place of torment." He knows that unless they repent they ought to come and must come to the same torment and doom which had unexpectedly fallen upon him. Men see clearer in Hell than they do on earth. When the rich man lived, he did not expect to go to Hell when he died; he did not see his own danger. But now that he is in Hell, he knows why he is there, and he is desperately afraid for his unsaved brothers who are not concerned about themselves!

The rich man in Hell had two concerns. First, he was concerned to know if there was some way to alleviate the awful torment brought on by his sin. Second, even his own torment could not

drown the cries of his scourging conscience. He felt accountable for his brothers and begged that they might be saved. We suppose that in Heaven there are two concerns: first, the unceasing joy and glory of a blessed salvation in the presence of Christ and the Father; and second, an interest in the salvation of men on this earth. So in Hell, we suppose there are two concerns: first, the awful realization and torments of the wages of sin; and second, a concern about those left behind on this earth. It becomes clear to the prayerful student of this account by Jesus, in Luke 16:19-31, that soul winning is a principal concern of those in Heaven and those in Hell!

Brothers! What a Tender Tie!

It is a part of the goodness and wisdom of God that children grow up in families. While beasts of the field are independent and self-sustaining in a few days or a few weeks after they are born, God planned that children should be under the nurture and care of parents for many years. Evolutionists are silly, illogical and blind when they say that marriage and the family are a product of evolution. No, marriage and the family are divine institutions! God gives time for the love and associations of father, mother, brothers and sisters to have their impact on character. God gives time for the ties between brother and sister, father and mother and the child to grow strong. Those tender ties ought never be severed. God meant the influence of brother on brother for good. We do not wonder that the rich man in Hell remembered his five brothers!

God intended that always in good or evil we should remember our brothers—those of our own family.

The ties of family are very intimate, very sweet, and very strong in lives that are truly Christian. The Bible teaches that children should honor their fathers and mothers and that they should requite or care for their aged parents. Among Jews, it

was the command of God that a man marry his brother's wife and care for his brother's children. Proverbs 17:17 tells us that "a brother is born for adversity."

God allowed the brother under Jewish law to be the avenger of blood for his brother and slay the murderer if he could catch him before the guilty one reached the city of refuge (Num. 35:21).

What lessons there are for us in the brothers of the Bible! The best and the worst of a man comes out in relation to his brother.

Cain, the first man ever born, in a frenzy of hate and jealousy, killed his own brother. Then Cain lied to God and said, "Am I my brother's keeper?" Cain *was* his brother's keeper. Every man to whom God has given a brother is his brother's keeper. Even the rich man in Hell realized that!

A brother can love or hate his brother with a terrible intensity. Jacob and Esau were twin brothers. Esau was born first, but by trading and trickery Jacob got the father's blessing, though God had already chosen to give him the birthright, and it would have come so much more happily without his sin. What God had promised to give him, he seized by scheming. Hatred flared up in Esau's heart, and he swore to kill his brother as soon as their father Isaac died.

Jacob ran away to the land of Padan-aram to his mother's people and was there for twenty years without a sight of his loved ones. It is a touching and beautiful story in Genesis, chapters 32 and 33, which tell of his penitence, his eager efforts to please and win the favor of his brother Esau, his long night of prayer, wrestling with the angel of God, and then of how he and Esau met and hugged and kissed each other. Jacob said that he had seen his brother's face, "as though I had seen the face of God."

What sadness and bitterness when brother hates brother! What joy when they make reconciliation! What a tie is that of brotherhood, and how great is the influence of a brother!

Who can read the story of Joseph and his brethren and not

weep, as Joseph wept when he sent everyone else out of the room and said to the brothers who had sold him into slavery, "I am Joseph!" How he yearned over his baby brother Benjamin and laded his banquet plate with five times as much as the portion of the others! It is God that puts it into the heart of brother to love brother.

Memories of Youth, Childhood, Brothers

Abraham said gently but sternly to the rich man in Hell, *"Son, remember!"* People do remember in Hell! I am sure that the rich man wished he could forget, but memory is part of Hell's haunting torment. The rich man did remember, and I am sure that in Hell today he still remembers, *remembers*, REMEMBERS! And memory could not go back far down the line, calling to mind opportunities wasted, sins committed, light rejected, gospel messages scorned, without coming face to face with the fact of his five unsaved brothers. Doubtless it was true, and doubtless the rich man knew it, that the five unsaved brothers were impenitent and lost because they followed in his footsteps.

I suppose the rich man was an older brother. He died first. This rich man had had his own mansion, his own wealth, and the beggar "was laid at *his* gate." But the five brothers are back at their father's home, and from Hell the rich man cried for Lazarus to be sent to "my father's house; for I have five brethren." This man in Hell was the oldest of six brothers; now he faces the tormenting realization that he has led his five younger brothers in the ways of sin; that probably they, like himself, will die impenitent, condemned, and spend eternity in Hell.

In Hell one has plenty of time to remember, and the memories of childhood are strongest. Doubtless he remembered when each baby brother was born. He remembered their childish ways, their growing minds and bodies. These brothers had worked

together, played together, and God knows that they had sinned together!

This writer has four brothers, one older and three younger than himself. We had a large family, and we five brothers had three sisters. I have thanked God many times for my brothers and sisters. The funniest things I ever knew to happen happened to us in the home on the farm. Many of the tenderest memories I have are of those early days with my brothers and sisters. My heart longs all the time for these who are mine by blood. We have the same childhood friends. We have the same ideals imbibed in the same home. We wept around the same graves. Our hearts are knit together by bonds that ought not be broken.

My two youngest brothers, Joe and Bill, were preachers. I think it possible, nay, probable, that had I not preached the Gospel, they would not have preached. An older brother has great influence. I well remember when I wrote my brother George, when I was in Baylor University, "Come on down to Baylor. You can room with me in this little attic room. I will help you through the best I can. And I have a girl picked out for you!" George came to Baylor, and we worked our way through together. I helped him all I could. A man is accountable for his brother. Incidentally, he married the girl!

When Joe planned to get married and didn't have the money, I raked up a few dollars for the necessary expense so that the boy might not delay his happiness. A brother is responsible for his brothers.

But with these memories are other memories which are sad. My brothers would have been better men had I been a better man. My influence has not been altogether and wholly good.

Brothers Should Win Brothers to Christ

The rich man in Hell remembered his brothers. He had lived his worldly, Christ-rejecting life before them. The five brothers

had followed the sixth, who led them wrong. Throughout the ages of torment in Hell that rich man will remember his sin against his brothers. If they went to Hell, as they may have done, can you imagine their meeting with the brother whose wickedness had led them to eternal torment? Perhaps a brother's love was turned to hate by the ruin which a brother's sin had brought. They sinned, and they deserved Hell, but perhaps they would have sought and accepted the free mercy of God but for the example of their brother.

Dear reader, if you have an unsaved brother, I beg you by everything that is holy, win him while you can.

People sometimes say, "Brother Rice, you know how it is. A man's own family won't pay any attention to him." Oh, yes, they will, if he means business. That thought is a deception of the Devil. Brother will listen to a brother quicker than he will to an outsider. The ties of blood are stronger.

To be sure, we cannot influence our brothers if we live in hypocrisy. Lot could not influence his own sons-in-law, but neither could he influence anybody else. Any man who takes Christ as Saviour and lives a transformed life can have influence over his own brothers.

When Andrew was saved, "he first findeth his own brother Simon, and saith unto him, We have found the Messias, which is, being interpreted, the Christ. *And he brought him to Jesus*" (John 1:41, 42). Old stubborn-hearted, loud-mouthed, blustering Simon Peter must have been a pretty hard man to influence. He wanted to lead, not to be led. This old cursing fisherman had his own opinions and was quick to express them. I have an idea that he was older than Andrew, though the Bible does not say. Certainly he had the stronger character of the two. But when Andrew came, the first thing after he was saved, and said, "We have found the Saviour," he brought Simon Peter to Jesus right away!

Oh, you can win your brothers in many cases, and I pray as I write these words that you will determine to do so.

One Sunday morning when I preached on this subject and asked how many in the audience had unsaved brothers, I suppose two-thirds of the congregation held their hands. If Christians who read this would win their own brothers at any cost, what a revival would sweep the land! What rejoicing, what hallelujahs, what happy homes, what glory to Christ!

"And Thy House"

God clearly intends that every human tie be used in soul winning. Mothers should use a mother's influence to win their children. So with the father. Sweethearts should win their lost sweethearts (though it is doubtful if Christians ought ever to have sweethearts who are unsaved. Certainly, the saved should never marry the unsaved). The teacher should win her pupil; the brother, his brother.

When the jailer came trembling and fell down before Paul and Silas and asked them, "What must I do to be saved?" the inspired answer of the apostles was, "Believe on the Lord Jesus Christ, and thou shalt be saved, *and thy house.*" The jailer was to believe, but the promise was not only for him; it was for his household! Even in the very act of salvation, the jailer was taught that he must win his family, he must tell them the same story and teach them to trust in Christ, as he himself had trusted Him. And the heart rejoices to read further on in the same chapter how that family, all saved and all baptized, gathered around the table past the midnight hour, after Paul and Silas had their wounds dressed, and ate their belated supper. The jailer and his family were happy, "believing in God with all his house."

There once came to my office in Dallas, Texas, a man from Fort Worth who long had been a Christian. When he attended

our Bible conference, he told how he had come to Dallas to see a lost brother and happily had led him to accept Christ. Now on this second trip, he told of the conversion of another brother. The second brother had been out in California, and the Fort Worth man, Mr. Conner, began to pray for his soul. He asked his Sunday school class to pray. On Monday night they had a special prayer meeting, praying that God would save Mr. Conner's brother. They prayed late and earnestly, and God seemed to hear. The next Wednesday morning, in California, the brother was strangely moved with a strong desire to see his loved ones back in Texas, so he got in his car and began the trip to Fort Worth. Now let Mr. Conner tell the story:

"I got him in my car, and we drove out on the Jacksboro highway. I asked him why he came back to Texas, and he told me he just suddenly became hungry to see his brothers. I told him how I had trusted the Lord, how our other brother had been saved, and how we had prayed for his soul. Then I took the Bible and showed him how to be saved, and there in my car he trusted Christ. We drove back into Fort Worth to tell the rest of the family." Mr. Conner's face beamed with joy as he told us the story of his brother's salvation.

Win your brother while you can. See him if possible. If not, write him. Begin to pray earnestly for his salvation.

Two other worlds are concerned about sinners. "There is joy in the presence of the angels of God over one sinner that repenteth." Heaven longs to see the salvation of your brothers. Christ longs to save them. This is the thing nearest His heart. He came to seek and to save the lost.

In Hell men are lifting their cries, begging that someone be sent to warn their brothers who live here unsaved. If in the eternal worlds of bliss and torment the principal concern is the salvation of sinners, surely you should win your brothers while you can. Do not depend on others; do your part today to win you own

brothers, and the brothers of others who are pleading for them in Hell.

Decide for Christ Today!

Dear reader, why not persuade some unsaved people to read these Scriptures, and urge upon them to confess their sins to God and trust Christ for forgiveness and salvation today!

"For God so loved the world, that he gave his only begotten Son, that whosoever believeth in him should not perish, but have everlasting life. For God sent not his Son into the world to condemn the world; but that the world through him might be saved. He that believeth on him is not condemned: but he that believeth not is condemned already, because he hath not believed in the name of the only begotten Son of God."—John 3:16-18.

My Decision for Christ

If you will here and now decide for Christ, taking Him as your own Saviour, will you not sign the following decision, then copy it in a letter and mail it to me? I will be so glad to rejoice with you over your salvation and will send you a letter of counsel and encouragement. Decide and sign it today and let us hear from you.

Dr. Curtis Hutson
P. O. Box 1099
Murfreesboro, TN 37133

Dear Dr. Hutson:

Realizing that I am a guilty, lost sinner, but believing that Christ died for my sins on the cross and rose again from the grave, I here and now accept Him as my personal Saviour, depending on Him to forgive all my sins, change my heart and give me everlasting life now, as He promised. I am glad to confess Him as my Saviour, and I sign my name to claim Him. I

intend to live for Him, beginning today, and rely on Him for help.

Date_____

Name_____

Address_____

_____

If you have taken Christ as your own Saviour, then be sure to confess Him openly before men (Matt. 10:32); get in with the people of God, read your Bible daily, let the Lord Jesus be the Master of your whole life, and set out to be a soul winner for Him.